CODENAME RYGOR

THE SPY BEHIND THE ALLIED VICTORY
IN NORTH AFRICA

CODENAME RYGOR

THE SPY BEHIND THE ALLIED VICTORY
IN NORTH AFRICA

MIECZYSŁAW ZYGFRYD SŁOWIKOWSKI

TRANSLATED FROM THE POLISH BY
GEORGE SŁOWIKOWSKI AND KRYSTYNA BROOKS

dialogue < >

First published in Great Britain in 2010 by
Dialogue, an imprint of
Biteback Publishing Ltd
Heal House
375 Kennington Lane
London
SE11 5QY

ISBN 978-1-906447-08-3

10 9 8 7 6 5 4 3 2 1

A CIP catalogue record for this book is available from the British Library.

Set in Sabon

Printed and bound in Great Britain by
CPI Cox & Wyman, Reading, RG1 8EX

CONTENTS

1

OUT OF THE SOVIET UNION

At the outbreak of the Second World War I was working in Kiev, the capital of the Soviet Socialist Republic of the Ukraine, as secretary of the Polish General Consulate. I was listed under an assumed name (Eugene Zarembski), and my real task was to gather Intelligence on southern Russia for the Second Bureau of the Polish General Staff. With the announcement of the Nazi–Soviet Pact, Hitler's next move was not difficult to predict. Nevertheless, his ruthless attack on Poland came as a shattering personal blow. I felt an all-pervading sense of helplessness and foreboding. Only the old ingrained sense of duty compelled me to continue with my work. It became more imperative than ever to attempt to fathom Stalin's immediate intentions. In the meantime, all our spare time at the Consulate was spent listening to war communiqués.

Perhaps surprisingly, the civilian population of Kiev and the local press came out strongly against the fascist attack on Poland. The Soviet authorities had introduced a blackout, anti-aircraft defences were in evidence and we were under intense surveillance by the NKVD (the People's Commissariat for Internal Affairs – the Soviet secret police). An unusual movement of population, usually the prelude to mobilisation, was particularly noticeable. This was confirmed by added difficulties placed in our way and, from 10 September 1939, we were forbidden to leave Kiev by car. It was obvious that Stalin was secretly concentrating his armed forces, while Polish and German troops were still locked in combat. This became more apparent during my journey to our Moscow Embassy on 12 September, since all the railway stations were crowded with young conscripts. Our Ambassador, Grzybowski, confirmed my belief that the USSR was going through a general mobilisation.

On 13 September there was a marvellous surprise. My wife Sophie telephoned from Kiev, having arrived there unexpectedly soon after I had left for Moscow. Sophie had decided to take a chance and had left Warsaw on the last train, which was attacked en route by the Luftwaffe, without any guarantee of finding me. George, our thirteen-year-old son, who was not on her passport, was waiting for me to collect him at the Polish border town of Równo.

I immediately returned to Kiev and, as anticipated, the Post Office refused to accept telegrams to Poland. As our Consulate radio did not receive signals, I was compelled (without much conviction) to despatch telegrams to our legations in Romania and Latvia in the hope that news of the military build-up would reach our authorities. Since this appeared doubtful, our Consul, Matusiński, agreed that I should travel to Poland to warn the authorities personally. It would also give me the opportunity to collect George at Równo at the same time. One of the young members of our staff volunteered to accompany me.

The Soviet authorities delayed our departure but we managed to leave Kiev on 16 September by the 00.15 train to Shepetovka, a southern Russian town very near the Polish border. Travelling through the night, we saw endless columns of trains packed with Soviet troops facing west towards the Polish frontier. The Red Army was ready and waiting for the order to attack.

We arrived at Shepetovka later in the day and Równo that evening, where I was reunited with George. As no higher Polish authority could be found in the town, all we could do was return to Kiev as quickly as possible. Early on the morning of the 17th, while we were enquiring about trains to Russia, the station-master informed us that news had just been received that Soviet tanks had crossed the Polish border. A fourth partition of Poland was now taking place.

On our return journey to Kiev we were arrested in Shepetovka on 21 September, interrogated by an NKVD colonel and accused of spying. Fortunately I was able to prove that the sole purpose of our journey to Poland had been to collect George. An elaborate cat-and-mouse game then followed. We were released, rearrested at Kiev station, then released again on 2 October and finally allowed to rejoin the Consulate. There we learned that Consul General Matusiński had been arrested in the middle of the night of 1/2 October, together with our two chauffeurs. The Soviet authorities then ordered the rest of the Consulate staff to leave for Moscow, demanding that all our diplomats should assemble at our Embassy there. The Kiev Consulate was, in fact, the last to join them.

The outlook for our diplomatic staff was bleak. Molotov maintained that, since the Polish state had ceased to exist, its Embassy no longer existed either, and its personnel, therefore, had no diplomatic rights. This meant that we could expect, at the very least, to be sent to a forced labour camp in the Arctic or Siberia.

Fortunately the Italian Ambassador was a personal friend of our Ambassador Grzybowski and learned about our plight from the latter's wife. She put considerable pressure on Schulenburg, the German Ambassador, the doyen of the diplomatic corps in Moscow. Schulenburg, in turn, demanded that Molotov reinstate our diplomatic privileges, especially our voluntary departure from the USSR and the immediate release of Matusiński and the chauffeurs. Molotov confirmed that while our Embassy personnel would be allowed to leave, as regards Matusiński he declared, 'in the name of the Government of the Soviet Union', that 'Consul General Matusiński is no longer within the territory of the Soviet Union'. After such an official reply, any further intervention was impossible.

We left the USSR by the northern route, through Finland, Sweden, Norway, Britain, Holland and Belgium, and arrived in Paris during the last days of October 1939 . En route, our Embassies in Finland and Sweden kept us informed of the situation in Poland. We learned that a new government-in-exile had been formed in Paris, with General Sikorski as Prime Minister and Commander-in-Chief of the armed forces and W. Raczkiewicz as President.

3

2

PARIS AND TOULOUSE:
THE BEGINNING OF THE EVACUATION
AND OF THE SPECIAL SERVICE

General Sikorski's headquarters were located at the Hotel Régina on the Rue de Rivoli. First impressions of the Polish community in Paris were depressing. Intense personal and political arguments had broken out, widening the split among them. Our previous Government and its leading politicians and soldiers were the obvious scapegoats for the Polish defeat. These internecine quarrels were seriously damaging our relations with our allies.

Amid this political turmoil, our army was gradually being rebuilt. Poles were being mobilised, with the support of the French Government, both from the previous waves of emigration and those escaping from Poland, which, it was estimated, would produce over 100,000 men for a new Polish Army. The 1st Grenadier Division was being formed under General Duch and an armoured brigade under General Maczek, and preparations were being made for the formation of three infantry divisions.

Unfortunately there were considerable problems. Our High Command was still under the spell of the victorious French Army of 1918 and accepted the outdated doctrines taught by French reserve officers. The newly learned techniques of modern warfare, painfully acquired by Polish officers who were the first to gain real combat experience in September 1939, were totally disregarded.

Leaflets were distributed to newly arriving volunteers at our outposts on the Franco-Italian border blaming the old regime for the Polish collapse, thus causing further demoralisation. The governmental commission to investigate the reasons for the defeat became a witch-hunt, where NCOs were ordered to report on errors committed by the commanders of army groups.

Furthermore many professional officers, who were considered to have been too closely connected with the previous regime, languished in French camps while their postings were deliberately delayed. All these activities only weakened the discipline and morale of our armed forces.

As for the average French soldier, he did not resemble the *poilu* of the First World War in any way. The French Army had lost its offensive spirit and, contrary to the expectations of the French General Staff, the Maginot Line would soon be bypassed by the Germans without a frontal attack. The majority of the French were opposed to 'dying for Danzig' while the extreme left sabotaged the war effort. The Third Republic was collecting the fruits of its labour. It would take some time before the French will to fight was reactivated, while the French Communist Party only actively joined in the struggle after Hitler's attack on the USSR.

Soon after my arrival in Paris, I requested to be posted to a unit at the front. After a long delay, presumably because of my connection with the former regime, I was appointed Deputy Commander of an infantry division under my old friend Colonel Kobylecki. It was being trained at Loudéac in Brittany, where the local vicar, who retained his rank of Major from the 1914–18 War, was in charge of the camp. He was a sympathetic character and well disposed towards Poles, but, apart from that, the military training was a huge joke.

Quite unexpectedly, in February 1940, our General Staff brought me back to Paris and into the Intelligence section. Experts on Soviet affairs were needed now that eastern Poland was under Russian occupation and the Russo-Finnish War was in full swing. The head of our Bureau of Eastern Studies, complying with a request from the French General Staff, asked me to elaborate a plan for conducting propaganda deep into the USSR. Leaflets were prepared but we were overtaken by events.

We also studied the Russo-Finnish War and the wealth of Intelligence material sent to us by spontaneously formed cells in Poland. We learned that Red Army units stationed in Poland were being sent to Finland and that fresh Soviet troops were replacing them. Colonel Skinder's report on the deportation and splitting up of tens of thousands of Polish families deep in the interior of Russia, under the most terrible conditions, made a profound effect on me and subsequently haunted my actions.

Meanwhile, in the west, the German offensive had begun on 10 May 1940, and the military situation deteriorated. Anticipating the worst, I sent Sophie and George to the south of France.

Early on Sunday morning, 1 June 1940, I was ordered to report to the General Staff, where I was informed that we were to be immediately evacuated to the south of France. I was responsible for a group of officers and suggested we should meet at Montparnasse station at 4pm. Taking only a small suitcase I arrived there early and was greeted by unbelievable scenes of chaos and hysteria. The station was packed with huge crowds fleeing from the Germans. We managed to squeeze on to the train but reached our destination, Saintes, only in several stages. Captain Jankowski and myself managed somehow to find lodgings where we could rest and consider our situation.

Jankowski had served in prewar Polish Intelligence in Germany and, like myself, had not hitherto taken an active part in the war nor directly experienced the defeat. The tragic French events were, therefore, a new experience and doubly depressing. We agreed that the sudden French collapse had taken our Intelligence chiefs by surprise. On the other hand, the Germans had not yet digested their spoils and there was a tremendous opportunity for successful Intelligence. Instead, practically everyone seemed panic-stricken and had only one thought – to clear out of France as quickly as possible.

Our Intelligence section was billeted in a former school in Saintes, and we began burning important documents. On 17 June General Dreszer, Commander of the 4th Infantry Division, arrived looking for General Sikorski or his Chief of Staff to obtain orders. All we could say was: 'General Sikorski went up north trying to save France while we were left down here at HQ without any orders or even a bloody clue what to do!' I also suggested that, as our troops might be shipped to England, his best bet would be to move his men to the nearest port.

Marshal Pétain announced on the radio that day that France had capitulated. It was the end of our fight in France – the struggle could only be continued from Britain. Jankowski and myself realised that a high proportion of officers would manage to get to Britain but there would be insufficient men for them to command. It would be more useful for us to remain in France and try to organise an underground movement. There would be considerable problems but perhaps our High Command would suggest something. In the meantime, I would allow myself to be swept along by events. Having obtained permission, we set off next morning by car to collect our families from Salies-du-Salat, a small town south of Toulouse. Our driver, Bernard Libermann, who came from a wealthy background, had volunteered to join the Polish forces in Paris and had served as chauffeur to Major Zarembski. He was a marvellous character with an inexhaustible supply of Jewish jokes, covering almost every conceivable situation, who never failed to keep us in high spirits. Ploughing slowly through the crowds of refugees painfully pushing their way south with the remnants of their possessions, we reached Toulouse on the evening of 20 June.

At the Polish Consulate almost everything had been packed away prior to an evacuation to Spain. As nobody appeared to be working, we issued ourselves with passports, which Consul Dygat duly stamped and signed.

By this time it was getting late, the town was swollen with refugees and we were anxious about our sleeping accommodation. Libermann solved the problem in his typically ingenious way – that night we slept in a brothel!

After a happy reunion with our families, the next few days were spent hunting for extra transport to take us to St Jean-de-Luz, a port on the Atlantic coast, north of the Spanish frontier. The evacuation to Britain turned out to be a problem. The Port Commandant, General Burchard-Bukacki, gave priority to airmen and soldiers, while officers and their families were at the back of the queue; everything was conditional on the availability of ships. During the next two days troops kept arriving, while officers and their families slept in the open, awaiting their turn. The weather was atrocious: continual heavy showers, fierce winds and a very rough sea. It was not very pleasant and food supplies were running low.

While awaiting embarkation we had a look at the Spanish border. At Hendaye a French Deuxième Bureau officer whom we knew disclosed to us the terms of the Franco-German armistice agreement. The Germans would occupy the Atlantic coast but there would also be a 'free zone' under a French Government, which would include several large towns. He advised us to return there, which coincided with my secret resolution to remain in France.

On our return to St Jean-de-Luz we were compelled reluctantly to bid farewell to Bernard Libermann, who, anxious about his property (which included a palace!), had decided to return to Paris. We admired the way he dismissed our fears with the retort: 'Don't worry, the Gestapo also loves money!' We were unaware at the time that he had forecast his own future. As the situation deteriorated and the possibility of embarkation dwindled, the knowledge that a 'free zone' existed prompted us to return to Salies-du-Salat where, luckily, our accommodation was still vacant.

Toulouse was packed with refugees; Polish could be heard spoken everywhere and Polish uniforms were in great evidence. I had gone there with Major Zarembski to find out whether our Consulate was active and to determine the situation of our nationals in the town. I bumped into an old Warsaw friend, Joe Radzymiński, a young journalist, who was delighted to hear that we might be in business again soon.

The Consulate was, in fact, overflowing with soldiers clamouring for documents and advice. They were extremely hostile to officers, especially those of higher rank, whom they accused of abandoning them without money or papers. They reminded me of the Russian troops during the 1917 revolution, and it was lucky for our Defence Minister that they couldn't lay their hands on him. Fortunately, with the appointment as our new Consul at Toulouse of Mr Bitner, whose devotion to their welfare gained their confidence, the situation was defused.

Newcomers were sent to the military barracks (the 'liquidation centre'), where those awaiting French demobilisation were organised into units and received rations and pay. There was a similar centre for officers where I recognised Mr Keplain, known to me in Warsaw as a French industrialist and now a captain in the French Army. We had a long chat and he paid our salaries and arrears, which was very useful.

Consul Bitner agreed with my proposal to organise the evacuation to Britain of our servicemen left behind in France. We would set up a verification and selection committee to prevent enemy agents slipping through. While promising to inform us when we could commence, his resentment when learning of our Intelligence connection was noticeable. Back at Salies-du-Salat, I met a radio engineer from our Foreign Office, Mr Dulemba, who casually mentioned his ability to construct a two-way radio. This was important news indeed. He promised to search for the parts and to inform me of the cost.

As there was no news from Consul Bitner, Zarembski and myself decided to pay him a surprise visit on 3 July. En route we bumped into my old friend Colonel Kobylecki, pushing his bike. He was exhausted after cycling from Brittany, dodging the Germans on the way, and I insisted on putting him up. Fortified by brandy at a local bistro, we swapped stories. Kobylecki had been the Commanding Officer of the Podhalańska Brigade, which, during the Norwegian Campaign, had encircled Narvik. Disembarking at Brest, and despite their lack of heavy weapons, they were ordered to advance towards German-held Paris. Compelled to withdraw under intense German fire, they were then ordered to make their own way to the south.

Two days later we both went to see Consul Bitner, who finally consented to the evacuation scheme. For obvious reasons I refrained from mentioning Intelligence at this stage. Major Zarembski readily agreed to join our new organisation and we began our daily trips from Salies-du-Salat to Toulouse, a tiring journey in itself. Our home was six miles from the nearest railway station and, with no public transport, we had to walk that distance twice a day in all sorts of weather.

On the way to Toulouse the next day a plan began to take

shape. Major Zarembski, as my deputy, would be responsible for the verification and selection of soldiers for evacuation. Joe Radzymiński confirmed that he could find us suitable people. Consul Bitner was reassured when I explained my concern to limit our organisation to military personnel and not endanger the Consulate. He did not raise any financial objections but merely insisted on limiting the number of evacuees for the present as his budget was overstretched.

The Polish captain in charge of the 'liquidation centre' allocated us three rooms, thus retaining our secrecy under cover of the Consulate's Military Office. Our next move was to revive the fighting spirit of our men by introducing propaganda for joining our forces in Britain. Radzymiński, as a journalist, was entrusted with this task as well as contacts in the town, while Captain Jagielski was responsible for our passport office.

The procedure was that soldiers wanting to return to northern France would receive their demob papers from the French. Those who preferred to remain in the 'free zone' would, after being cleared by verification, be issued with Polish passports. During this phase we received considerable help from Captain Keplain, who was invaluable in informing us, well in advance, of any impending French directives. He warned us not to expect any help from the French (Pétain was now 'the saviour of France'), and advised us that the French authorities would not object to the departure abroad of men over forty-five. We were very grateful to him and established a method of keeping contact. Joe Radzymiński proved to be invaluable, recruiting all our personnel and arranging our contacts at foreign consulates. He had the happy knack of making friends and luring people to our side – invaluable attributes in our trade – and many joined our group as a consequence of his efforts, including Henry Łubieński. Finally, as a camouflage, the obsessive Polish mania with military titles was abolished and we all became 'civilians'. I became 'Doctor Skowroński' and henceforth was known in France under that name.

3

TOULOUSE AND MARSEILLES

The main purpose of our organisation was for our troops to reach Portugal. Evacuation from France consisted, therefore, of two simple alternatives, both involving travelling through Spain – either a legal departure from France or by human contraband across the Pyrenees. One could leave France legally after obtaining an exit visa from the Prefecture, which was conditional on having previously obtained a visa to a country of destination. Armed with both visas, the Spanish authorities would then consider issuing a transit visa. This method required an adroit manipulation of our contacts at the various foreign consulates.

Unfortunately, the main problem was that all our men were under the age limit. In order to pass them 'legally' into Portugal, we had to doctor their passports by entering false dates of birth and adding photographs making them appear much older. The usual disguises were employed – beards, moustaches and dyeing their hair grey.

Obtaining visas soon became routine work. Regular contacts were established at foreign consulates, the amount of the bribe depending on the number of 'heads' that required to be evacuated. By these methods we obtained destination visas to Brazil, Shanghai and other exotic places, and it was undoubtedly the easiest method of evacuation. Evacuees received passports, visas, money and instructions, and left in batches of ten. On arrival in Spain, they reported to our Embassy in Madrid. The first group was despatched on 10 July 1940 and, to my great relief, the pre-arranged postcard arrived from Madrid confirming their safe arrival.

However, with increasing German influence in Spain, the situation on the Franco-Spanish border changed. The Spanish authorities began refusing admission and raised the age limit. Evacuees refused entry returned to France, creating additional problems and adding to our expense. We therefore established one-man outposts near border crossings, which reported changes by telegrams in code, which compelled me to recruit extra people. Zarembski agreed that the increased work required our continual presence in Toulouse, which became the new HQ of our organisation.

New difficulties arose. Following resolutions by the Vichy Government under Gestapo pressure, the French created additional problems in the form of limitations and refusals. Soon only human contraband would be feasible and we would have to assure ourselves of co-operation from the other side of the Pyrenees. The indispensable Radzymiński knew the right person with good Spanish contacts – Lieutenant Popławski, who had been a correspondent there during the Spanish Civil War. Popławski assured me that he would be able to organise the reception in Spain and establish contacts with our Embassy there. After obtaining visas and travelling expenses, and accompanied by his wife, he left for Spain in mid-July 1940.

Hitherto we had no contact with London and our work was slowed down by lack of funds. Consul Bitner, who served as our paymaster, could never have been described as over-generous, and the number of men (mainly officers) seeking our help was increasing daily. Priority went to privates and NCOs, while officers were only evacuated proportionally to the other ranks.

By early July Dulemba had found the parts and the radio was ready to work, but we were still unable to contact London without the necessary data. However, Dulemba, who knew almost all our Foreign Office radio operators, remembered the wavelength and began listening. One day, recognising the wireless operator's touch as that of a friend, he identified himself and, using a simple code, joined in the radio conversation. His correspondent, fearful that the enemy was posing as Dulemba, immediately broke off radio contact and our transmitted signals remained unanswered. Other methods had to be sought to obtain the elementary data vital to a radio correspondence with London, and this proved to be extremely difficult.

The end of 1940 saw the return of the Polish Embassy with General Kleeberg as our new Military Attaché to Vichy France. The consulates began receiving orders from London regarding the evacuation. Mine did not recommend specific individuals but merely stipulated the order of priorities. This period also saw the beginning of demobilisation. Centres were opened in towns with large Polish populations, where officers and men received money and civilian clothing in return for submitting their personal data. The casual way in which this was conducted by the French authorities led to some abuse. Some individuals demobbed themselves at several centres, collecting sums of cash which they later shared with ladies from the reserved quarters on special streets. The French authorities also formed labour battalions for our men while officers were to receive a monthly 'allocation'. On the whole, the French tried to solve the problem of the excess Polish ex-combatants in a fair manner.

With the evacuation network functioning smoothly, I hoped we could prepare our next important step – an intelligence service. This was impossible, however, without solid financial backing and radio contact with London. We could only make certain rudimentary moves, in connection with which I thought we had found the right person in Captain Czerniawski. He was an enthusiastic young air force officer, very ambitious, and only lacked experience of life and of general military matters. I met him in Toulouse while he was on his way to Britain and offered him a job in espionage. As he had no Intelligence background, I thought it useful for him to work in evacuation to gain some experience.

In late July 1940, I sent him to Paris to report on conditions under the German occupation, to explore the possibility of infiltration into the occupied zone, to renew old acquaintances and, if possible, to make new contacts. He was sent a second time in August to explore further possibilities. The results of both visits were highly satisfactory. He found our old friend Bernard Libermann and made new contacts among Poles still living in Paris. The passage between the two zones had not presented any serious problems.

Towards the end of July 1940 General Kleeberg paid us a visit and appeared impressed by our evacuation progress. Privately, he outlined his own scheme for evacuating several hundred soldiers at once. He had purchased a cargo boat and asked me to move 250 men from my district to Marseilles prior to the sailing date, which was in a few days' time. I organised those from the Armoured Brigade and those from Toulouse. Groups of ten were smuggled on board the trains under the noses of the gendarmes. The reception party then smuggled them into the 'English Hospital', the reception centre for our men arriving for demobilisation.

General Kleeberg based his plan on official approval by the French High Command. Instead of granting permission, General Dentz, the Commander of the South-Eastern Military District of France, threatened to arrest Kleeberg or anyone else using the ship for a similar purpose, and ordered the port police to keep a close watch. The enterprise was a fiasco. The ship remained in port, and the soldiers at the 'English Hospital' gave one more headache to the Commanding Officer there.

With hindsight, one should not have expected the French to give it their official blessing. We had many friends among them who turned a blind eye to our illegal actions. Asking them to legalise it was a very different kettle of fish.

After a period of chaos and disorder, the French authorities began to act. Directives were issued limiting the movement of population and introducing detailed surveillance. Foreigners were forbidden to change departments and required a special police pass, the *sauf conduit*, for travelling long distances. Police patrols on roads and railway stations were stepped up and the Gestapo kept observers in the Prefectures. These restrictions added extra hazards to our plans. On German instructions, the Prefectures practically stopped issuing exit visas. To add to our problems all the foreign consulates in Toulouse also refused to issue visas.

Fortunately we had made preparations for human contraband. Our outposts on the Franco-Spanish border, at Cerbère, Banyuls,

Bedous and Andorra, were each directed by a fluent French speaker whose function was to contact smugglers on both sides of the border. The latter would then escort our men deep into Spain where police pressure was less intense. With human lives at risk, the operators did not have an enviable task. They had to select the most comparatively reliable ruffians from a gang of cut-throats. The smugglers also demanded to be paid by piecework – per number of Polish heads to be escorted.

The network was organised sooner than expected. Surprisingly, in late August 1940, the outpost operators reported that they were ready. However, there was no news from Popławski, who was on the other side of the Pyrenees – a mystery that was only solved some eight months later.

After the naval fiasco, General Kleeberg offered me command of Polish evacuation for all of France. First, I visited our centres in Marseilles, where I met Consul Lisiewicz, the Polish military camp of Carpiagni, and Lyons, to check on co-operation. Finally, I reported to General Kleeberg at our Embassy at Vichy that the change from Toulouse to Marseilles – which was ideal for sea evacuation – should be effected at the end of August 1940. This necessitated a complete reorganisation. Łubieński was assigned to the newly formed outpost at Perpignan to keep an eye on our Cerbère and Banyuls outposts. Czerniawski was left in charge at Toulouse and moved into our flat. Consul Bitner was informed of the impending changes.

At Marseilles, Consul Lisiewicz had funds allocated to the evacuation and made regular payments to Colonel Stafiej, the organiser there. It looked as if Dr Skowroński's arrival would be resented in certain quarters. General Duch, commander of the Grenadiers, told me that nobody had hitherto left Marseilles for Spain and was naturally impatient to see his soldiers on the move to England. He ordered Stafiej to stop his activities and the Consul was advised not to pay out any funds without my permission. I requested a report on his endeavours. Almost 300,000 francs had been spent on 'research' but as yet nobody had actually been evacuated.

Apparently one of his officers was organising sea evacuation consisting of a motor boat to ferry evacuees to Gibraltar, but this was 'still in the project stage'. After further investigation I advised him to stop and report on its cost and the results, which he ignored. He sent a handful of officers by motor boat to Gibraltar while he himself preferred to be evacuated through our organisation into Spain. Before leaving he claimed in his report to have been robbed at gunpoint by the Frenchmen who had helped purchase the boat and, for obvious reasons, had been unable to report the matter to the police. He then reproached me for forbidding evacuation by sea, claiming that, by sending the motor boat to Gibraltar, he had proved it was possible. I greatly regretted that he was never informed that it had been intercepted by the French Coastal Police and its occupants sent to Guirs, the special penal camp in the Pyrenees notorious for its harsh conditions. We managed to free them but it took some time, and they paid for their recklessness.

The fifteenth of September was a turning point. Consul Lisiewicz informed me that two officers had arrived from London with orders to contact an unknown organisation operating a radio transmitter. Unable to find me in Toulouse, they returned to Marseilles the following day and introduced themselves as Lieutenant Jekiel, Polish Navy, assigned to our Consulate in Nice, and Captain Korwin-Szymanowski, assigned to the Toulouse Consulate. Fearing problems at the border, they had left their small radio in Madrid. In any case, they knew that we possessed one already. This was strange since nobody outside our small circle knew about it and we had been unable to make contact with London. Jekiel had brought a cipher book, codes and radio instructions. The following afternoon we successfully contacted London and made our first report:

To the Chief of Staff of the Supreme Commander of the Polish Forces: Situation Report no 1. Marseilles, 16 September 1940. I hereby inform you that a secret organisation has been set up for the evacuation of our troops to England from unoccupied France and Intelligence work has begun in the German zone of occupation. The composition of our organisation is as follows:

Commanding Officer: Major Mieczysław Z. Słowikowski
Deputy Commander: Major Wincenty Zarembski

Directors of evacuation outposts:
Lyons: Captain Jan Kamiński
Toulouse: Captain Pilot R. Czerniawski
Perpignan: Lieutenant Henryk Łubieński
Andorra: Cadet Officer J. Roztworowski

Headquarters of the organisation: Marseilles.

Special units are operating in Marseilles for the production of
exit visas in the Prefectures and visas in the foreign consulates.
Financial, technical assistance and instructions are requested for
the start of the Intelligence operations. Preparatory steps have
already been taken.

Major M. Z. Słowikowski, Commanding Officer.

On 17 September 1940, the first message from London with
initial orders for the organisation of all our work in France
was received. By this order my deputy, Major Zarembski, was
nominated Chief of Intelligence in France with the *nom de guerre*
TUDOR, while I was nominated Head of Evacuation, both functions
to be carried out separately. The TUDOR network would cover
immediately. He was allocated two new officers – Jekiel (in Nice)
and Korwin-Szymanowski (in Toulouse).

Our orders were clear, but there was only one snag. How
was TUDOR supposed to organise Intelligence work without any
financial support? It was somewhat confusing – even a layman
should have realised that espionage, above all, is based on gold.
We discussed our respective functions and, as his was obviously the
more important, I felt obliged to help him out. I put my transmitter
at his disposal and persuaded an unwilling Dulemba to change
organisations. TUDOR was offered the choice of my officers and
200,000 francs in cash. He chose Czerniawski, Kamiński and Joe

Radzymiński, later supplementing them with others, and had good reason to be pleased. We continued to maintain close contact, which was not difficult as our two families continued to share the same apartment.

With so many officers leaving for Intelligence, the evacuation had to be remoulded. New officers were admitted and Major Gustowski became my deputy. Sea evacuation appeared feasible and a suitable outpost was set up by Lieutenant Kiersnowski who had come from Argentina to join our army in France. After Czerniawski's departure, the Toulouse outpost was abandoned and its work was taken over by Łubieński in Perpignan. Around mid-September the Prefectures stopped issuing exit visas and the Spanish authorities, in turn, practically closed the border.

Our soldiers from the labour battalions (forced upon us by the Vichy authorities) now arrived in civvies at the 'English Hospital' in Marseilles. There they were issued with our forged passports, then sent to Perpignan and the border outposts, where they were smuggled over the Pyrenees. The smugglers guided them deep into Spain, bought the tickets and ensured that they boarded the Madrid train. Orders were given not to drink too much wine, smoke French cigarettes or speak Polish while in Spain. They were not to loiter in large groups and were to comply with the instructions of the guides. Group leaders were instructed to send a postcard on arrival in Madrid to the Polish Consulate in Marseilles. The names of the addressees were frequently changed to avoid associating them with too large a correspondence from Spain.

Despite our dwindling funds the evacuation ran smoothly, but gradually individuals, then whole groups, were arrested by the Spanish police and sent to the concentration camp of Miranda de Ebro. I discovered that the reasons for some of the arrests lay in the total disregard of our safety instructions. Some of our men, after finding themselves in Spain and in comparative safety far from the border, had got drunk on cheap wine and had even provoked incidents on trains and at railway stations. Others, having successfully passed through Spain, wrote letters from Portugal to their colleagues in France detailing the route and encouraging them to try their luck without waiting their turn. Arriving in the Pyrenees, without proper guidance, they fell easy victims to police traps. Their confessions incriminated the smugglers, who either refused any further association with us or demanded increased payment.

It was evident from Łubieński's reports that border controls were being tightened and that the number of arrests was increasing. I was reluctantly compelled, therefore, to order the suspension of evacuation through Spain except for the handful over forty-five who could continue to do so legally. Miranda de Ebro, first used as an internment camp when armed and uniformed Polish groups crossed the frontier in June 1940, after the French collapse, was now swelling with our men. The Spanish Government wanted to maintain their neutrality but were subject to increasing German pressure. Obviously they would not tolerate the foolish behaviour of our young men travelling on forged passports. The information reaching us spoke of hard and brutal conditions at Miranda de Ebro, including shootings, together with a total lack of interest by our Embassy in Madrid. The only other evacuation method was by sea and I was compelled to turn in that direction.

Our cargo boat, the *Panama*, bought by General Kleeberg for the evacuation, still lay abandoned in the port of Marseilles and the French port police had lost interest in it. I thought it opportune to return to the same idea but this time without asking anyone's permission. Lieutenant Niemiec, who had worked for a shipping company before the war, knew all the legal procedures. It was registered at the Panamanian Consulate, partly because of its name but also for their facilities, and with modifications it could be used for the evacuation. The port authorities were advised that the wooden bunks were needed to transport oranges. We even engaged a French captain and were enlisting a crew. Niemiec achieved the seemingly impossible feat of buying sufficient food and wine to last a considerable time and work on the ship progressed well.

The *Panama* would have picked up the evacuees at night on the coast outside Marseilles, taken them to Gibraltar and, on her return, loaded cases of oranges on board from one of the Spanish ports.

In spite of our strenuous efforts to keep it secret, our soldiers, very gifted on such occasions, somehow managed to discover our plans. News of the *Panama*'s departure spread like wildfire throughout Marseilles and eventually reached the ears of the authorities. The port police immediately sealed the ship and only allowed the crew on board. The boat was now useless. At least we managed to sell it and make a small profit.

4

UNFORESEEN EVENTS – SEA EVACUATION – NEW ORGANISATION IN NORTH AFRICA

One day my deputy, Major Gustowski, introduced me to a Czech acquaintance, Mr Bauer, whom he had mentioned frequently as having good contacts with the Marseilles police. He made a profound impression on me as an extraordinarily intelligent and gifted person. I was delighted when he volunteered to join us, and he was given the code name 'Bartek'. Through him I became acquainted with the Czech Consul in Marseilles, and with Commissaire Dubois who became one of my closest friends.

Marcel Dubois, Deputy Commissaire for Public Security in Marseilles, was a huge, powerfully built northern Frenchman in his middle thirties who hated the Nazis and was a good friend to the Poles. It was heartening to find a patriotic Frenchman in such a responsible position while most of the French were staking everything on a German victory. Dubois helped me obtain a safe conduct pass, without which it was impossible to travel extensively by railway in France. This enabled me to travel to Vichy, where General Kleeberg, who was unaware of the impending changes, gave me US $20,000 for the evacuation and a cipher book for TUDOR.

On 1 October 1940, the Germans struck all legal Polish activities in France, ordering the French to close our Vichy Embassy and all our consulates. With the Ambassador's departure, General Kleeberg lost his diplomatic status and only remained in France as unofficial head of the Polish forces by fully utilising his personal friendships with high-ranking French officers. Our consulates became 'Polish Offices' and the Embassy 'Head of the Polish Offices'.

With General Kleeberg's arrival in Marseilles, I suggested the creation of a clandestine headquarters to maintain our troops as a close military formation. It was soon reactivated, giving orders and lectures, and I was able to change the evacuation system. Our underground military HQ was now informed of the numbers to be assembled at the 'English Hospital'. They chose the candidates and ordered our battalion commanders to bring them to the assembly point at a given time, thus relieving us of an excess of activities. It also enabled me to increase our security precautions, a move which, given continual attempts by the Germans to infiltrate our organisation, had become imperative.

In one case a Polish artillery officer reported that he had heard that a colleague from his regiment had escaped from a German POW camp and was in Marseilles demanding a speedy evacuation. He warned us that his regimental friend, who had been badly wounded, had died in German captivity, and that this 'officer' must therefore be an impostor. Commissaire Dubois confirmed that, if he was unmasked as a German spy, he should be speedily liquidated. Our plan was agreed.

The 'escapee' would report to me together with two of my officers posing as evacuation candidates, and the artillery officer (his 'regimental friend') would also be present. I would check his Polish officer's identity card and see whether he recognised his 'old friend'. All three would then adjourn to await further orders. Dubois, at an arranged time, would send a taxi to my office. My two officers and the 'escapee' would go to Carpiagni camp to be demobilised by the French authorities. The road ran through a forest on a precipitous and rocky coastline. The taxi would stop near the coast, and they would shoot the German and throw his body over the cliff. In the event of his body being recovered, Commissaire Dubois himself would officially take up the case.

The three officers duly reported and the interview took place. The 'escapee' failed to recognise his regimental friend and the artillery officer swore on oath in an adjoining room that he was an impostor. The 'escapee's' identity card was genuine but the stamp on the photograph was forged; he spoke fluent Polish but with a very slight foreign accent. The plan was therefore carried out. Our officers immediately left for Perpignan and crossed over the Spanish border the same night. Thus only two men were left in Marseilles who knew about the incident – Commissaire Dubois and Dr Skowroński.

Our border outposts were also exposed to dangers. Sometimes the commander, identified by the police, had to be hidden in Marseilles until he himself could be evacuated into Spain through a different outpost. In October 1940, the young commander of the Andorra outpost requested orders for dealing with someone who was continually following him. My advice was that there were many dangerous passes in the Pyrenees where an accident could easily occur; if he was positive, then the solution lay in his own hands. He returned to Andorra and never asked for a similar order again.

We were threatened not only by the loose tongues and indiscreet letters of the evacuees but also by various types of speculators. There were a flock of these vultures in Marseilles, who, boasting of their contacts in consulates and prefectures, cheated naive soldiers out of large sums of money. They caused unpleasant breaches with our foreign consulate contacts and made it more difficult to obtain visas. Others, always managing to find gullible customers, organised motor boat expeditions to Gibraltar from the port of Sète. Once the money reached them it was found that the police had uncovered the enterprise and confiscated the boat, which usually had a different owner anyway.

There were other types, comparatively less harmful, who exhibited a great desire for speedy evacuation. Having received the necessary documents, information and, of course, money, instead of crossing the mountains, they enjoyed themselves at good hotels in the Pyrenees. Our border outposts never failed to report these acts of treachery. On their return to Marseilles they would tell stories about the impossibility of crossing the border, or of arrest, and demand to be re-evacuated. I was able to trump their stories with some of my own and inform them that they had forfeited their chances of further evacuation. It was particularly despicable as they were officers and, as such, had to be evacuated individually.

There were also cases of nervous breakdowns where the evacuee had to remain at the border outpost for some time. I well remember one Major who, arriving in Perpignan, refused to leave his hotel room for several weeks. Łubieński, anticipating action from the local gendarmerie, came to Marseilles seeking my personal intervention, and I had to travel a considerable distance in order to beg him to cross the Pyrenees. Later, this same Major passed himself off in Britain as a hero who, unaided, had surmounted all the problems.

During our search in Marseilles for alternative methods of evacuation, we contacted a Spanish refugees' organisation ('the Red Spaniards') and discovered that the Mexican Government had promised to accept them all. We came to an agreement by which a large group of our men would be able to leave for Mexico by posing as ex-members of the International Brigade. They received special identity cards (the Vichy Regime were glad to get rid of them), and were to sail from a southern French port. Their departure was conditional on the approval of the German Armistice Commission; it was refused and the project fell through.

By late autumn 1940, rumours of an impending German occupation of the 'free zone' were extremely strong. The Perpignan outpost was closed down and Łubieński was transferred to Vichy to cultivate friendly relations with French officials and to obtain information given to them by the Germans. As a journalist, he was ideal for such an assignment, and we were soon kept informed of political news in Vichy government circles.

Among much important secret information from Łubieński's 'special outpost', two items were directly connected with our organisation. Firstly, the Germans were pressing the French to get rid of General Kleeberg, who was now in hiding in Marseilles. Secondly, Commissaire Dubois had been placed on the blacklist as an anti-collaborationist and his dismissal was imminent. Dubois, who was immediately informed, went to Vichy and with the help of a highly placed colleague verified the information. He managed to secure a transfer to Rabat, in a similar post but in a higher grade. He assured me of his everlasting gratitude, later confirmed in a letter from Morocco. His departure meant the loss of a true and devoted friend. I had no idea that quite soon I would urgently need his help.

TUDOR informed me about the reappearance in France of Stefan Olpiński. Olpiński was a German agent, a fact that was unknown in prewar Poland; on the contrary, he was popular in some Warsaw circles because of his judicial attempts to incriminate M. Starzyński, the Polish Minister of Finance. Later he owned a publishing house in Paris, which published General Sikorski's works. During the war Sikorski wanted to take him into the Polish Army in France with the rank of Lieutenant-Colonel and make him head of Polish Intelligence. Fortunately for us, the French arrested him and he was charged with spying for the Germans. After the French collapse, however, he was set free.

London was alerted by TUDOR, who was ordered to liquidate him immediately. It was discovered that Olpiński visited his French mistress near Lyons. A trap was set that misfired. Bartek reported in due course that the Gestapo had sent him to Poland. The Polish Home Army finally caught up with him at Auschwitz concentration camp where he was poisoned while serving as a confidant of the Nazis.

Sea evacuation was extremely difficult. Boats could not be purchased without being cleared by the port police, who kept a tight control over the coastline. The German Armistice Commission's permission was required before any craft could leave a French port. Furthermore, there was a shortage of motor fuel even on the black market.

I was convinced that the road to evacuation led through North Africa and that its strategic value would induce the Allies to occupy it first, in which case our soldiers would automatically find themselves among friends. In October 1940, Lieutenant Kiersnowski, commander of our naval outpost, was ordered to fraternise with merchant seamen on the Marseilles–North African run to ascertain the possibilities of their taking stowaways. He knew the argot of the waterfront bars and soon gained their confidence. The price was 100–300 francs per transportee, depending on the number of stowaways.

The next step was to organise a network of outposts on the

North African coast to receive arrivals and direct them to our safe houses prior to their being transported to Casablanca, the safest port, at the discretion of the local commanders. Given the distances involved, their task would not be easy. The administrative division of French North Africa into three separate parts – the Protectorate of Tunisia, the General Governorship of Algeria and the Protectorate of Morocco – added to the hazards. The borders of these territories were guarded and a special travel permit was needed.

Success also depended upon picking the right people for the outposts. Krasiński (Tunis), Krzesimowski (Algiers), Gordon (Oran) and Tonn, Krzyzanowski and Badeni (Casablanca) were chosen. They left for French North Africa in November 1940, with orders to report on the local situation. Our aims, methods of communication between the outposts, contact with the Evacuation Command, and the ways in which to approach the French authorities had all been explained to them. The rest was left to them, the entire evacuation programme being dependent upon their reports. We also organised outlets to French-held Syria and the Lebanon, which were used sparingly because of the vast distances involved.

Around this time TUDOR received an order from London to organise an Intelligence outpost in Casablanca. He accepted my suggestion that Captain Tonn, whom I had already designated there, would be an ideal choice. Having two very talented officers with him, he would be able to combine his Intelligence and evacuation functions, and TUDOR gave him special instructions before his departure. The North African reports were very satisfactory. Our officers had made the right contacts in the ports and elsewhere; the local authorities were more lenient and friendlier than those in France; conditions for the evacuation were excellent. I reported all this to General Kleeberg, who gave his consent.

Kiersnowski provided the departure details of the cargo boats sailing from Marseilles and the numbers to be transported. Our clandestine military headquarters then arranged for them to arrive at the 'English Hospital'. Kiersnowski had the lists of payments to the sailors and for the evacuees' maintenance in North Africa. He usually collected the group from the assembly point late at night and guided them to the rendezvous where the boats awaited them. In order to avoid detection by the port police, the ship was approached from the starboard and boarded by rope ladders. The stowaways were immediately ushered to their hideouts where they had to remain while the boat was at sea and in the port. The entire operation had to be effected quickly, in complete silence and under cover of darkness.

The hideouts were very uncomfortable, usually in those parts seldom visited by the ship's officers, such as coal bunkers and boiler rooms. Great physical stamina was required to remain constantly in the same place in a foul atmosphere and tremendous heat. The disembarkation also took place at night. The stowaways were guided to a secret rendezvous where the outpost commander awaited them. The actual size of a stowaway group varied but often reached forty. The effort involved in boarding such a large group can be imagined. Thanks to Kiersnowski's marvellous efforts we managed to transfer a few hundred soldiers to North Africa by the end of February 1941, which was quite an achievement.

With continually increasing numbers of our men in French North Africa, I felt it necessary to send a higher-ranking officer there to assume command. General Kleeberg recommended Major Wysoczański, who was unknown to me. His duties were explained to him and he was expected to report to me on his progress and on the local situation. He was provided with funds and a list of officers already actively engaged there. I had no objections to his own choice of associates.

Wysoczański and his group arrived in North Africa around Christmas 1940, and he immediately changed most of the existing outpost commanders including replacing Lieutenant Gordon in Oran with Captain Szewalski. He forbade Captain Tonn in Casablanca to involve himself in Intelligence work, ordering him and the other two officers to Kasba-Tadla camp, some 200 miles south of Casablanca, where our soldiers were assembled. In the event TUDOR never received any messages from Tonn, and his Intelligence cell at Casablanca had to be closed down. Despite his precise orders, Wysoczański never sent a single report to either

27

General Kleeberg or myself. Instead, he sent telegrams to my secret office demanding money. General Kleeberg agreed that it was unwise to send money for totally unknown purposes.

Otherwise the evacuation went reasonably well until mid-March 1941, when disaster overtook us. I had tried to group our armed services together. Thus, our airmen went to Tunisia where we had good quarters, as Admiral Esteva, the head of the Tunisian Protectorate, was very favourably disposed towards us. The Polish commander of our airmen's camp outside Tunis had celebrated festive occasions with military parades, which came to the attention of the Italo-German Armistice Commission. They asked Admiral Esteva the reasons for the Polish airmen's presence in Tunisia. Under German pressure, French officials began to investigate and discovered the illegal traffic and the illegal camps in Tunisia. Many French officials were dismissed; the airmen were returned to France and then sent to a penal settlement. Even more depressing was that our soldiers (and the sailors) on board the ships were arrested. The French authorities tightened control of shipping and the ports, and I was reluctantly compelled to abandon sea evacuation.

Kiersnowski wanted to go to Britain and was passed into Spain. I was very sorry to see him leave. In the spring of 1941 I met the representative of the Polish Government to French North Africa, Count Hutten-Czapski, on his way there via Marseilles. He promised us further assistance, and our men in North Africa owed a great deal to his strenuous efforts on their behalf. My deputy, Major Gustowski, also decided to go to Britain and was replaced by Major Mizgier-Chojnacki.

5

CO-OPERATION WITH AGENCY TUDOR –
OUR ASSOCIATE BARTEK

TUDOR and I continued to share the same apartment in Marseilles and he frequently discussed his work in Paris where WALENTY (alias Czerniawski) was sending back very valuable information. TUDOR's network in the 'free zone' was functioning well, with cells in Toulouse and Nice, and one in Marseilles which he directed himself.

As there was only one cipher book, we frequently coded our messages together. While studying WALENTY's reports we tried to understand the purpose of certain German activities. Why were Panzer Units training in tropical uniforms on the sandy dunes along the northern French coast? What was being despatched in giant crates to Atlantic ports in such secrecy? Why were a large number of German soldiers in specially marked units badly burned and wounded? In September 1940, all this was still covered in a veil of secrecy.

With the increase in Intelligence activity, TUDOR experienced an *embarras de richesse*. He had amassed a considerable amount of material and was badly in need of a courier to London. I approached the United States Consulate in Marseilles and inquired whether they would carry our pouch in their diplomatic bag to London. They excused themselves by quoting a State Department order forbidding such actions.

During our discussions, the question of women agents cropped up. There were some on WALENTY's list, and I questioned the wisdom of employing them. TUDOR did not mind and even praised Mathilde Carré, whose reports 'were better edited than any staff officer'. He could not conceivably have known that she would eventually betray them all and that Czerniawski would become a German agent in Britain and then a double agent in the British 'double-cross system'.

In early November 1940, TUDOR received a message from London ordering him to report to the Spanish border town of Canfranc to receive money and a cipher book from our Madrid men. He could not obtain a travel permit for such a long journey and was unable to comply with the order. As I had the one that Marcel Dubois had obtained for me, which was valid until the end of December, I went instead.

Canfranc is in Spain, on the southern approaches to the Pyrenees, and is joined to France by a tunnel some 14km long. The railway station was divided into French and Spanish sectors; the hotel and restaurant were shared but under Spanish administration. The train arriving from the last French station, Bedous, entered the French section where, after completing customs and visa formalities, one crossed into the Spanish sector where the same formalities were completed. It was necessary to change trains at Canfranc since Spanish (like Russian) railways had wider gauges. The station was, therefore, ideally suited for meetings without attracting too much attention.

We had a lucky break. One of TUDOR's officers in Toulouse made a routine report mentioning the departure for London of Minister Morawski and his daughter. TUDOR obtained the Minister's co-operation and his daughter agreed to pose as my fiancée whom I was escorting to the frontier. My third travelling companion was Vice-Consul Morozewicz, who had excellent relations with the Spanish officials at Canfranc. This was important as Morawski had also volunteered to take TUDOR's Intelligence pouch with him to London. I took it to Toulouse, where I joined my companions, and the four of us departed for Canfranc.

There were no problems on the French side of Canfranc railway station and we crossed into the Spanish sector. There the Vice-Consul introduced me to his close friend Señor L. (the customs official) as 'the fiancé of the minister's daughter'. He allowed me to remain on the Spanish side until my 'fiancée's' departure on the train arriving from Madrid with (unknown to him) our Embassy people on board.

While waiting, I invited Señor L. and the Vice-Consul for a drink, the French train left and everything seemed to be working to plan. The Madrid train arrived on time but there was an unpleasant surprise – our people were not on board. An hour later, and after a warm send-off, the train made its return journey with the Minister, his daughter and TUDOR's pouch all safely on their way to Madrid.

Prompted by the Vice-Consul, Señor L. obtained the Falange Captain's permission for me to spend the night at the hotel awaiting the next train to France. I was not too worried – at least TUDOR's pouch was on its way to London and I had made friends with local officials at Canfranc. Perhaps our officers were coming by car; far safer than rail considering the merchandise they were carrying.

In fairly good mood, therefore, I invited Señor L., the Falange Captain, the French Commissaire of Police and, of course, Morozewicz to a good dinner liberally seasoned with wine and brandy. We had a wonderful time and before we realised it, it was daylight. God knows how they knew, but I could swear that they all called me 'Major'! The Falange Captain stated that the Falange were pro-Polish; Señor L. promised to facilitate everything, while the French Police Commissaire declared that he was anti-German and swore passionately, '*Mon Commandant, à vos ordres, je fais tout.*'

The dinner party was fairly expensive but paid back dividends, and from then onwards Señor L. was known as 'Louis'. The people from Madrid failed to arrive. I returned to France with Morozewicz without accomplishing my mission. All I had to show for it were some good friends on the Spanish border.

At Bedous, the first railway station in France, the same two gendarmes checked my papers. One asked the reason for my journey. I replied that this could only be known to the officer who signed it and to myself. The gendarme saluted and handed back my travel pass. I had no idea then that my impromptu remark would render me a great future service. We alighted there and Morozewicz introduced me to an eighty-year-old Basque, a hotel proprietor, who was completely trustworthy and could be used in emergency situations. TUDOR was dismayed at the result of my journey. I asked him to make a strong protest to London but, as they failed to reply, we never knew the real reason why Madrid had failed us. One thing I did know, I had to bloody well finance our Intelligence service!

Our contacts with the International Brigade brought us in touch with the Catalan Separatist Organisation aiming at an independent Catalonia. I discovered their sentimental connection with Poland, which they regarded as a symbol of freedom, and was deeply moved when they showed me their newspaper with a picture of the Black Madonna of Czestochowa. I used them to send TUDOR's pouch to our Madrid Embassy and, as its arrival remained unconfirmed, we surmised that it had either been lost or had fallen into the wrong hands. We later discovered that the courier was recognised by a fascist on the train and had thrown the parcel out of the window. It was found by the Catalans and delivered safely to our Embassy but we could not afford to take a similar risk again.

When, in January 1941, Mrs Januszewska (a member of our group) was leaving for London with TUDOR's pouch, I gave her a note and a souvenir for Louis. At our meeting in London in 1943, she recounted how delighted she was with Louis, who had dealt with her customs formalities extremely quickly, very politely, without checking her suitcases, and how very happy he was with his new gold Parker fountain pen. In early March 1941, TUDOR moved to Villa Mimosa, taking the radio station and the Dulembas with him. The villa could have been under surveillance and our contacts became more sporadic.

I mentioned Bartek before. He was the only Czech I knew who became a fully fledged member of our group, speaking perfect Polish and indistinguishable from any of us. He was a real live wire, exceptionally intelligent and cunning, very friendly with a variety of officials and the police (especially Marcel Dubois), with the knack of appearing to be everywhere at the same time. He was always the first to report the arrests of our men on the cargo ships and always the first to help with their release. Through him I made contact with the Czech Consul in Marseilles. As a member of the Czech Social Democrat Party, he had many friends among the German socialists who were refugees in Marseilles. They had contacts among their relations, sympathisers and friends in the German bureaucracy and the German armed services who provided him with valuable information. In brief, within a short space of time he became our most valuable colleague.

TUDOR, however, did not have much confidence in him and was surprised at our friendship. Nevertheless, Bartek, aware of the problem of forwarding TUDOR's Intelligence pouch, reported to me that his friend, the Secretary of the Yugoslav Consulate, regularly sent their diplomatic pouch to Lisbon and would not be averse to adding one small packet to it. He arranged a meeting, we came to a mutual understanding, and our Intelligence documents were able to reach our Lisbon Embassy – an arrangement that lasted until the German invasion of Yugoslavia and the closing of their Marseilles Consulate.

In December 1940, Bartek discovered a German refugee being hunted by the Gestapo – a talented engineer who had designed a revolutionary new gyroscopic bomb-sight. Without any financial means of support, he was being kept alive by the other refugees. Bartek would find out whether he would co-operate and provide us with a general description of his device, which could be appraised by our experts in London. In the meantime, we would take him under our wing. The description was radioed to London and we also sent in TUDOR's pouch. A positive reply was received in March 1941, with a request that he be delivered to the British Embassy in Madrid. A few days later he was smuggled over the frontier into Spain.

Towards the end of December 1940, Bartek brought me extraordinary information concerning the transport by sea to Tripolitania of crack German Panzer units, trained and commanded by Rommel. I immediately reported this to TUDOR who discarded it. However, I advised Bartek to obtain the names or numbers of the divisions and their exact route to North Africa. In January 1941, our indefatigable Czech brought new details. The convoy had left southern Italy under cover of darkness, crossed the Straits of Sicily, and was proceeding up the Tunisian coast to Tripoli.

He repeated this information, adding fresh details each time, which could now be tied up with WALENTY's earlier reports of

German armoured units training on the sandy dunes of northern France. The pieces were falling into place. I was convinced that Bartek's reports were accurate and that we were dealing with a powerful German Army on its way to Africa.

I tried to convince TUDOR that the information should be sent to London immediately, and that he was taking a great responsibility on himself by not informing them. Reluctantly, around mid-February 1941, he started sending them radio messages (without, however, showing them to me), but there was no confirmation that they had been received. This silence was unusual since it was a well-established practice that all messages from the field to HQ were answered. After a few weeks of continual silence I was completely baffled, while TUDOR was convinced that the information had proved false and had been discarded. He let me know, in no uncertain terms, that he greatly regretted having allowed himself to be pressurised by me.

On 1 April 1941, the morning editions of the French press reported the British defeat at Agheila in Tripolitania. A British Army communiqué stated that, under pressure of German armoured divisions, their forces had withdrawn from the Libyan town of Agheila. I went to TUDOR's villa with the newspaper in my pocket. He grinned broadly, giving me the impression that he had also heard the news, disappeared into another room and emerged handing me London's reply. The radio message, dated 30 March 1941, stated that 'according to the information available to the War Office, there is no evidence of the presence of any larger German armoured units in Libya, there might be the presence of one German brigade only.' I showed him the newspaper; he was stunned. I told him, 'The information was correct. If I were you, I'd ask the War Office who pushed the British out!' I knew that he would never send such a message.

It took me nearly ten years to discover the reason for the delay in answering TUDOR's messages concerning the movements of the Afrika Korps. Churchill in his war memoirs related that 'our intelligence reports' from February 1941, regarding the 'arrival of German armoured formations and aircraft in Tripolitania' alarmed the Chiefs of Staff, who sent General Wavell (the British commander) a message. Wavell stated in his reply, dated 2 March 1941, that there was no evidence of large-scale German reinforcements to Tripolitania, which were 'estimated at maximum of one armoured brigade group'. During March the evidence increased and on the 26th the Prime Minister telegraphed a personal message to Wavell, who, in his reply of 27 March, again reaffirmed the lack of evidence.

Probably London had only answered TUDOR's messages after receiving Wavell's final reply. Ironically this reached us at a time when Wavell, attacked by Rommel at Agheila, was in total retreat from Cyrenaica almost back to the Egyptian border. If TUDOR had sent the information earlier, and immediate counteraction could have been effected, the whole course of the war might have been changed. This may serve as a classic example of a failure of perception, illustrating the consequences of not acting on Intelligence at the right time.

Soon afterwards, Bartek brought us equally extraordinary information. The Germans were transporting small submarine parts by rail and assembling them at French Atlantic ports. These pocket U-boats would operate in 'wolf pack' formations supported by a normal submarine (code name 'Mother'), which would act as a floating depot supplying them with fuel and torpedoes. It introduced totally new tactics into submarine warfare, using vessels hitherto unknown to us, and confirmed WALENTY's reports of mysterious crates arriving at French ports. After a long delay, London's reply to TUDOR stated that according to the British Admiralty the information was false since such operations could not be performed successfully on the high seas.

A few months later, immediately prior to my departure to Algiers, we heard of the heavy Allied losses in the Battle of the North Atlantic. TUDOR received an urgent message from London ordering him to supply plans of the German pocket U-boats in the shortest possible time, regardless of expense. Unfortunately most of Bartek's friends who had provided him with the original information had already left Marseilles. In any case, their own contacts inside Germany or in the German armed forces had been

transferred or had disappeared. In other words, his contacts had
been broken off, his source of information had been lost and the
data was now virtually unobtainable. I never knew whether TUDOR
was successful as I left Europe for North Africa.

Bartek also provided us with confidential political and economic
data on the mobilisation of French industry for the needs of the
Wehrmacht. This reached us just after the secret conferences of
the German High Command in Paris, and in most cases appeared
in the French press a few months later as decrees of the Vichy
Government.

6

THE SECOND JOURNEY TO CANFRANC AND THE END OF MY EVACUATION WORK

TUDOR unexpectedly visited me in early April 1941. London had ordered him to collect US $50,000 and cipher books from our Madrid people. As the meeting would be held at Canfranc, he obviously wanted me to accompany him. In the event I agreed, and hoped that it would be more successful than on the previous occasion. This time, however, it would be even more difficult. TUDOR did not have the necessary travel documents and mine had expired the previous December. What we needed very badly was a plausible excuse.

Dulemba, our first radio operator, had passed through Spain (disguised as a priest) and reached Britain. His wife, now pregnant, had all the necessary visas and was awaiting her departure. Agreeing to act as our cover, she arranged for it to coincide with our rendezvous at Canfranc. TUDOR, never missing an opportunity, made her carry his pouch.

Our plan was simple. Mrs Dulemba would appear so weak that two men would have to accompany her during the complicated part of her journey, namely at Canfranc. This seemed fairly convincing, especially when one of them was her 'brother'. The only other 'genuine' things missing were the travel documents. My deputy, Major Mizgier-Chojnacki, suggested half-jokingly that he would issue us with the necessary documents. He gave each of us a pass to Carpiagni issued by the Franco-Polish Friendship Society at 'Labour Battalion no. 25' on the assumption that its enormous official stamp would be sufficient to take us both to Spain and back!

We met at Marseilles station and bought tickets to Toulouse. TUDOR and I arrived on the platform by shinning over a wall (thus dodging the gendarmes) while Mrs Dulemba entered in the more conventional way. I took a very nice radio set which TUDOR would present to Louis in the hope that it would facilitate Mrs Dulemba's custom formalities, help her to board the Madrid train and allow TUDOR to slip her his Intelligence pouch. I would stop over at Bedous and wait for TUDOR at the old Basque's hotel. If he made contact, we would return to Marseilles the following day. Otherwise he would stay at the hotel and I would try my luck.

As arranged, Korwin-Szymanowski met us on the platform at Toulouse station with the tickets to Canfranc. There were an unusually large number of soldiers and police at Pau – apparently Pétain had visited the town the previous day, but fortunately the alert was now over. After a farewell to Mrs Dulemba and a 'good luck' to TUDOR, I alighted at Bedous and immediately made for the exit. The gendarmes did not check my papers, I heard the train move off for Canfranc and, without looking back, went straight to the old Basque's hotel.

While waiting for TUDOR, I brooded on our situation and what could go wrong; everything depended on luck and chance. His sudden arrival, considerably earlier than expected, dispersed my thoughts. He was pale, visibly shaken and breathless: 'I was arrested and searched by the Spaniards. Nobody came from Madrid; you needn't go. It was a miracle that I got away!'

I made him sit down and have a brandy. It appeared that even at Bedous he had noticed the gendarmes pointing at me as I left the station, and he was convinced that I had been arrested. En route to Canfranc he had managed to convince the police that he was accompanying his sick, pregnant sister. After passing into the Spanish sector he had recognised Louis and handed him the radio but was arrested on the orders of the Falange captain for not having a Spanish entry visa.

The captain ordered a personal search. The pouch was in TUDOR's overcoat pocket ready to be handed to Mrs Dulemba. He took off his coat quickly and threw it over a chair. An official made a personal search and looked at his papers without touching the coat. He was ordered to say goodbye to his 'sister' and leave immediately. While embracing her 'brother' in a fond farewell, Mrs Dulemba, who had kept her composure throughout, slipped the pouch into her handbag. The officers from Madrid never came.

Let's see [I replied], I wasn't arrested and the officers could have arrived later since the exact time wasn't fixed. The officials I met are obviously still at their posts. I wasn't arrested or searched last time – far from it! I'll have to go and try my luck; meanwhile you stay here at the hotel. If I'm not back soon that means that I've either met the Madrid people or been arrested. If everything goes OK, I'll be on the first morning train. Get on it, and if you don't find me there notify London of my arrest!

At the railway station at Bedous I recognised the two gendarmes from my previous visit. While ordering a ticket to Canfranc, the booking office clerk told me, 'The phone call from Canfranc must have been from your friends who are waiting for you'. He let me use his telephone and I spoke to Popławski, who was awaiting my arrival. I told him I'd be on the next train and gave the booking clerk a generous tip.

The two gendarmes boarded the train as it departed. One entered my compartment, smiled, and I offered him a cigarette. He thanked me, saluted and, without looking at my papers, wished me good luck. A very strange development indeed!

In the Spanish sector at Canfranc Louis thanked me for the radio, without mentioning how he came by it. He invited me to the restaurant, where the Madrid people were waiting – Popławski and two other men. All three appeared nervous. Popławski pointed out someone who had been watching them closely since their arrival, who they suspected was a plain-clothes Gestapo agent. I told them not to worry, he would be reporting to us soon. It was only my French friend from my previous visit, the Commissaire of Police. He approached our table, shook my hand and exclaimed in a loud voice, 'I am very happy to see you here, mon Commandant!' I invited him to join us, which obviously surprised but greatly relieved my Madrid colleagues.

While our French guest was quietly sipping his drink, I treated them to a short lecture in Polish: 'Nothing will be achieved with one glass of brandy. If you want to have good future relations here you ought to invite all the station personnel to a good dinner!'

They promptly acted on my suggestion, and after the dinner party, with the French policeman, the Falange captain and, of course, Louis as the guests of honour, we retired to our hotel rooms where I received five cipher books and US $50,000 in mixed banknotes. Years of experience had taught me to be careful in situations inspiring one with a sense of false security. I noticed that one of my Madrid colleagues had an overcoat similar to mine. We swapped coats and he wore the one with the dollars and the cipher books. They would be exchanged again on the train in the morning, immediately before its departure.

Popławski told me in confidence what had prevented him from fulfilling his original orders and why he failed to contact us. He had established good relations with the Spanish police and had even arranged to pay them an agreed amount for evacuees passing through Spain. As soon as this was discovered by Ambassador Szumlakowski at our Madrid Embassy, he was forbidden to maintain contact with the Spanish police or with our organisation. Instead, he was immediately appointed to Polish Intelligence in Spain.

Popławski was aware of Szumlakowski's connection with extreme left-wing Polish elements during the Spanish Civil War when the latter was an envoy in Portugal. It looked as if the Spanish police had tightened their grip on the frontier, resulting in the mass arrests of our men, because of the non-fulfilment of Popławski's agreement. They regarded it as a double-cross. Polish evacuees were trying to get through Spain without paying their 'just' dues. It was also obvious why Szumlakowski had not helped our men in the camps. He wanted to avoid any involvement with the Spanish police and the Gestapo because of his previous Spanish and Portuguese connections.

My departure from Canfranc was a happy one. Louis, the French police commissaire and the three officers saw me off in style; the exchange of overcoats went unnoticed. The gendarmes on the train to Bedous asked whether my journey had been successful. I replied that I was very happy with its outcome – which was, of course, the absolute truth.

Being in a playful mood, I decided to play a little joke on TUDOR. I hid in a corner of the compartment and, unobserved, watched a worried-looking TUDOR gazing intently into the coaches as the train slowed down. Boarding my coach by accident he found me 'asleep'. His first words were, 'Did they come?'. I remarked sadly, 'We travelled hundreds of kilometres, exposed ourselves to danger, and what do we have to show for it?'

TUDOR, nervous and furious, launched into a string of invective, threatening to send a very sharp message to London. After I while, I added, 'Listen, there's a bottle of brandy in my coat pocket. Let's have a swig to cool ourselves down!' His face was a real study when, instead of a bottle, he pulled out the dollars and the cipher books. His obvious relief soon allowed him to forgive me my exuberance. Years later, well after the war, he would gleefully relate the same story whenever we met, with its unchanging refrain: 'I'll never forget how you took me for a ride!'

Our return trip to Marseilles was an uneventful and happy one. We concluded that our success lay in my first journey to Canfranc when I had valid travel documents. The gendarmes remembered my reply and were under the impression that I was someone very important in the service of France.

Our journey illustrates the difficulties facing agents in the field working on what appears, at first sight, to be a simple assignment. The officer issuing the order from the comparative safety of London had no conception of the conditions under which it would have to be fulfilled. He was unable to sense a dangerous situation, as he had probably never been in one himself. We had to travel hundreds of kilometres to execute our order, without documents, breaking the regulations of two police states. Only luck and favourable conditions permitted us to fulfil it without grave mishap. On arrival in Marseilles, we returned to our separate duties.

TUDOR told me that there were continual requests from London for information from French North Africa and, as yet, he had not received a single communication from Captain Tonn. Knowing Tonn to be a very conscientious officer, I was convinced that he must have encountered serious problems. Meanwhile, as my men were already there, and as I was familiar with the area through their reports, TUDOR thought that I should organise the North African Intelligence network myself.

He admitted that London had sent him the address of a retired English Major, ex-British Intelligence, now residing in Marseilles, and that he had contacted him. The Major had agreed, providing he received £100,000 in cash and at least a year in which to get organised, which the War office found 'unacceptable'. Realising his inability to run a North African network from Marseilles, TUDOR wanted to put my name forward as 'the only person capable of organising such work'. I gave a cautious and noncommittal reply.

On 1 May 1941, TUDOR handed me a message from London. I learned that as from that date I was nominated Chief of Intelligence Agency 'North Africa' ('Agency Africa'), and was ordered to proceed there to organise the network as soon as possible. The area of the new agency stretched from Dakar to the borders of Tripolitania. TUDOR would give me 500,000 francs, and the next financial allocation would come directly from London. I was to supply a codename and to inform them of my departure date. The next message would contain orders for my first Intelligence assignment. Thus ended the first message received in my new capacity. A happy TUDOR warmly congratulated me on my new appointment. He had rid himself of an enormous problem, while mine were only just beginning!

I saw General Kleeberg the next day. My deputy, Major Mizgier-Chojnacki, was the obvious choice as my successor. All our archives were transferred to him but for security reasons he preferred to have them destroyed. A final glance at the documentation, however, revealed that between June 1940 and May 1941 almost 3,000 men had been transferred to Britain where they joined the Polish forces.

My successor was warned that financial management was his

most difficult problem, and to guard against all sorts of pressures and favouritism. I suggested employing a totally fictitious character, 'Colonel Hugo', sent from London to replace 'Dr Skowroński', who had been recalled. 'Colonel Hugo' would be working incognito and in complete secrecy, with Major Mizgier-Chojnacki acting as his representative. Thus all responsibility for refusing dubious requests would be borne by the Colonel. Curiously, his arrival was accepted as a true fact, and there were even people who admitted knowing him rather well!

Fearing gossip above all, I disappeared from Marseilles. Preparing at home, and looking back over the past year, I realised how badly the Polish Government had organised the evacuation. Attempts were made after the war to create the impression that it ran to a specified plan. In reality, Jankowski's cryptic comment, 'chaos and escape', was a considerably more realistic assessment.

7

A CHANGE OF WORK

On 1 May 1941, returning home from TUDOR with London's radio message in my pocket, I knew that a new chapter of my life was about to begin. They had handed me an enormous task – total responsibility for building up an extensive network from scratch, in a vast territory, completely on my own, and in the shortest possible time. Obviously outside help could not be expected; in any case, it had not been mentioned in the message. All I could rely on was my own initiative and luck.

Gradually a plan took hazy shape. It was imperative to obtain permission to leave France. Only then could the other problems be tackled. I confided to Sophie, my closest comrade, that my departure must be secret. It would have to appear that 'Dr Skowroński' had been recalled to London; our appearances in town and contacts would have to be avoided and we should move to another address.

Up to now my stay in the 'free zone' had been illegal. The only papers that could establish my identity were an old Polish officer's identity card and the passport I had issued to myself at our Toulouse Consulate about a year ago. This state of affairs caused Sophie to perform miracles in procuring ration cards, without which life would have been impossible in France.

The year 1941, in fact, brought a further deterioration in the conditions of everyday life, with a drop in industrial and agricultural production. Rationing had been introduced to cover all essential commodities and there were long queues at restaurants. The problem of buying food and drink was a superhuman task, especially for our soirées, which were an essential aspect of our contact-making activities. The black market was dangerous – one could easily be arrested, with unforeseen consequences. The large number of plain-clothes police on the streets on the look-out for Gaullist sympathisers made even harmless conversations dangerous and created a tense atmosphere.

We found a flat in a house with two entrances in a busy street in Marseilles. Our former acquaintances confirmed that Dr Skowroński had left for London. Only TUDOR and my successor, Major Mizgier, visited us. Leaving Bartek in Marseilles was a great wrench but he was an invaluable source of information to them. France was his natural hunting ground and, besides, he had no contacts in North Africa. I felt guilty about concealing my departure from him but it was safer to work to the old dictum, 'The less people know, the better.' My plan was based on a legal departure with all the necessary permission granted. At the moment, though, I didn't even possess a French identity card. The authorities in the 'free zone' had all Polish officers on their demob files and issued them with green identity cards carrying the obligation to report twice monthly to the local police station. I had hitherto managed to conceal my presence in France but my clandestine status was now hindering me. In order to leave France legally, I would be compelled to legalise my stay. The irreplaceable Bartek fixed it all up with his pals in the police. Within days a green identity card was officially stamped '1 June 1941' during my first-ever visit to a French police station. I then discussed with TUDOR how he could supply me with London's radio messages relating to my future work in North Africa.

My plans were prepared according to the order of priorities. First was the question of my safe arrival in North Africa; its solution would influence the rest of my actions. Second, independent and uninterrupted radio contact with London, technically difficult, was an absolute necessity. Then, of course, I had to acquire some knowledge (however superficial) of the vast territory in which we would be operating.

London's radio messages only indicated the nature of the tasks to be fulfilled, and were orders of a strictly military nature, e.g. identification of units, military garrisons and commanders of all the armed services presently in French North Africa (no. 1786). They also supplied me with a French Order of Battle prepared by British Intelligence which was somewhat out of date. One message urgently sought the proposed codename of my new agency, which would be a closely guarded secret between Central Office and myself; another concerned radio linkage (3512). In all they totalled twenty-five.

Legalising my departure was vital in order to minimise the risk of being arrested while carrying a great deal of cash and incriminating documents. If I made an illegal entry into French North Africa without proper documents, the shadow of arrest would always be hanging over me. It would deprive me of the opportunity to obtain adequate cover, without which I would be unable to justify my stay there. Cover could only be decided on after my arrival in Algiers and after exploring the local possibilities.

To leave France legally for French North Africa one required: (a) a French exit visa issued by the Prefecture; (b) landing permission for Tunisia, Algeria or Morocco issued by the respective French colonial authority; (c) agreement by the Italo-German Armistice Commission to leave France. The last was the most essential, and the Commission were against allowing males between eighteen and forty-five to travel to French North Africa. Added difficulties arose from the personal whims of the German members of the Commission; even after obtaining all the relevant documents, permission could still be refused.

The first obstacles were the French prefectures and the Vichy authorities. Łubieński was to report to me in Marseilles on my chances of obtaining a French exit visa. He had frequently hinted that he wanted to work with me even if it meant going abroad. His personality and journalistic abilities made him ideal. I therefore took him into my confidence and asked him to accompany me to Africa.

In order to lessen the suspicion that might arise from Łubieński's sudden departure from Vichy France, I suggested he spread the news among his friends that he wanted to write a book about French

North Africa. He should also obtain from his French friends all the information he could about their acquaintances in North Africa, including their political affiliations, and get them to provide letters of recommendation, which would be of great value.

His colleague, Jordan-Rozwadowski, also wanted to work with us and would have no trouble getting into Algeria; General Weygand, the Governor General, had been a family friend since 1920. On 24 May, therefore, a radio message was sent to London with a request to confirm them both as Intelligence Officers of Agency Africa.

Browsing through the cipher book for a possible cryptonym for the agency and myself, I accidentally spotted the word 'RYGOR' which seemed highly appropriate. Yes, I thought, in my new agency rigour must prevail!

Linkage from North Africa to Central Office was discussed by radio with London. As yet, however, we had neither a radio nor an operator, and I had no real idea of local conditions. According to Central Office, contact would be maintained by WICHER until we set up our own station in Algiers.

WICHER was the cryptonym of a clandestine radio intelligence outpost at Uzès, near Nîmes in southern France, headed by Lieutenant-Colonel Langer. He had been my colleague at the Higher Military Academy in Warsaw, and became chief of BS (Biuro Szyfrów – Cipher Bureau) of the Polish General Staff. Its function was to monitor and decipher radio traffic. I met him again in Paris in early 1940 but at that time knew little about his work.

After the fall of France in June 1940, this Franco-Polish centre, formerly located at Gretz near Paris, continued to operate in the free zone in total secrecy and isolation. Only one leading high-up Vichy official, Colonel Rivet, the head of Vichy's Intelligence Service, knew of its existence, and he protected it from the French collaborationists.

Part of Colonel Langer's unit was transferred to Algiers in autumn 1940, with Major Maximilian Ciężki as its head. This then was the secret Polish radio link that began working soon after the French collapse and, unknown to the French, would now be used as a means of communication between Agency Africa and London.

I was to supply Major Ciężki in Algiers with ciphered messages, which he would then transmit to WICHER in southern France, who, in turn, would radio them to London. The same operation was reversed for messages intended for our Agency in North Africa. This type of radio link would cease once our own radio station became operational.

I discussed the composition of our Intelligence Department in London with TUDOR. It was vital for me to know who ran our Central Intelligence Office and who, therefore, would be my chief. I discovered that Colonel Stanisław Gano (STANISŁAW) was the head of our Military Intelligence (the Second Bureau), while I received my immediate orders from Major Jan Żychoń (codename JANIO), the director of Secret Intelligence. I knew neither of them personally.

TUDOR had the radio transmitter prior to my departure, which had to serve us both. We discussed more efficient methods of co-operation. Despatching my Intelligence material was most important. I anticipated that, with the development of the Agency, certain documents, such as bulky reports, confirmation of short radioed signals and plans, would have to be delivered to London by secret pouch. I would send them to TUDOR through merchant seamen on the Algiers–Marseilles run or other reasonably reliable individuals who happened to be travelling there. This was not a particularly satisfactory arrangement but it would have to suffice temporarily.

TUDOR handed over to me two of his Intelligence Officers – Lieutenants Jekiel and Rombejko. Jekiel was keen to work in Casablanca and wanted to take his agent Dr Marion Gallois (codename GYNAECOLOGIST) with him and open a doctor's surgery as a cover. Jekiel's contacts could easily provide him with a French passport while Gallois, as a Frenchman, would have no problems whatsoever. I knew the second officer, Rombejko, from my prewar service in the USSR, where he had been employed as a minor official and Intelligence 'technician' at our Moscow Embassy. Agency Africa needed someone with technical knowledge. Furthermore, Rombejko was married to a French woman, a Breton countess, whose relations resided in Algiers, which could be very useful to us.

Since Major Wysoczański had been sent to French North Africa in December 1940, reports from the commanders of the evacuation outposts had failed to reach us. Thus my knowledge of current conditions in these French territories, especially local attitudes towards Vichy's collaborationist policies, was meagre. As an introduction I bought the *Guides Bleues* to French North Africa and then began a more detailed study of its administrative and political divisions, its ethnic composition and its economy. As I pored over the maps, concentrating especially on the industrial areas, mines and ports, road and rail communications, a picture of French North Africa gradually grew in my mind.

An important aspect was that Morocco, Algeria and Tunisia each had a separate currency, valid only in that country. I therefore asked TUDOR to hand over to me the funds earmarked for my Agency, in order to change it gradually into North African currencies. The total amount was rather large, and changing it suddenly would have been highly suspicious.

In early June 1941, Łubieński invited me to Vichy to attend his wedding to Marta Biskupska, who had been a courier in our evacuation organisation. I went there with General Kleeberg, who was also one of the guests. Discussing our future assignment, Łubieński said that a French higher civil servant had told him that I would not be allowed into French North Africa. As for himself, he was promised a visa for 'a journalist to collect material for a book', and had also obtained letters of introduction to various influential people in Algeria and Tunisia who were secret Gaullists. Although I was pleased with his success, the information concerning my own chances was depressing. It was not going to be as easy as I had thought.

I returned home in a very pessimistic mood, seriously doubting my chances of ever getting there. Then Sophie suddenly reminded me of Marcel Dubois. We agreed that she should write to Lucienne, Marcel's wife, complaining about the harsh conditions in Marseilles and expressing our desire to join them in Morocco. Within a very few days a telegram arrived: 'Entry visas to Morocco for all the family under the no. 8126 were sent to Prefecture in Marseilles on

16/6/1941, a letter on the way, Marcel.' I took this as a good omen, but there was even more earth-shaking news to come.

On 22 June, while queueing for the cigarette ration, I saw the morning headlines: 'Germany declares war on the USSR – German Army and Air Force destroy Red Army troops – enormous number of prisoners and war equipment taken'. I was shaken to the depths. At last the world's two greatest criminals were at each other's throats! I had no idea how this new situation would affect the French attitude towards Pétain's collaborationist policies or its consequences for French North Africa.

A week later, inquiring at the local Prefecture about my French exit and Moroccan visas, I showed the telegram to an official who could not remember receiving any information from Rabat. He asked me who 'Marcel' was. I replied in deadpan fashion that 'Monsieur Marcel' was the Deputy Head of the Service Securité Publique at Rabat. The official suddenly became more polite and decided to check again. Returning with some papers, he looked even more bemused and told me that he had just received entry visas for two adults and a young man. As for the exit visas, we would require permission from the Ministry of the Interior.

A few days later we received our exit visas, and a radio message was sent to London informing them of my departure for French North Africa. We would leave during the second week of July 1941.

8

THE JOURNEY TO ALGIERS –
FIRST STEPS THERE

Passenger crossings to Algiers were infrequent and I was advised to book immediately for the first available date on the *Ville d'Oran*, a fast and comfortable ship. Sophie and George would join me in Algiers in a month's time, giving me the opportunity to organise our household. They would go to Nice for a holiday, breaking contact with our acquaintances in Marseilles, and then leave immediately for Algiers. Mizgier would take over our flat in Marseilles. Łubieński reported that he was ready to leave and I booked two adjoining cabins for 19 July.

Cook's would notify me in advance when to submit my passport. My entry visa, issued in Rabat, was valid only for Morocco, which was stated as the country of final destination. London had, however, ordered that Agency Africa's HQ should be in Algiers, presumably because of its geographical position. This would be complicated, and I would have to plan my next step on arrival there.

Customs inspection in Algiers was causing me considerable anxiety. French acquaintances, asked discreetly, all gave the same answer – some had to undergo a body search while others just went straight through. I would be carrying roughly 400,000 French francs plus a considerable amount of Algerian and Moroccan currency. Even more dangerous were the cipher books and London's messages with their Intelligence tasks. My arrest, with all that incriminating evidence, would not only be disastrous for our future work in North Africa and the Polish network in France but would also expose Marcel Dubois to grave consequences. Unfortunately, there was no other way out; I would just have to take the risk.

TUDOR was informed of our departure date, as were all Agency Africa's officers – they would receive my orders through him. On 5 July Cook's confirmed our reservations and told me to submit my passport and identity card. The Łubieńskis arrived the following day and would board the ship separately. TUDOR at long last gave me Major Ciężki's address in Algiers (Hotel Arago, no. 6 Arago Street) and his 'new' name (Monsieur Miller). I reserved a room there by telegram while the Łubieńskis booked into another hotel on the Boulevard Briand.

While I was collecting my passport from the Prefecture on the 12th, the official told me that my wife could collect her visas any time she wished One sensed that he was being considerably more polite than usual.

Meanwhile, on 1 and 15 July I reported to the Special Commissariat of the Gendarmerie. During my first visit they made an error and put '1 June' on my identity card. This was immediately corrected but it was to cause an unpleasant incident later on in Algiers. After my final visit there on 15 July, I changed my name on the card (and on my passport) from 'Słowikowski' to 'Stowikowski' before handing it to Cook's. Possibly the Gestapo were unaware of my real name. Nevertheless this slight precaution would not do any harm.

Cook's obtained all the necessary permissions at the Commissariat Special du Port without my obligatory presence, thus sparing me a thorough scrutiny by the Gestapo. The 18th was spent on a final check on my luggage. At 18.30 on the 19th, after farewells to Sophie, George and the Zarembskis, the *Ville d'Oran* departed southwards carrying me into the unknown.

An indefinable sensation grew inside me, my agitation subsided and I became calm, even happy. I was sailing to the continent of my childhood dreams but under very different circumstances from those I could have imagined. On deck, as land disappeared slowly from view, I suddenly knew that I would never see my own country again.

In my cabin I succumbed to further meditation. I have always been someone who deeply believes in fate. So far my good luck had spared me. During the war with Russia in 1920, in Soviet prisons, and elsewhere in my life, my escapes from danger appeared as if guided by an invisible hand. The last time was a car crash in Marseilles, with Marcel driving, when we hit a wall head-on at top speed. We emerged unscathed. The crash bound us closer together and, as a result, I was now safely on my way to Algiers. Wasn't there a touch of providence, somewhere, in all this?

Lying in bed that night, I resumed my meditation. Not knowing the real conditions in North Africa, I would not plan anything for the future. Otherwise it would only be a fantasy, devoid of realism. First I would need to create cover, then all the rest would emerge. After all, the old English major wanted over a year to get organised so one shouldn't expect miracles. Perhaps I could do a lot better. Much would depend on any help received from Central Office. The steady and monotonous rocking of the boat at last brought me sleep.

I awoke early, dressed hurriedly and went on deck. It was daybreak, with not a living soul to be seen. Somewhere in the East the sky began to redden imperceptibly, and its colour reflected a tranquil sea as if in a crystal plate, refracting the rays of a rising red ball. The ball grew in volume, changed colour from blood-red to gold, and finally remained silver. The sea now sparkled with billions of lights, so strong that it was blinding. All this marvellous apparition lasted less than half an hour.

The beauty of the sea reminded me of the journey Sophie and I had made from Odessa to Sevastopol on the Soviet ship SS *Abhazia* in February 1939. What a difference between those two seas! The Black Sea waters moved from dark green to indigo and black. The sight of the black-green waves furiously striking against the ship filled one with anxiety and fear. The fathomless mysterious depths induced a feeling of dread. Here, the Mediterranean had the blue of the sky under the sun, evoking calm and the sheer joy of being alive. The other passengers emerged on deck, including the Łubieńskis. I teased them for sleeping during such a beautiful sunrise. But what can you expect from a newly married couple?

Still the sea gave the impression of a huge lake, without even the slightest ripple, and so it remained throughout our journey. All Sunday except for meals (which we fell on as if half-starved) was spent soaking up the sun. I repacked my suitcases. Customs officials usually looked at the bottom for suspicious objects. The messages from London were hidden in my French books (among which were the cipher books), and placed on top. My camera, spare film and field glasses went to the bottom. I kept my small Browning automatic pistol in my pocket. Worn out by exposure to the sea air and the sun, I fell asleep immediately.

The next day, Monday, 21 July, through the bluish haze one could make out distant lights twinkling like small stars, far above the horizon. As the boat came closer to shore, the fog began dispersing and one could see Algiers, its whiteness dazzling, descending in large steps to the sea and the port. Far on the right, high up, one could see a beautiful church, the Basilica of Our Lady of Africa. Nearer were the slender turrets of the minarets, while the entire town appeared to be dominated by Fort Empereur with its tall obelisk, monument to the fallen soldiers of the African Army. The green of parks and squares was everywhere, contrasting with the whiteness of the town. I stood on deck, apprehensive.

A motor boat carrying the pilot and the port police sped to the ship. Loudspeakers ordered the foreigners to report, documents ready, to the second-class drawing-room. There were only five of us – the Łubieńskis, myself and two others. Some civilian officials entered, recognisable as German and Italian members of the Armistice Commission. A Frenchman approached our group asking for passports and identity cards. Keeping my documents, he said, 'Your identity card is not in order. I am compelled to detain you. You must go to the office of the port police!' Inquiring about my luggage, I was told sharply, 'There's no need to worry. It won't get lost. You'll get it back!' Łubieński, who was supposed to meet me at my hotel at 4pm, looked surprised and deeply worried. It was 8am.

I was left alone in a small room and told to wait. Through the windows I could see my fellow passengers leaving the port. The gendarme's words nagged at me: 'Your identity card is not in order!'

Was it my change of name? Had I altered it too clumsily? As time passed, all sorts of doubts began to assail me. Were they waiting for information from Marseilles? After three hours, my nerves were nearing exhaustion point. My luggage kept creeping into my mind. Surely they must have found everything by now? I tried to keep calm and prepare myself for the inevitable questioning, reminding myself that I had been in much more dangerous situations. Gazing through the window at the ship, I saw that the sun was already high in the sky; the heat was unbearable. My watch showed noon.

At that moment the Commissaire entered holding my passport and identity card. It's going to begin, I thought. Approaching, he said, 'I beg your pardon for such a long detention. Everything is, of course, in order. You reported to the Gendarmerie on 15 July so the correction of the date on the 1st in your card is irrelevant. You are free to go, Monsieur.'

Collecting my wits after the sudden anticlimax, I replied, 'If I'd known what it was all about, I could have explained on the ship.' He then asked me whether I knew Yugoslavia, as he had served in Belgrade before the war, liked the country very much and had friends there. He was delighted when I replied in Serbian (his own was quite good), was very pleased to have met me, and wished me 'bon voyage' to Morocco. For my part, I would sooner have made his acquaintance under different circumstances.

I rushed to the customs office. All the passengers had gone through, and the customs men, having nothing to do, might have been tempted to look at my suitcases, if only out of boredom. I braced myself for a new encounter. My suitcases stood in the middle of the office, which was deserted. An elderly cleaner brandishing a broom asked whether they were mine: 'They told me to wait for you. Please take them away, Monsieur, so that I can close the place for the day'.

No need for her to repeat herself. Although my luggage was heavy, I positively flew through the exit, only stopping to rest a good twenty yards away from the gate. I was soaked with sweat. The heat, the weight of my suitcases and nervous exhaustion had finally taken their toll.

Suddenly, as if from nowhere, a hazy shadow appeared in front of my sweat-smarting eyes. It was a young Arab porter. I asked him for a taxi. Instead, he wanted to know my destination and on hearing 'Hotel Arago', advised me to walk with him as it was very near the port. So it was, and in about ten minutes we were there. My room, no. 4, awaited me on the first floor. The young Arab brought the suitcases. I gave him a large tip and after a few minutes I was alone.

Covered with perspiration, I locked the door, removed my clothes and threw myself on the bed. The terrible heat, to which I was unaccustomed even though I had lived in Marseilles, finished me off completely. I only had a hazy recollection of a very narrow escape. After resting, washing (there was no shower in the room) and putting on lighter clothes, I searched the room thoroughly and found a safe place to hide the papers, ciphers and money, keeping only the Algerian currency on me. The *Guide Bleue* advised me to lunch at the Café Etoile on Rue Isly.

Algiers descends towards the sea in the form of terraces, shaped like a huge amphitheatre, rising to the south-west and descending to the north-east. The little streets, parallel to the sea, are on different levels and connected by stone steps. Others rise to the top by large or small serpentines. I gravitated towards the centre of the town. The Arab women in their long white flowing robes, smouldering eyes peeping out of their veils, were mysterious and attractive. The Arab men, on the other hand, were dressed in European style except for a fez, and were frequently ragged. In the area situated between the Embankments and Rue Isly, mainly populated with small Moslem grocery shops, the crowds, clamour and heat were terrific. The nearer to the centre, the more Europeans could be observed. Rue Isly resembled Marseilles except that the shops and big stores, full of goods, had low prices and ration cards were not needed.

Since leaving the hotel I noticed that I was being regarded with curiosity, particularly when walking through the centre of town. I suddenly realised that the men wore short-sleeved shirts, while I was dressed *à la marseillaise* and wore a sun helmet. It was a sharp reminder of how important a knowledge of even the most trivial social customs are in Intelligence work. I immediately bought all that was necessary to pass myself off as an ordinary European resident, and continued my stroll.

After a magnificent meal at the Café Etoile, I gave the waiter a generous tip to establish myself as a regular. Returning to the hotel by a different route, I familiarised myself with the cafés and bars. The suitcases had not been touched and my hiding place was intact. Tired out, I fell asleep.

Łubieński arrived late at exactly 5pm. He was convinced that I had been arrested and had himself been subjected to a thorough search. Fearing a trap, he had been uneasy about meeting me at the hotel. We discussed the situation. The Polish official representation in French North Africa included two Consulates – in Algeria, the General Consulate at Algiers with Mr Friedrich as the General Consul; in Morocco, an Honorary Consulate in Casablanca with a Frenchman, M. Thor, as the Consul. Recently, there was a representative of the Polish Government in Algiers – Count Hutten-Czapski.

I told Łubieński that I would not report to the Consulate; my presence was to remain unknown, and should not be discussed with anyone. Tomorrow he should visit Consul Friedrich, explain why he was in Africa (along the lines that we agreed), and try to learn anything about the Polish colony, their organisations and leading personalities, as well as anything concerning the Frenchmen to whom he had letters of introduction, their attitudes and social positions, to determine whether they were worth contacting. I also wondered whether the Consul knew about our evacuation work and whether there were any officers engaged on it in Algiers.

The latter was particularly important if my presence was to remain secret. In the meantime I wanted to familiarise myself with the port and the town before starting work and he and Martha should do the same. We should not be seen together in town. In conversations with casual acquaintances false names and addresses should be given. Such conversations should be conducted so as to extract the maximum personal and general information without revealing one's own views. We would meet again tomorrow evening.

Around 6pm I went for a stroll in the direction of the port, following the Boulevards Carnot and de la République up to Government Square. I gazed at the buildings – the magnificent Hotel Aletti with its casino, the Banque d'Alger, the so-called Assemblée Algérienne and the offices of various shipping companies – until I reached Government Square through the built-up area, where pillars following the pavement protected it from the sun. Opposite there was a magnificent view of the sea, the port, the railway station and the streets below. Beneath were huge warehouses. Sloping roads, stairs and large lifts connected the boulevards with the streets at a lower level and with the port.

The *Ville d'Oran*, on which I had arrived, was leaving the harbour and returning to Marseilles, which gave me a strange feeling. This last symbol of Europe was disappearing, emphasising my isolation and the realisation that I was now trapped in North Africa. Leaning against the balustrade, I had a view of the entire port, la Gare Maritime and the Admiralty. To the right, far away but visible, was Port Agha and Mustapha, the huge merchant port with its many docks. One could also see the marvellous, huge bay of Algiers screened from the south-east by Cap Matifou and from the north-west by Point Pascade.

At the Café-Restaurant Terminus on the corner of Boulevard Carnot and Briand Square, one met a totally different type of Arab – the Arab aristocracy: sheiks and kaids decorated with French medals. They were in their beautiful multi-coloured national costumes, embroidered in gold and with turbans, which reminded me of the historic dresses of the Polish nobility. These Arabs, moustached and frequently blond, gave one the impression of old Sarmatian figures. Doubtless, the costumes of the Polish nobility were strongly influenced by the Islamic Mediterranean.

I remained in the café for some time, observing the military men and the other habitués and memorising the army badges and regimental numbers. Late in the evening, on my return to the hotel, tired out after a hectic day, I soon fell into a deep sleep.

9

ALGIERS: PREPARATIONS AND THE CASBAH

On 22 July 1941, my first full day in Algiers, I took a tram ride across town to look at the Government buildings and the barracks at the Place de General Sarrail, Place Bab El Oued, d'Orlean and le Fort Empereur. Afterwards I scanned the local French newspapers, making notes on military and political items. What a difference from the Soviet press in Kiev! There, even the most trivial military information was designated by letters, e.g. 'MN' regiment or 'NN' town, while factories appeared as numbers rather than names. Here, many names and details were given. What an Intelligence feast – I would save a great deal of time.

Łubieński reported at 9pm. His conversation with our Consul had been useful. There was a large Polish community in Algiers with a chairman, Lucian Godziszewski, an elderly lawyer, who apparently enjoyed very good relations with the local administration and the police. Due to his efforts in 1940, a large group of Polish families was brought here from Romania. As for the French personalities, some were not worth approaching because of their political views, while the others could be seen later on. First, he wanted to call upon M. Malvy, a senior civil servant at the Prefecture, of whom the Polish Consul had a very favourable opinion. Regarding our officers engaged in evacuation work, Gordon and Krzesimowski were here; the others had left for Morocco. I advised him to visit M. Malvy at the Prefecture tomorrow, and also call on Chairman Godziszewski.

I wanted to devote the following day to analysing how an Intelligence network could be set up over an area as vast as French

North Africa. Obviously, only those who appeared respectable would find doors open to them. Becoming a businessman would be my best cover – not easy, however, as any commercial or industrial venture would have to have a large initial capital and the Germans and the Italians were milking the economy. It would have to be postponed until influential contacts had been made. At the moment my finances were insufficient and I was afraid of committing a serious blunder at such an early stage. I didn't want any venture into which funds from Central Office would have to be invested to fizzle out quickly, and any precipitate entanglement with the local business community could be disastrous. On the other hand, the current political situation in French North Africa was better than in Metropolitan France and more conducive to economic stability.

True, there was an Armistice Commission, with its apparatus of agents, and the Gestapo as well as the German and Italian consulates. But there was no danger of an immediate German occupation of French North Africa. It was, after all, defended by French forces, whose strength was as yet unknown to me. From my chats with waiters, I understood that the local populace had faith in their Governor, General Weygand, to maintain their independence. My own view was that Weygand, as a soldier, would sooner or later bow to Pétain and introduce Vichy policies into the country. At the moment the Légion was not yet strongly organised but the Free French Movement was being officially persecuted here as in Metropolitan France.

French attitudes towards the Allies varied. Those towards Britain were decidedly hostile, a feeling reinforced by the actions of the Royal Navy at Dakar and Mers-el-Kébir and by the recent campaign in Syria. While the British had a Consul General in Tangiers (which was a free, international city), and a Consulate in Tetuán in Spanish Morocco, they had neither diplomatic nor consular representation anywhere in French North Africa. The Americans, on the other hand, enjoyed friendly relations and had a Consulate General at Algiers, Consulates in Oran, Tunisia and Casablanca, and representation at Vichy in Metropolitan France itself. There was also sympathy for Poland as a faithful ally of

France. At the moment Arabs, Berbers and blacks had no influence whatsoever on the development of political events. Since the French defeat, however, their attitude had become markedly disrespectful and French prestige had undoubtedly suffered. Most probably, opinion in Dakar differed little from that in Algiers.

My conclusion was that our work should proceed slowly and prudently. The initial emphasis should be on important centres such as Algiers and Oran and only later on Tunisia, Constantine, Morocco and Dakar. It was imperative to find good French commanders for these outposts who would bring in their agents. They would have to cover all the ports and places with military garrisons. Then the network would spread its antennae into the main railway centres, mining districts, industry and agriculture until it covered all the military and economic life of French North Africa. The Agency itself had to remain completely secret. Its chief would not be known to any of its agents, even the most successful ones. He would reward, praise or condemn them, but his identity would always remain unknown.

During the recruitment of agents, it would be emphasised that they would be working for France against Nazi Germany. Primarily they should be ideologically motivated and only later would some of them be placed on the payroll of the commanders of the Intelligence outposts. While the search for agents could only be effective in the political context of the anti-fascist struggle, known supporters of General de Gaulle would be avoided. The authorities were deeply hostile towards them and suspicion would only be aroused. Liaison between the outposts and the centre in Algiers was of the utmost importance. These, then, were the basic organisational principles of Agency Africa. Other problems could be settled in due course.

Central Office had already supplied me (in message 3512) with a series of numbers ranging from 1800 to 1990 for marking my future agents, which would be allocated after proving their value. A few good agents would be better than several mediocre ones. A meeting with Major Ciężki (alias M. Miller) to discuss ways of passing on messages was imperative. Doubtless WICHER would have informed him by now of my arrival and he was awaiting my move. I noticed that there was a letter addressed to 'M. Miller' sticking out of letter box no. 16 near the hotel reception. It was essential to keep our contacts secret.

At the Café Etoile the waiter entertained me with some interesting gossip about Weygand. Vichy wanted to recall him but his friends feared that he would never return and advised against it. Nobody knew what he would do. I thought, 'He'll go.'

Afterwards I went to the Hotel Aletti for coffee. In the cafeteria one encountered German and Italian members of the Armistice Commission, consulate employees and, inevitably, Axis agents. The Germans could be spotted a mile away; the Italians, on the other hand, assimilated well into the local French and Arab population, as indeed I did myself. My own appearance – darkish complexion, black hair and suntan – gave me the appearance of a typical southerner, and my regular appearances at cafés would help me blend into the background.

The Arab population fascinated me, and I took a ride on a tram – dubbed by the local French *sac à puces*, or fleabag – to look at their quarters. The narrow, crowded Casbah streets, with their gesticulating merchants, provided an animated scene. Piles of rotting vegetables and fruit lay on the ground. This noisy humanity was submerged in an atmosphere of unwashed and sweaty human flesh mingled with the fragrance of perfumed oils used by the Arab beauties that were present in abundance. To this already intoxicating air were added other aromas from makeshift foodstalls – mutton roasted on spits, sweetmeats, dainty titbits fried in oil, with the place of honour given to dried locusts. All this in a temperature of almost 90°F, where the stillness of the air was only agitated by the buzz of swarms of flies. It induced queasiness and was definitely not to be recommended to those of sensitive dispositions.

On leaving, quite by accident I found myself in the 'reserved quarters'. Here the priestesses of love sat on the doorsteps of their houses enticing the passers-by. Again, the hot air was filled with a sickly odour and the hum of bargains being struck.

Further down, on my way to the European district, I met an unusual sight. Across the road about fifteen men, including Arab soldiers and some Senegalese blacks in French Army uniform, were queueing up outside a small, ordinary-looking Moorish house. They were staring attentively at a dirty, greasy blanket hanging across the porch, which served as a makeshift door. The young civilian Arab heading the queue was very agitated, constantly moving the blanket aside, glaring in and shouting '*Dépèche-toi*!' ('Hurry up!'). I soon realised that this was a makeshift brothel and the gentleman inside was overstaying his time, much to the indignation of the others.

I was not all that sorry to leave the Casbah and was certain that I would not return there again, except, like the legendary Pépé le Moko, to hide from the police. Nobody could ever be found in that maze of twisting little alleys, where one could walk along the tops of the flat roofs as easily as on the ground. It was a relief to be in the open spaces again. I took the tramcar along the coastline to its terminus, Point Pascade, with its fabulous view of the unending sea, then walked the rest of the way back to the hotel. All along the coast, a distance of about five miles, I did not notice any fortifications or military installations. Tired, I awaited Łubieński.

Łubieński reported on the outcome of his visits. M. Malvy had impressed him as a straightforward and highly intelligent person. The letter of introduction from his friend had inspired Malvy with confidence and he agreed to co-operate with us. He gave Łubieński the names of other Frenchmen in Algiers and Oran who were completely trustworthy, and they fixed a date for their second meeting. I was delighted. Malvy, as a high official in the local administration, was a very valuable acquisition.

The other person he visited, Chairman Godziszewski, was a sly old fox, extremely cunning, who liked to advertise his achievements in North Africa. He boasted of his excellent relations with the police, the Prefecture and the General Governorship of Algeria, which could be just right for us. To give him credit, he had brought several hundred refugees into Algeria. His final ambition in an already adventurous life was to make a great deal of money. He envisaged a lucrative business but the one ingredient that was missing was 'someone of vision' capable of financing his venture. The Chairman and his much younger wife kept Łubieński for dinner, asked him to call again and offered help with his North African literary efforts.

The possibility of starting a business was the most interesting part of his report. Łubieński was told to pay the Chairman a second visit in a couple of days' time. I wanted him to raise discreetly the business topic, and to mention very casually that 'one of his friends' from the diplomatic service was expected quite soon (say, from Switzerland) who had a fair amount of capital and was in search of a sound investment.

The next step was for Łubieński to meet all the new people recommended by M. Malvy and to continue visiting the others recommended at Vichy. He would go to Oran in early August, after first establishing more contacts in Algiers. Łubieński was doing excellent work and proved to be first class in his contacts and the way he had handled M. Malvy. I congratulated myself on having chosen him as my right-hand man, and expected that he would soon have quite a few reliable Frenchmen on our books. The time was right to use a cardinal rule, 'Thou shalt not use thine own name'. Łubieński became BANULS, and M. Malvy PIERRE, and as such they will be known henceforth. These code names were only to be used in our Agency's inner circle and would not be known to anyone else.

Tomorrow, the 24th, I planned my first meeting with Major Ciężki . BANULS's next visit to me would be on the 25th. I wrote a short note to 'M. Miller' inviting him to dinner tomorrow, asked him to visit me in room no. 4 between 6 and 7pm and pushed it unobserved through the door of room no. 16. Today was my third day in Africa, things were going well, and we had accomplished far more than I had expected. Let's hope it stayed that way.

Studying the local press took up most of the following morning. There were several interesting bits about the movement of French troops and the industrial production of wine and spirits, doubtless for German use. The Allied war communiqués were few; the Germans by contrast boasted about their victories in Russia and those of the Afrika Korps in Libya.

The Eastern Front was always good news. Hitler had already committed his greatest blunder by attacking the Soviet Union while

Britain remained undefeated and the West African coast remained in French hands. Knowing the USSR, I realised that the German successes could be expected to last until the weather changed in the autumn. Mud, and then deadly frost, along thousands of miles of unfriendly territory would help the Russians as it had against Napoleon in 1812.

After lunch at the Café Etoile, where they now treated me as a regular, I returned slowly to the hotel. The heat was increasing by the minute. The waiter told me that it usually precedes the North African wind known as the sirocco. BANULS was not coming today, which gave me a few hours of relaxation. I was full of foreboding. Ciężki – what was he like, would we be able to co-operate? PIERRE – is he as safe and certain as BANULS thinks? What kind of business is the Polish Chairman after? Is it safe to get involved with such a slippery customer? There was no answer to all these nagging questions. Dozing, I fell asleep.

'Miller' – Ciężki – came at exactly 6pm. He was small with blond hair and blue eyes, very gentle and extremely polite. He made a rather sympathetic impression, which gave me hope for a friendly working relationship. A native of Western Poland, from the Poznan district which before 1918 had been occupied by Prussia, he had been conscripted into the Imperial German Army during the First World War, and had acquired a perfect knowledge of the language. Informed by WICHER of my arrival in Algiers, he had been very disturbed by our lack of contact, especially as he already had several messages for me.

First things first. We agreed that I would push messages for London under his door between 11pm and midnight when the hotel had settled down for the night, while he would drop into my room at 10pm. We hoped that this discreet method would help keep our relationship secret, at least temporarily. WICHER had notified him of my code name; his was MACIEJ.

We went to Les Deux Moulins, a restaurant overlooking the sea, leaving the hotel separately. There we exchanged our different stories as to how we had been brought together in Algiers. MACIEJ's life and military career were extremely unusual. Stopping him at one point, I told him that the technical side of radio Intelligence fascinated me, and that his commanding officer, WICHER (Colonel Langer), was an old friend of mine. Could MACIEJ put me in the picture, as I knew almost nothing about this intriguing subject, which surely, now, could no longer be regarded as a military secret?

MACIEJ interrupted: 'Your assumptions are wrong! Radio Intelligence is still the greatest secret of our time.' He then went on to describe it.

It all started during the Russo-Polish War in 1919–20. At that time the Polish Army's Signals Corps operating the radio-telegraphic monitoring stations intercepted many Red Army messages including the operational orders of Trotsky and Marshals Budyenny and Tukhachevsky. They were deciphered and Marshal Piłsudski and our General Staff knew of the Soviet intentions.

After the war, Colonel Wyżel-Ścieżyński wrote a book entitled *Radio Telegraphy as a Source of Information about the Enemy*. In the early 1920s the Polish General Staff formed the Biuro Szyfrów (Cipher Office), continuing the work of radio Intelligence, i.e. intercepting and decoding messages. Its first head was Major Pokorny, followed by Langer.

Polish radio Intelligence, especially codebreaking and cryptology in the 1920s, was also successful in breaking many German military ciphers. The situation changed in 1926–28, when the German army and then the German navy introduced cipher machines. This, however, was kept strictly secret except for those Cipher Bureau officers directly concerned with the problem. Today we know from numerous publications that the German cipher machine, Enigma, had been 'broken' and that all the sophisticated equipment and knowhow used in deciphering Enigma was passed on to our Allies, Britain and France, in late July 1939.

MACIEJ mentioned a case where a German radio message to their resident agent in Egypt was deciphered, which ordered him to poison all the fresh water supplies in Alexandria with typhoid. London was immediately informed. A second identical message to the same agent was intercepted; again London was alerted. These two communications from MACIEJ, transferred to London by

WICHER, helped to arrest the German agent, who could have dealt an enormous blow to the Allied forces in the Middle East. A BBC news bulletin informed the world that the British authorities in Egypt had frustrated a Nazi attempt to poison the water supplies.

Since joining the French radio Intelligence station, the 'Equipe Z' team had deciphered well over ten thousand different German operational orders. After the French defeat and their concealment in the south, thousands of messages of inestimable value to the Allies had been decoded and passed to London by WICHER.

MACIEJ's story was finished. I sat quietly digesting the enormity of what had just been confided to me. We had forgotten the time and managed to slip back into the hotel unobserved. Sleep did not come easily to me that night.

10

THE FIRST MESSAGES FROM LONDON –
MY COVER AND THE AGENCY'S FIRST MEETING

On 25 July I deciphered Agency Africa's first messages from London – requests to report on the anti-aircraft defences in French North Africa (3511); shipments of war materials to Germany and on the state of the Algerian railway network (3495); whether work had started in Dakar and if a 'hurdy-gurdy' (a two-way radio receiver) could be set up (3225), and what cover Lieutenant Jekiel would use (3502). The last was a strange request since Jekiel was still in France. Central Office's demands were amazing. Did they really expect me to set up an espionage network all over French North Africa in a few days? The morning press contained information about General Weygand which would supply material for my first message to London (41/001).

BANULS came much earlier than usual; his new contacts in Algiers appeared promising. MACIEJ arrived at 10pm with new messages, and we dined together. He had left his wife and children in Poland; there was no news from them and one could sense his profound loneliness.

In the morning I decoded the previous night's messages, which contained a new assignment relating exclusively to Dakar (3705). London asked for a mere trifle – to ascertain the condition of the battleship *Richelieu* anchored in the harbour and report on the thickness of her armour-clad turrets and the calibre of her guns; the position of the coastal defences around Dakar; the type of shore batteries and the calibre of guns, and whether there were any armoured vehicles or tanks in the vicinity.

What credence could I possibly give it? I had only been here for five days, hadn't yet been able to begin work, and was not even certain whether it would be possible at all. Dakar was over three thousand kilometres away, accessible only by air and to those holding special French permits. Obviously vast distances are unimportant to the desk officers in London. They had no conception of the dangers involved in working in enemy territory. These assignments could only be treated as exercises in wishful thinking. I was puzzled, though, at the nature of the Intelligence assignments, as they must have come from the British. After all, since our defeat in 1939, we Poles were taking a back seat. They must have known, if only from their retired Major in Marseilles, that organising a network all over French North Africa would take slightly longer than five days.

Here's a new one: message no. 3726 from General Malinowski to a Pole in Algiers. I neither know nor do I wish to meet this individual. Furthermore, I have no desire to reveal my radio contact with London to anyone. Perhaps they want me to dress up in a postman's uniform and deliver it. It was very difficult to understand their mentality.

BANULS brought some unwelcome news. He had bumped into Lieutenant Gordon (the head of our Oran evacuation outpost) on the Rue Isly who claimed to have recognised 'Dr Skowroński' and was curious. BANULS disposed of this as being highly unlikely and said it must have been someone resembling him. He was not certain whether Gordon was convinced. His other news was about his visit to Chairman Godziszewski. The business the Chairman had in mind was to open the first factory in North Africa to manufacture oatmeal. He was supposed to have obtained all the necessary planning permission and a promised allocation of barley at local government prices. The impending arrival of BANULS's wealthy friend had produced its intended effect. The Chairman wanted to meet us both as soon as possible.

In the meantime, I gave BANULS General Malinowski's message to the Pole to be delivered via our Consul with a request for secrecy as 'it was received through the Gaullist underground'. His visits to me would be restricted to those where he had important information, in case suspicion was aroused.

MACIEJ brought only one message (3704), which I decoded immediately, a request to supply maps and plans of the towns and ports, telephone directories, and a description of the Allied ships requisitioned by the Vichy authorities, together with their new names. It looked as though British demands were increasing the scope of our work. I was still optimistic that we would eventually find the answers somehow.

I was free during 27 July until the evening. This welcome interlude gave me the opportunity to consider the problem of Gordon's reappearance and also the Chairman's oatmeal project.

Immediately after breakfast, and forsaking the morning newspapers, I went straight to the peaceful Marengo Gardens to think things over. The Chairman's project to start a new factory was just what I was searching for as cover as it would turn me into an industrialist. The fact that he was in favour with the local police and civil service was also of the utmost advantage. Furthermore, his partners would be completely above suspicion, a state of affairs that certainly appealed to me.

Would the factory be profitable? The answer was that it did not really matter as Intelligence cover could be expensive; the commercial risk was, therefore, unimportant. More serious was the personal risk. As a cunning lawyer and inquisitive character, the Chairman could eventually see through my double game and guess my real occupation. Possibly he might be afraid of my downfall because of its consequences for him and his business. On the other hand, what sort of capital would he want? Would my limited funds cover this new expenditure as well as running the service until new funds reached me from London?

The big risk was its duration. If it collapsed quickly there would be no benefit to the Agency. Nevertheless, I took this unexpectedly speedy crystallisation of my thoughts and plans as a kind of good omen. A visit to the Chairman would allow me to draw a final conclusion. Gordon was another matter. It was possible that my arrival in North Africa was no longer a secret. He might have told Major Wysoczański, and Polish gossip may have ruined my chances. Although I did not wish to recruit any of my previous officers into the Agency, he would probably have to be made an exception. To put it bluntly, by taking him in I could order him to keep quiet.

Refreshed by my sojourn in the garden, I strolled through the centre of town searching for maps. There were a great many relating to Algiers and its environs, which I purchased in double quantities, for London and for myself. The others could be bought later and would form a substantial collection. At the moment I had no idea how or when they would be sent to London.

BANULS had seen PIERRE. They discussed Oran and he was provided with names of new contacts, together with their passwords, as previously arranged. I asked him to inform the Chairman that we would like to visit him on the 29th between 6 and 7pm, and to tell Gordon that 'Dr Skowroński' wanted to see him on the 29th between 3 and 4pm.

No MACIEJ today. He has nothing for me and I have nothing for him, which may well be an ideal arrangement. The local French press reported further German successes on the Eastern Front and the bombing of British towns.

The next day, 28 July, was free of visitors and messages. It was devoted to private matters.

Lieutenant Gordon arrived at 3pm on the 29th. He was pleased to see me and began reporting on Major Wysoczański's activities and the evacuation work. I was no longer interested as I had been ordered to other duties to which he had also been assigned by our General Staff in London. It was Intelligence work and highly secret. He must immediately break off all contact with the evacuation people but in such a way as not to arouse their suspicion. Fortunately, he had not informed Wysoczański of my arrival as he was not absolutely certain that he had recognised me in the street.

I appointed him officer of the Algiers Intelligence outpost with a monthly salary of 7,000 francs as from 1 August and the codename RENÉ. He was delighted with this new turn of events and added that he was very happy to be working with me again. I concluded that if he had any reliable people working for him whom he would continue to use, he would let me know. He would receive instructions and assignments during our next meeting on 31 July. After RENÉ left, I drafted a message for London to confirm Gordon as an Intelligence Officer of Agency Africa (41/006).

BANULS came at 5pm to take me to the Chairman. I told him about Gordon and that their first briefing would be on the 31st, after which he could go to Oran. En route, it was agreed that he should introduce me as 'Stawikowski', a Councillor of the Polish Foreign Office coming from Geneva, and I'd do the rest.

The Chairman and his wife awaited their guests. Our introductions were high-flown. I, of course, had the great privilege of meeting such a meritorious Chairman of the local Polish community etc., etc. He, on the other hand, was happy and very honoured etc., etc. The Chairman was over seventy and still in good shape, with sharp features, narrow lips and high forehead. His hands, with their long bony fingers, were perpetually moving while his quick and piercing bluish-grey eyes gave one the uneasy feeling that he was trying to penetrate one's innermost secrets. One sensed instinctively that he was devious and insincere and that one would have to be on guard and be careful what was said.

At first we discussed the political and military situation, Poland and the USSR. Later, the Chairman treated us to a very graphic description of his experiences as a lawyer in Czarist Moscow. Wishing to know his opinion of local conditions, I steered the conversation round to Algiers and mentioned casually that I would like to settle somewhere in North Africa. The Chairman believed that this was the promised land for business opportunities. The holy trinity for success was a business brain, capital and the necessary contacts. He himself was well on the way to starting a profitable concern. I did not question him about it, nor did I exhibit any interest in his future enterprise.

After an hour we thanked the Chairman and his wife for their hospitality and bade them farewell. He gave us a warm invitation to visit him again tomorrow evening. I excused myself on the grounds that I had a prior appointment and we agreed on 31 July. Once outside, I confided my observations to BANULS, reminded him of the briefing on the 31st and told him to prepare himself for his Oran trip. Next time, it would be better for me to see the Chairman alone. MACIEJ came with two messages, received mine in exchange, and as a return service invited me to dinner.

The following day was left free to prepare my first briefing with BANULS and RENÉ. First steps are always the most important and determine one's future self-confidence. The simplest error committed now would gradually be magnified and could prove disastrous. My first two Intelligence Officers were novices and needed to learn the main principles of their craft before receiving detailed instructions. The rest of the day was taken up with deciphering radio messages from London. They wanted to know the Agency's financial situation as anticipated on 15 August and the budget estimates for the next quarter.

The next day, 31 July, was my tenth in Algiers. So far everything appeared to be going well. A bottle of wine and three glasses were ordered to be brought up to my room at 2.30pm. In the event of unwelcome visitors, a small party of friends would suffice as an excuse. BANULS, RENÉ and myself immediately settled down to work.

As an introduction, I acquainted them with the cardinal rule – not to keep any notes and, above all, no names and addresses, as it could betray the entire network. One must learn to memorise. They must hammer this inflexible rule into all their future agents. Secondly: no women agents. Not that I am against the fair sex (on the contrary) nor do I discriminate against them on grounds of adaptability – they are as good at espionage as any man. But when men and women work together, sooner or later a physical attraction may develop between two agents. This could produce jealousy among the others, which, in turn, could cause unnecessary conflict and friction in work which should otherwise run smoothly.

Real names are never used in the Intelligence Service. As this is the Polish service, Polish methods of work would be used. Only Poles would be appointed Intelligence Officers, directly responsible to me, and they alone would know my identity. Once an agent was accepted after an initial period, he would receive an agency number. He would be known henceforth under that number, but only to Central Office and myself; the agent himself would not know it. Any unusually efficient agent could become an outpost commander. Thus selected, the outpost commander would be responsible solely to the Intelligence Officer for whom he was working, and would not be known to any of the other Intelligence Officers. The outpost commander would pick his own agents, who, if found useful, would receive codenames, which would only be used at work.

All expenses incurred during work would be reimbursed. The expenditure should be presented quarterly by the Intelligence Officers for settlement. The identity of the head of the Agency must be maintained in strict secrecy. It is possible to refer to him as 'the Chief', but nobody knows him or his whereabouts. 'Our organisation', the name to call our Agency, should be presented (even to those participating in it) as all-powerful and operating everywhere with the fight against Nazi Germany and the liberation of France as its primary objectives. A patriotic line should therefore be followed in any approach to a prospective agent, but direct links with well-known Gaullists should be avoided as they could be under police surveillance. Any contacts with them should be maintained secretly. We should not admit any connection with the British, since, after the events at Dakar and Mers-el-Kébir, they are hated here.

During conversations with future agents they should be told only the minimum they need to know, i.e. matters connected with them individually or with their assignment. The less people know, the safer it is for them and for the entire network.

'Following this principle,' I said, 'even I, who have complete faith in you both, will in future only discuss matters relating to you individually, in confidence and separately from each other. Please do not ask me for any other information.'

All direct contacts between agents were dangerous. Unfortunately, for the moment, it would be the only means available to us for obtaining information and handing out assignments. When written materials needed to change hands, a system of 'post office boxes' would have to be organised. This meant that a third person would be recruited to serve as a link between agents. He must not know anything about the Agency or its purpose but merely act as a post box – receiving letters and packages from an unknown person giving a certain password, and passing them to another unknown person producing a second, different, password. In this way contacts between agents would be broken. Obviously the individual operating such a box must be reliable. Furthermore, due to his profession or trade, he must be frequently visited by other people, thus allaying suspicion.

Boxes could be arranged in a double-ended way. For example, a courier agent from Casablanca, bringing information in the morning, would make contact again during the day to collect new instructions before returning home. For security purposes, different passwords would be used for these two separate meetings. Boxes should be organised in Algiers, and by the outpost commanders, for agents to deposit their reports. The strategic position of the port and town of Oran, with its naval base at Mers-el-Kébir, required our priority. The post boxes for the couriers from Oran should be the first to be organised.

As this was the beginning of their Intelligence work, there were specific points which their future agents must pay special attention to, when reporting on the various armed services or different localities:

1) Agents must be made aware that when identifying Army units, the following information is required:
i) name of town of stationing garrison;
ii) name and number of the unit;
iii) size of the unit, with composition: regiments, battalions, companies and batteries;
iv) armaments: in the case of an artillery unit, the type: heavy, field, anti-aircraft, anti-tank, calibre of the guns and type of traction; for armoured units, the weight of tanks and armoured vehicles;
v) munitions: type and quantity;
vi) morale of the soldiers and their political orientation.

2) For Air Force identification, the following specifications are required:
i) type and number of aeroplanes;
ii) stock of bombs, munitions and fuel;
iii) hangars;
iv) type of runways.

3) Naval assignments are divided into navy, merchant marine and port. Until our naval expert arrives from Marseilles, the work should consist of monitoring the movements of ships in and out of ports. The numbers and names of vessels and all markings and names on sailors' caps should be noted. In the case of merchant cargo:
i) name of the ship;
ii) time of arrival;
iii) from which port;
iv) time of sailing;
v) destination;
vi) cargo being loaded.

Very important were descriptions and plans of ports, the entry to the ports and the nightly locks. The information would be particularly useful to BANULS, as he was about to depart for Oran.

My two Intelligence Officers were then given their individual orders. RENÉ: reconnoitring and pinpointing all the military garrisons in Algeria and in the town of Algiers.

BANULS: making contacts in Oran with people willing to work for us and supplying them with military and naval assignments. Setting up a post box for Oran in Algiers and choosing and conveying the passwords. Making initial payments to our first recruits.

I reminded them to buy maps of the towns and ports visited as they were required both for London and for ourselves.

There were no questions; everything was understood. RENÉ already had a few people to work with but would only name them after a trial period. He and BANULS received their salaries for August with a little extra for their expenses. Their reporting times were established — RENÉ at 7pm and BANULS at 9pm each day; in emergencies any morning before midday. Wishing them luck, I parted with them. Now I had to prepare for my second meeting with the Chairman.

He seemed mildly surprised at seeing me by myself. I excused myself for disappointing him: my friend's absence was due to a very urgent meeting connected with his research. He immediately invited me into his study for a chat. As usual when two complete strangers meet, general topics were at first discussed. The Chairman, a well-seasoned lawyer, was beating around the bush and trying to force me to disclose the reason for my visit. This, of course, would have put him in a stronger bargaining position as my benefactor. He was obviously waiting for my questions.

Finding the situation amusing, I decided to force his hand and make him lay his cards on the table. I mentioned casually, among other things, that last night a local industrialist had interested me with a lucrative business offer but that, not knowing him, I had to be cautious. This spur must have dug deep as it produced the anticipated reaction. Without further prompting, he revealed his plan (which I already knew from BANULS) to start a factory producing oatmeal, the first of its kind in North Africa.

The project had the blessing of the local government, which agreed to allocate a monthly quota of barley. For his own reasons he wanted to sell his product through chemists' shops. Presumably by doing so he expected that it would add to its commercial prestige and he could raise the price. It had taken him some time to draw up production plans – everything was ready except the money; he needed a partner with the ready cash.

While my host was busy replenishing my glass with brandy, the slight interlude gave me the opportunity to reconsider the risk that might be involved. The project was based on food produce, and in the event of shortages it would always sell. After a moment of deliberation I assured the Chairman that the idea appealed to me, provided it could be made to work.

In my opinion, the barley flake factory would resemble a kind of flour mill, where the barley was first cleaned, then broken, and finally pressed into the necessary shape. I wondered, however, whether it would be possible to buy such machines in Algiers.

My host expressed his amazement and delight at my 'excellent knowledge' of this type of industry. As far as production was concerned, there was nothing to worry about. The French had offered him new (or almost new) machinery, and he even had the lease of premises for the factory. Labour would not be a problem as there was an unlimited supply. Arab women would be best since they were more reliable than the men.

I only had one question – 'What sort of capital outlay would be required to get the whole project going?' The Chairman lowered his head over his papers and after a while answered quietly, '150,000 francs.' He was very tense awaiting my reply.

Instead of giving it to him immediately, I took him into my 'confidence'. Up until now my stay in Algiers was temporary and, not having a permanent residence permission, it was difficult for me to make any decision. I heard him say that this should not cause any problems as he had excellent connections with the police and in the Governorship. I sensed that, having convinced me that I should join his venture, he would never let me go. Mentally summarising, it was clear that 150,000 francs was a small price to pay for a cover that eventually might even pay for itself. Without further hesitation, I took his hand and said, 'I agree to join you as a partner and will supply the necessary capital!'

It would be virtually impossible to describe all the expressions of admiration uttered by the Chairman at my wisdom. His wife, brought in by him to be informed of my decision, sealed the deal by ushering us in to dinner. At the table, while toasting each other and our future success, we also discussed the organisation of our new enterprise. The Chairman made me agree to join him in our daily work in his office. To him, of course, it was the most important thing in life, and he would suspect me of having other vested interests if I did not spend any time at his oatmeal venture. Willy-nilly, I was led to promise him three hours of my time, from 3 to 6pm each day.

After dinner, over delicious coffee, we were like old partners and, in a relaxed atmosphere, discussed some of the influential personalities in French North Africa. His shrewd descriptions convinced me that he was a very clever man and that one had to be careful when dealing with him. On the other hand, he struck me as being a fervent patriot with a dose of gold fever.

I returned to my hotel in the early hours of the morning in a marvellous mood. After all, why not? For a small sum, I had acquired the status of an industrialist, in the highest stratum of local society, and a perfect cover for my work for the Allies. I took the decision quickly and without seeking approval from London, which would have involved a lengthy radio correspondence, wasting too much valuable time. In any case Central Office in London, to whom the whole business of cover was not as essential as it was to me, might have wanted to save a few thousand francs. The unexpectedly speedy purchase of cover made me believe that luck was with me.

11

AUGUST, SEPTEMBER AND OCTOBER 1941

August 1941

Despite the rules of caution obligatory in the service, especially in wartime, that I had laid down to my officers, I was compelled to break them all myself. To have kept all the various facets of the economic and military aspects covered by Agency Africa in one's memory would have been an impossible task. Furthermore, my officers were new to the service, and I knew that the entire responsibility for the work would be placed on me. I therefore kept, as future evidence, all the radio correspondence with London. Given our uneasy relationship with some individuals at Central Office, it was also prudent to keep account books, which are normally forbidden. I had no desire to be accused of unjustified expenditure at some later date.

Despite the obvious risks, I was compelled, therefore, to organise a miniature office in our Agency. One rule, however, was observed. There were no names or addresses of the participants, only their numbers. In the event of a mishap, I alone would bear the responsibility.

While going to town to buy stationery and a typewriter, I bumped into the hotel proprietor, M. Caucasse. I told him that I was going into a partnership and was expecting my family's arrival soon. Could he find us larger accommodation? The hotel was very comfortable and I would be reluctant to move. Delighted, he promised to provide it for us and assured me that my new business venture would be 'a great success'.

Back at the hotel, I began my office work and opened three notebooks. The first was our accounts book in which the two radio messages concerning June and July's expenditure were entered. The second was a register of incoming and outgoing radio messages with London; the third, a similar book for the Intelligence Officers and outpost assignments. A fourth book, which at the moment remained blank, would contain all our Intelligence reports which I hoped would soon be forthcoming.

My working day was beginning to be crammed with activities and occupations, and it was vital to set up a routine. My timetable was as follows:

9 am–12 noon: Office work at home including coding and decoding of radio messages; filing and classification of Intelligence reports received; elaboration of assignments for the outpost; agency accounts.

12–2pm: Daily observation of the port and the Admiralty; personal contacts; business in town; lunch.

2–3pm: Additional office work and/or period for relaxation.

3–6pm: Work at the Chairman's office.

6–7pm: Dinner.

7–10pm: Receiving Intelligence Officers' written and oral reports; MACIEJ with radio messages.

10pm–1am: Editing and coding of urgent messages from reports received and passing them to MACIEJ for transmission.

Back at the oatmeal factory, something was bothering our Chairman and I prayed that he had not decided to withdraw from the company. Apparently the local administration would look more favourably on our venture if we took in a Frenchman as a third partner. He had someone in mind, from an old family of *colons*. I agreed, much to his relief, and even suggested that I had thought of the same thing myself.

Cheerfully, he mentioned M. Delfau, who, besides being the son of the famous local lawyer, was wealthy and – the Chairman added in a crescendo of triumph –was also an engineer. As I was supplying all the capital, the decision was up to me. Realising that this would save me a third of that amount, I readily agreed, adding that I did so only for the sake of the company. He was delighted, and would invite Delfau to a future meeting to draw up a contract. I excused myself as I was very pressed for time.

BANULS called in the evening before his departure for Oran. A post box inside the Prefecture for the reports from Oran would be very convenient (providing PIERRE agreed), and would not attract attention. They would have to arrange two sets of passwords. MACIEJ brought me one message and received two in return.

Between 1 and 13 August RENÉ brought me very detailed information on the military garrisons in the Algiers district and other towns, which provided sufficient material for several messages. Checking the French Order of Battle supplied earlier by the British, I found great discrepancies in the number of regiments and their deployment. Among MACIEJ's messages was confirmation of Gordon's appointment to our agency and a new despatch from General Malinowski for the Pole in Algiers who, apparently, was acting as a guardian for Polish widows and orphans in the area. Now that this had been clarified, I would be willing to act as a postman.

On the 6th I met M. Delfau, a pleasant engineering student, and the contract was signed. Our business name was Floc-Av ('la première fabrique d'avoine à Alger') with the Chairman as General Manager, M. Stawikowski as Commercial Manager and M. Delfau as Technical Manager. The business was proceeding normally.

Our long-awaited naval expert, Lieutenant Jekiel (codename DOKTOR), arrived from Marseilles on the 8th, posing as a Frenchman with a passport issued by the Prefecture in Nice. His agent, GYNAECOLOGIST, who, as mentioned previously, was indeed a doctor, would come next month, and open a surgery in Casablanca. DOKTOR's first assignment was to observe Algiers port and to look for possible contacts in the town. If we obtained valuable contacts in Tangiers, he would go to Morocco. Until then he would report to me daily at 8pm.

BANULS returned on the 12th bringing information from Oran and the military garrisons of Sidi-bel-Abbès, La Sénia and Tlemcen

(41/018). The important news from Oran concerned a shipment of lorries from France to be transported to Tunisia (41/025). We would check on where they went; most probably the Germans would take them to Tripoli. He had also found a new associate who was given instructions and a first Intelligence assignment. The Oran post box would be at PIERRE's office, and for the time being BANULS himself would collect the reports and place new assignments.

All this was material for several messages. DOKTOR supplied me with an accurate plan and a description of the port of Algiers, together with the movement of ships (41/031). The work was expanding. At the moment our finances were 272,814 francs, which would be reported to Central Office (41/023).

BANULS received the first reports from the Oran post box on the 15th – initial information from our new agent, as yet without an agency number, from the ports of Oran and Nemours and the naval base of Mers-el-Kébir (41/026) with interesting data on the cruiser *Dunkerque* (41/027) and from the port of Arzef, the military hydroplane base (41/028), also a fascinating but incomplete description of the coastal defences in the Oran and Mers-el-Kébir regions (41/020). Again: sufficient material for several messages.

The result was that MACIEJ was now receiving an increasing amount of work for his radio while he himself delivered only one or two messages, and not always every day. In their last message Central Office demanded information on the Intelligence outpost in Casablanca and the fate of Captain Tonn (4310). This was difficult. I could provide it only by going to Morocco and carrying out an investigation on the spot. At the moment this was impossible.

BANULS brought new reports from Oran. The most important concerned Nemours port, the centre for the shipment of iron ore to France (41/034). Also, that the Germans in Oran were awaiting a shipment of rubber latex from Dakar. Our new agent in Oran was doing well and would receive an Agency number soon. RENÉ reported information leaked from the staff of the Oran Division on the concentration in strength of infantry and tanks in Spanish Morocco (41/037). This sounded dubious as there was no apparent reason. However, London would be able to check it against their other sources of information. As anticipated, the work was increasing. It took me until well after midnight to transcribe all the reports into messages and then code them for MACIEJ. And this was just the beginning, with only two districts working.

On the 21st Sophie and George arrived in Algiers, having managed to leave France unobserved by our friends. A German port official had tried to make difficulties by directing her to Morocco through Oran. It was only at the last moment that she managed to make him alter his decision. Her nervous exhaustion, the Algerian heat and the pressing throng in the street all combined to make her immediately dislike the town. After a rest, the three of us left for dinner at the Café Etoile. The good food and the sight of the cheerful stores on the Rue Isly brightened her up. Back at the hotel, I found an added distraction by asking them both to try to discover my hiding place. After a long search, they gave up and admitted that it was 'absolutely unimaginable'.

Sophie was intrigued by our future visits to the Chairman and the Floc-Av Company. Knowing my officers from Marseilles, she volunteered to receive written reports from them in my absence and met MACIEJ in the evening, who would be delivering messages to her as well. Her presence gave me greater independence of action. I was no longer tied by a timetable to my hotel room. After a short time, she mastered the ciphering technique and helped me to code and decode messages.

The presence of my family in Algiers, together with my business connections, gave me the reputation of being respectable, well-heeled financially and with high social status, attributes that placed me well above suspicion. We visited the Chairman and his wife on the 23rd, and Sophie also met M. Delfau. It emerged that the Chairman had a grandson about the same age as George, and promised to place them both at the Lycée du Maréchal Bugeaud, a very good local school.

On the fourth day after his arrival, George became ill and Dr Gozland, a Jewish physician, diagnosed pleurisy after a neglected pneumonia. The illness was protracted and dangerous and required long, careful medical treatment, and a prescribed diet. It was a blow to us, and required a great deal of self-control to maintain the calm so necessary in our circumstances. George's illness, the doctor's daily visits (and those of my new acquaintances), my work, both at Floc-Av and on the Intelligence Officers' reports and MACIEJ's coded messages, all made it difficult to adjust to life at the hotel. It was made worse by Sophie having constantly to cook special dietary dishes on a paraffin stove.

George's illness also upset my plan to travel to Morocco. By this time I was only too conscious of the fact that the Chairman's boast that he could obtain a permanent residence permit for me was empty bombast. Our current permits were valid for only three months, and any longer stay in Algiers would cause unwanted complications. In retrospect, this difficult period through which we lived, happily without any permanent mishap, conformed to the pattern of my previous experiences and proved salutary to the Agency in the long run. Again, one could ascribe it either to providence or simply to luck, or to both.

Nevertheless, the work continued according to schedule. PIERRE's post box was working well. Four newly recruited agents, who had proved their value, were given agency numbers (1800–03). The first three had succeeded in unravelling a mystery that had puzzled the British Admiralty. They discovered that ships whose names began with *Saint* were Allied ones requisitioned by the Vichy Government (41/044). Furthermore, they established that the cruiser *Dunkerque* was unfit for combat, had a greatly reduced speed and her mechanical steering was non-operational (41/047). They also supplied data on navigational charts for French ships relating to the African coast (41/050). RENÉ conveyed interesting information from Tunis regarding the secret unloading of German military aeroplanes in the port of Bizerta (41/052).

During the last days of August Central Office presented us with many new demands, ranging from acquiring exact data on any transports of iron ore to France or Italy (4441) and on shipments of liquid fuel (4489) to the reasons for the suspension of shipping between North Africa and France (4471) and collecting information on German 'tourists' travelling to Morocco from France (4375).

My records for August 1941 showed that we received sixteen messages and transmitted sixty to London, which could be considered a good start for the first four weeks of our work.

September 1941

General Weygand, the Governor General of Algeria, returned from Vichy bringing food restrictions with him similar to those prevailing in Metropolitan France. Rationing and the cuts in wine consumption hit restaurants and shops. French North Africa was forced to export large quantities of fruit and vegetables to France, which everyone knew was for the benefit of the Germans. Because of the traditional diversity of trading outlets, the authorities found it difficult to contain the black market. Sophie depended on it to provide a suitable diet for George, who was still very ill.

Our departure for Morocco was further delayed and Marcel Dubois had been impatiently awaiting our arrival. Sophie wrote to Lucienne informing her that we were bogged down in Algiers because of George's illness.

The atmosphere was becoming very unpleasant. Pro-German propaganda and the rapidly expanding activities of the pro-Nazi Vichy organisation, the Légion, was increasing. Most striking was Pétain's slogan 'Family, Work and Country', painted in huge letters on the port jetty. The police tightened their grip; listening to the BBC was forbidden and carried severe penalties and an officially inspired anti-Semitic campaign was stepped up in the press. Despite this, a secret pro-Gaullist movement flourished in Algiers led by Professor René Capitant, editor of the underground paper *Combat*. This group recruited its supporters among the youth, both inside and outside the university, and was persecuted by the authorities.

PIERRE, worried by the possibility that his pro-German colleagues might become suspicious, asked BANULS for different people to do the collecting from the post box. I suggested utilising our wives' services, as the sight of a woman was liable to evoke feelings other than suspicion.

Our work in the Oran department was spreading with

astonishing speed. Our agents were in all the ports, in La Sénia airport, and in the various government offices. They were very efficient, passed their probationary period, and Central Office were informed that numbers 1804–16 had been admitted into the Agency. This state of affairs allowed me to organise our first Intelligence outpost in Oran. Robert Ragache (agent 1812) was selected as commander of the outpost; he was a French merchant navy man, whose rank bore the impressive title of 'Captain, 1st Class of High Seas Navigation'.

BANULS was sent to provide him with a general outline of the duties of a commander for the whole of a department, who was also responsible for his own Intelligence expenditure, that of his agents and their salaries, which he would estimate himself. He would make a monthly financial account to BANULS, and his own salary was set at 15,000 francs.

In order to relieve PIERRE's post box from the extra work, a second box was organised at a local doctor's surgery. At the same time, thanks to RENÉ and DOKTOR's efforts, the Algiers network itself began to take shape.

An immediate problem was temporarily solved. Only a summary of the most important reports reached London via radio messages; their elaboration, plans and detailed descriptions had to be sent by a courier. I was reluctant to send them to TUDOR through unreliable merchant seamen and our material accumulated. DOKTOR was eager to make a trip to Marseilles; he had a French passport, and did not need visas or permits. He took all the material required by Central Office and they were informed on the 19th (41/093) that our post had been delivered to TUDOR, who would send it on to Madrid with his own pouch.

Meanwhile, thankfully, George's health improved slightly, the organisation of the factory was proceeding well, and we hoped to start production soon. The only real worry was the lack of news from Marcel Dubois.

His sudden appearance at our hotel on the afternoon of the 22nd, therefore, was a marvellous surprise. He was in Algiers for a special meeting with the Governor General and had found a solution for the problem of our stay in Algeria. His suggestion was that we should 'come to Morocco' for a holiday a few days before our visas expired, stay at his home, and he would then issue us with new Moroccan visas and those for a three months' stay in Algeria. The arrangement could be repeated ad infinitum. It sounded ideal as I could travel between Algeria and Morocco as often as I needed. I owed it not only to Marcel but also, paradoxically, to George's unfortunate illness. We spent an enjoyable evening together. Among other things, he wanted me to be godfather to his baby son Philippe, while Josephine Baker, the famous singer, would be his godmother. The baptism was planned for mid-October.

Having organised an outpost in Oran, I now turned my attention eastwards towards Tunisia. BANULS had letters of introduction to some people there, and went to try his luck with them. He found one, who became our associate, and after a time Tunis began to work. Bordering on Italian-held Libya, Tunisia had immense strategic value for Rommel's Afrika Korps, and was also the German supply base.

Towards the end of September GYNAECOLOGIST, who was earmarked for Casablanca, paid me an unexpected visit. We discussed Morocco, and my letter recommending him to Marcel. Learning of George's condition, he examined his lungs and assured me that the worst was over. He paid me a lightning visit a few days later before returning to France and looked extremely happy.

During September, MACIEJ brought me twenty-seven radio messages and received eighty-seven. Our messages to London reflected the expansion of our work in new areas and the increasing variety of our interests. Among our more important reports concerning military questions were:

September 1941

Military

Detailed plans for the defence of Morocco drawn up by the French and Germans (41/086); transfer of regiments to Dakar (41/111–2); further data re the military units and garrisons (41/059); plans of the airports of La Sénia and Blida (41/094); description of coastal fortifications and batteries at Cap Matifou (Algiers) and 210mm guns (41/091); air bases in North Africa (41/098).

Naval

Movement of French Naval vessels (41/123 and 41/124); further data on the cruiser Dunkerque (41/088); condition of the battleship Richelieu anchored at Dakar (41/089); plans of Port Arzev, the hydroplane base (41/108); ships at Oran awaiting convoy for Marseilles (41/106).

Economic

Division, between Germany and Italy, for the exploitation of North African mines (42/083); ascertainment of supplies of American petrol from Tunisia to the Axis Forces in Libya (42/099); German demands for supply of 2,000 French road tankers (250 were driven to Tripoli) (41/072 and 41/126); French permission for German war planes to land at La Sénia aerodrome for two hours' duration (41/081).

London was also made aware of our shortage of funds, which on 1 September amounted to only 173,772 francs (41/057). As the number of agents increased, our cash reserves dwindled proportionally. Central Office's earlier promises, assuring the necessary flow of funds, failed to materialise.

October 1941

DOKTOR returned from France on 29 September with 50,000 francs from TUDOR, sufficient to bridge the financial gap for a few weeks. He also reported that he was continually being shadowed by two men whom he pointed out through the hotel window, and said that if he had a motorcycle he could easily shake them off. I gave him my immediate consent, and the cash to buy one. Later, they tried to keep up with him in a car, but in the maze of narrow streets his motorbike was too nifty for them. Nevertheless, I ordered him to be very careful and only to report to me on important matters.

On 1 October, having been briefed by BANULS, our new agent 1820, Maxime de Roquemaure, was appointed commander of the Intelligence outpost Tunis. He had excellent contacts in the High Command of the Army of Tunis and knew its Commanding General. Among his important reports were

> the transfer of 300,000 tons of wheat from Tunisia to Tripoli (41/178); the opening of the Tébessa–Kasserine railway sector with its extension to the southern port of Gabès (41/125); tankers shipped from France via Oran–Algiers–Tunis–Gabès continued by road to Tripoli (41/126); a further 600 tankers on their way from Algiers (41/127); the SS *Strabon* and *Faason* sailing from Oran with armaments for Dakar (41/160).

Central Office were notified on 1 October that our funds were dwindling rapidly (41/143). Their sole response was to send soothing messages. Receiving a new allocation of funds now became a vital problem. I began thinking about exploiting my position as a local industrialist and approaching the banks or even the local money-lenders. During my earlier exploration of Algiers, I had noticed a huge building belonging to the Compagnie de Shell. They must have links with their main office in London, however tenuous. If this was the case, then there might be a possibility of obtaining our money from London. BANULS was instructed to find out the political convictions of the Chairman of North African Shell, while I would also make discreet inquiries about him myself.

While extending Agency Africa's work, both territorially and into new fields of interest, I suspected the presence of another Allied Intelligence Service with whom collision had to be avoided. Furthermore, sometimes the same agent may attempt to work for more than one service, passing the same information to them both. To avoid unnecessary expense and other problems, I asked Central Office to request British Intelligence to allow me to contact their man in French North Africa. They replied that British Intelligence were unable to contact me as, at present, they did not have any representative there (4932). It looked as though I was completely alone.

Besides the usual military information on the French Forces, RENÉ reported the displacement of Polish soldiers (evacuated from France) from Kasba-Tadla camp in Morocco to Mascara in Algeria. The officers were kept in a hotel while the other ranks were in a camp under very harsh conditions. I requested London to order our Government representative in Algiers, Count Hutten-Czapski, to co-operate with me. Knowing him quite well, I was certain that he would agree (although he did not know of my presence here), but I preferred the request to come from above. I also reported the presence at the officers' hotel of Captain Tonn, the subject of a previous message from London. This was the first news concerning his whereabouts since TUDOR had sent him to Africa.

Our Tunis outpost reported further large transports of American petrol and oil to the German forces in Tripolitania (41/148). This was a matter of some urgency with which I had to get better acquainted and which could not be allowed to continue.

As mentioned previously, US representation in French North Africa consisted of two General Consulates (in Algiers and Casablanca), and two Consulates (in Tunis and Oran). Robert D. Murphy was their diplomatic head with the rank of Minister. Relations between the American representatives and the Governors of French North Africa, General Weygand (Algeria), Admiral Esteva (the Protectorate of Tunisia) and General Nogues (the Protectorate of Morocco), were good.

General Weygand, who really represented the whole of French North Africa, realised that the economic life of their vast domain largely depended on obtaining supplies from the United States. He tried to keep French North Africa economically independent from Metropolitan France and proclaimed that its integrity would be defended.

The Americans were, to a certain extent, willing to maintain the independence of Algeria, Tunisia and Morocco, and to continue providing them with the economic means. The economic life of French North Africa depended primarily on the availability of fuel. This huge territory had no coal mines or large water reservoirs to drive its turbines producing electricity. There was an oil well in Morocco producing a few thousand tons a year, which was insufficient for the demand. The Army and Navy had reserves of petrol and diesel oil but the authorities were unwilling to use them for domestic purposes.

Fuel was necessary for the exploitation of the natural wealth of its territories, which were rich in iron, manganese, cobalt and copper ore, and for its as yet underdeveloped heavy industry and numerous small factories. Agriculture depended on motors pumping water from the depths; without irrigation the land would return to a desert.

General Weygand gave Minister Murphy his personal guarantee regarding the integrity of French North Africa, which was confirmed by the Vichy Government. This resulted in the Americans supplying 53,000 tons of oil, diesel and petrol up to the end of October 1941. (I was unable to estimate the tonnage of coal and other by-products.) To safeguard American fuel from being transferred to the Axis Forces in Libya, a special commission kept a check in the ports; it included American Vice-Consuls John C. Knox and John H. Boyd in Algiers, Harry Woodruff in Oran and David King in Casablanca.

Weygand had many enemies in Government circles at Vichy. The Germans exerted a formidable pressure on the Pétain regime and were dissatisfied with the number of American diplomats in North Africa and their too close relationships with the local authorities and with the Governor General. I feared that this heavy-handed American diplomacy in North Africa was infuriating the Germans and would make Weygand's position untenable. In my opinion, his days were numbered.

Although London did not expect us to report on political and economic matters, I felt it was imperative to furnish them with my observations. Having been taught a lesson in Marseilles regarding their unfriendly attitude towards our work, I was reluctant to maintain any contact with the Americans. My first priority was to build up our network wherever possible and to make it efficient, before relations with them could even be considered. I did not wish to play the role of their poor relation.

This is why BANULS, in his persistent attempts to get me to meet the Americans, repeatedly received a negative reply. He was, however, allowed to cultivate friendly relations with them, providing they were free of political connotations. We were also keeping an eye on them. Knowing most of the American Consulate's personnel, we checked their activities to ascertain whether we were sharing the same agents. We soon realised that, from the Intelligence standpoint, we were wasting our time as they were behaving as diplomats really should behave.

On 12 October Lieutenant Rombejko arrived from Marseilles with his wife Aliette and stayed at our hotel (41/151). The following day he was given the code name MUSTAFA and introduced to MACIEJ and the three other officers. He brought with him a letter of resignation from a young cadet officer who had changed his mind and left for Britain instead of following us to Africa. All my officers were now present.

A few days later MACIEJ warned me about the unusual interest being shown by the French commander of their radio Intelligence group. He wanted to know the reason for the greatly increased radio correspondence between the group and France. MACIEJ tried to placate him by blaming it on an internal reorganisation but was not certain how long it would satisfy him. Now I had a very difficult problem – how to organise Agency Africa's own radio communication with London.

My departure for Morocco was approaching. Although I wanted MUSTAFA to accustom himself to Algiers first, I also had to think about organising the office work in my absence. In the event, he was given responsibility for all internal cipher work, keeping records of messages and receiving reports from our other officers and the outposts. BANULS was in charge of the outside work – liaison with the outposts, operating the post boxes and helping MUSTAFA prepare messages for London. The arrangement should be ideal – MUSTAFA knew the ciphers from his prewar service in Moscow while BANULS had controlled the agents right from the beginning. Before handing over the Agency to their safekeeping, I held a short briefing and wished them all luck.

George's health was no longer causing concern. In any case, he was left in the safe care of Dr Gozland and Mme Aliette. Having cleared the decks, I purchased tickets to Morocco for 16 October. Before leaving, however, I issued Agency number 1819 to a new agent in Oran.

12

MY FIRST JOURNEY TO MOROCCO –
IN ADVERSITY – IN DETENTION

On arrival at Rabat, the Moroccan capital, after a long but uneventful journey, we were met at the station by Marcel, who escorted us to the Hotel Balima. Later we met Josephine Baker, the American star of French cabaret, who would be godmother to my godson Philippe; she was then recovering from an appendicitis operation. Unlike some of her contemporaries she had refused to perform in occupied France, and she had settled in Rabat. A staunch French patriot, Josephine was one of the sweetest and most beautiful women imaginable. As for Marcel, being a well-seasoned spy-catcher, he obviously knew the reason why I was in North Africa, but never once mentioned it. He deprecated his invaluable assistance by describing it as 'helping out an old friend'. Marcel and his wife were, in fact, the most marvellous friends. I knew, however, that he could be completely ruthless when it came to German and Italian agents. Incidentally, he too was keeping a close eye on the American Consulates.

Marcel drove me on a sight-seeing tour of the large Moroccan towns and military centres, where I noted the numbers of the units. Everywhere, he introduced me to sombre-faced French security men as his 'greatest friend', urging them to assist me in the event of my travelling alone. These contacts were of enormous importance as they were in southern Morocco, which was out of bounds to those not possessing a pass from the French or German authorities.

Philippe's christening gave me the opportunity to meet Marcel's boss, Colonel Herviot, who was also staunchly anti-German. I could imagine the tightrope tricks those two were compelled to perform in order to retain their posts. Their personal convictions were totally opposed to those of General Nogues, the French Protector of Morocco, whose policy was collaborationism.

Soon, Sophie began worrying about George's health. We agreed that she would return to Algiers alone, and that I would follow her in mid-November. At the station, Marcel whispered to her, 'In case of trouble, see Monsieur B. from Security and refer to me.'

Alone, I could move around more freely. I wanted to explore Casablanca, which at that time had a substantial Polish community, and to discover the truth about Captain Tonn and Major Wysoczański. Marcel told me that it was started by denunciations that someone had a radio transmitter. He arrested a Pole but quickly released him on the grounds of insufficient evidence. He gave me the address of a Polish woman, Mrs Goworowska, who could tell me more. Mrs Goworowska ran a pharmacy and was as brave as she was energetic; it was she who had hidden our evacuated soldiers at her house. She told me that Wysoczański had ordered Tonn to hand over the transmitter, stop his work and join the rest of our men interned at the Kasba-Tadla camp. Wysoczański was still posing as head of the International Brigade in Morocco and continuing to receive funds from our man in Lisbon. I could only marvel at the way French Security tolerated all this nonsense.

While in Casablanca, I surveyed the port and the French naval base. It was difficult not to admire the newest French battleship, the *Jean Bart*, as yet without her heavy armaments. I took photographs of the airfield and the military garrisons. Towards the end of my stay, I visited the ports of Mogador and Mazagan with their relics of Portuguese colonial rule.

It was (and probably still is) impossible to acquaint oneself with all the rich diversity of Morocco within the space of a short visit. Its modernity (including its technology) was the result of French innovations introduced after 1912. Traditional Morocco and its old Moorish culture could be seen more obviously in its cities and large towns – grandiose palaces, magnificent mosques and medieval living quarters, twisted mazes of alleys and passages. Its traditional craftsmen worked publicly in the colourful souks. On the narrow streets, an eternally noisy crowd reigned from dusk to dawn.

I explored Rabat. The European part dated from Marshal Lyautey's time, and its spacious, tree-lined streets, flower-beds and modern white buildings had a prosperous French colonial look. The old Moorish town, Kasbah Ouda, with its medina and souks, dated from the twelfth century. I also visited Chella, the Roman imperial town that was transformed during the thirteenth century into a fortified Moslem monastery containing the tombs of the Marinid Sultans.

MUSTAFA had not contacted me and I presumed that the Agency's routine was proceeding normally. I discussed with Marcel the advantages of having a business in Morocco that would serve as a pretext for my travels, and he promised to look out for any possibilities, especially on the Atlantic coast. In the meantime, he returned our passports with visas stamped for the next three months.

On the 13th, having been seen off by the Dubois family, I departed from Rabat. I greeted my colleagues in Algiers on 14 November and reported my return to Central Office.

The radio correspondence files revealed that during October 1941 we received thirty-five messages and sent sixty-five. The latter covered a variety of military, naval and related problems, including:

October 1941

Military
The transfer of two companies of the 1st Regiment of the Foreign Legion to Dakar (41/112 and 41/157); full data on the dept. of Constantine military garrison (41/150); detailed data on La Sénia airport (41/149); fighter squadron transferred from Maison Blanche airfield to Blida airfield (41/185); Italians using El Aouina airport north of Tunis (41/180); data on the coastal defences at El Metline, east of Bizerta, with batteries of 340mm guns (41/210).

Naval

Further details on the cruiser *Dunkerque* and the battleship *Jean Bart* (41/188); battleship *Richelieu* at Dakar ready for combat with speed of 21 knots (41/146); Bay of Hammamet in Tunisian territorial waters patrolled by Italians (41/181); the tanker *Le Tarn* left Oran, direction due east, with a cargo of 3000 tons of oil (41/172); movement of the French Fleet and Merchant Navy in North African ports (various).

Various

Transportation of Belgian gold to Maison Blanche and its delivery to Marseilles (41/131 and 41/190); the internment of twelve British airmen in Tunisia (41/183); La Sénia airfield: Gen. Weygand discussed the defection of French airmen (41/192).

Central Office continued to send us new assignments including further information on military units and naval vessels and, importantly, detailed plans of Bizerta port. Their message no. 5404 congratulated us on the work that we had accomplished and the news was circulated to boost the morale of our workers.

Several important matters needed to be discussed with BANULS. The routine of the couriers bringing reports from the new post boxes at our Oran and Tunisian outposts would have to be changed. In future they would spend the night in Algiers and collect their assignments from the post box the following day, immediately before their train departed. I also had to find a room suitable for me to use as an office, preferably among the local Jewish population, who were the most reliable and the staunchest anti-Nazi elements in Algiers. There was far too much Intelligence material piling up in my hotel room, not exactly the most private place for it to be stored.

BANULS reported on his investigation regarding the director of the local Shell Company, which confirmed my own information. It appeared that we were dealing with a Frenchman, Jean Lacaze, married to a Polish woman, Halina Domańska, who had been General Kleeberg's secretary when he was Polish Military Attaché in Paris. Lacaze was a French patriot, anti-German and very reliable. BANULS's next report concerned his own private English lessons given by an English woman, Mrs Tuyl, the wife of a Dutch industrialist called up into the Army. The important aspect was that he had met the American Vice-Consul, John Knox, at her home, and that she also seemed to be on good terms with other Americans. This was very interesting information. Mr Knox was unaware that we knew a great deal about him; it was worthwhile continuing friendly relations even though we could not expect to reap any benefits from it immediately.

DOKTOR brought news of the movement of ships and merchant cargoes in North African ports during the past two days. Doubtless, my description of Casablanca port would be passed on to GYNAECOLOGIST. RENÉ had new information on Major Wysoczański's latest activities. He had organised an abortive evacuation of our men at Mascara camp and the officers' hotel from the Bay of Arzev. They were arrested by the French and sent to another camp further south, in Mecheria. Only Wysoczański and a few of his officers had safely boarded the ship from Gibraltar. One of his officers, Captain Szewalski, was arrested but, according to RENÉ, soon released. This new problem would have to be discussed with Hutten-Czapski, and Central Office were informed.

Meanwhile, eight new agents were admitted to our outposts in Algiers (1841–3) and Tunisia (1821–5). An important achievement was that Maison Blanche airfield was now under our surveillance. This was the landing place for aeroplanes flying into North Africa, which meant that, from now onwards, we would have reports on all Germans, Italians and important Frenchmen arriving there.

During my absence in Morocco, the Algerian armed forces had been inspected by General Huntziger, Vichy's War Minister, and the occasion was used as an ostentatious display of French military might in North Africa. Its effect was somewhat marred by Huntziger's death on 12 November, when his aircraft crashed while on its way back to France.

With new agents being admitted, the question of funds, now visibly melting away, continued to plague me. TUDOR and WICHER confirmed that nothing had arrived for us and Central Office continued to prevaricate. Drastic action would soon be required. Having considered the reports about M. Lacaze and Shell, I decided to take a risk. A message (41/231) was radioed to Central Office asking them to send our next financial allocation through Shell's offices in London to Shell in Algiers.

I was also worried about the lack of news from DOKTOR, and BANULS tried to reach him by telephone. When he rang the hotel, a man's voice imitating DOKTOR's invited him to call there and see him. It was obvious that he had been arrested and a trap had been set up at the hotel for his colleagues. It was imperative to warn all his agents. Before we could do so, however, one of them was arrested as he entered DOKTOR's room. Fortunately, he was only a courier passing reports who did not know anyone else from our network. Nevertheless, although nothing incriminating was found on him, he had been arrested and his whereabouts were unknown.

We knew nothing of the actual mishap that had caused DOKTOR's arrest or the place of his detention, and our search proved fruitless. We had no idea, therefore, from which direction the threat came. Central Office were informed on 19 November of the arrests of the previous day (41/229).

It was only several days later that London informed us that DOKTOR's network in Nice and Marseilles had been uncovered when a civil servant from the Nice Prefecture, issuing passports to foreigners, had been arrested (5785). Typically, this message and other warnings came well after the damage had been done. Had they been received earlier, possibly our men could have been saved. It did, however, take off some of the heat as we realised that the arrests had not been sparked by a failure in our Agency. This meant that our network and the post boxes could carry on normally, as neither DOKTOR nor his agents knew anything about them. As to our three Intelligence Officers and myself, we were positive that he would never betray us and that he knew we would do everything in our power to secure his release. At the moment we had no idea of the charges that would be brought against him. It was possible that they would only be connected with his activities in France.

It was therefore with considerable foreboding that, early on the morning of 26 November, we were awakened by the hotel proprietor, who told us, 'There are two gentlemen downstairs in the hall who want to talk to you.' Such an early visit did not augur anything good. Although incriminating documents were hidden away, a search could always turn up some trivial item that could give them a lead. I tried to put on a brave face, urged Sophie to keep calm and tried to convince her that everything would be all right.

Playing for time, I went down in my pyjamas. Two men in plain clothes were standing in the hall, and identified themselves as police officers. They informed me that I was arrested. I pointed out that I needed time to wash and dress, to which they replied that they 'had all the time in the world'. I told Sophie to awaken MUSTAFA, tell him to follow me and find out where they were taking me. They should get rid of all the documents and warn BANULS and RENÉ not to visit the hotel until further notice. After embracing Sophie and George, I was led away.

I noticed that MUSTAFA was following us. We boarded a tram in the direction of Maison Carrée; he mounted the second carriage. We alighted near the Central Police Station (he was still there), then we crossed the road and I lost sight of him. I was led along the Rue Sadi-Carnot until we reached a tall private building and taken up to the fourth floor. Here was the heart of the fight against espionage in Algeria – the Office of Public Security.

Entering an empty office, which they had unlocked, the security men sat down at a table and read the morning newspapers, leaving me to my own devices. Sporadic snoring could be heard from the adjoining room. The office was rather small and appeared to be the 'common room'. The room from where the snoring was emanating was, presumably, for the detainees. The walls were festooned with notices, and on one of them hung a large map of the USSR. There were tiny red flags pinned to it, presumably indicating the front line. At that moment the two security men went out, locking the heavy door behind them.

Meanwhile, life returned to the detainees' quarters. The door must have opened, as the sound of audible conversation made me look in that direction. Good God! DOKTOR was standing in the middle of the room gazing at me with astonishment. He greeted me as 'Director', moved quickly towards me and pulled me into the room. There were some young people who, I discovered later, were Gaullist supporters, arrested for arriving from France without papers.

DOKTOR told me that he had been interrogated on the 23rd by Special Commissaire Leonard from Marseilles, who was in charge of the investigation. Leonard had asked him about Marseilles and Nice, his contacts with Dr Gallois (GYNAECOLOGIST) and his visits to me at my hotel. He told them that he knew me as a Pole from a restaurant in Marseilles and, having recognised me in Algiers, paid my wife and myself a few courtesy visits at our hotel. He also reported that all the Inspectors were anti-German, and their chief, Commissaire André Achiary, was the person for whom I had received a password in Marseilles.

> Yes, you are right [I said]. But I didn't want to use him just yet as there was no reason to. Your replies to Leonard were good. I'll adopt the same line so that our testimonies agree. It would be better, however, if you exhibit complete ignorance about my relations with the GYNAECOLOGIST. I'll also adopt the same story – that I know him from a Marseilles restaurant. It sounds convincing and I'll make up the rest as they question me.

It was time to return to the common room, now almost full of security men assembling for their daily duties. I tried to memorise their faces. About 9am someone brought the post and what they described as 'military information' – a copy of an official, typewritten communiqué giving the latest information from the Russian front. An inspector was having great difficulty with the Russian names while the others were unable to locate them on the map. Apparently it was the beginning of the first Soviet winter counter-offensive. One could see their delight at the Red Army's success.

Approaching the table, I told them that I could draw the line of the Russian front as I had spent some considerable time in Russia and knew the country quite well. They made room for me while I briefly sketched the war situation. Then, reading from the communiqué, I placed the little red flags on their new positions and explained the direction of the Soviet offensive, its presumed aims and the towns that should be captured next. I also gave them my opinion that the German Army would be unable to withdraw intact from the Soviet Union and that, in the end, Hitler would be defeated. Obviously, this was something they wanted to hear. Lunch, for which we had to pay ourselves, was then brought in from a restaurant.

About 2pm I was 'invited' into the Commissaire's office. Two men were present – Achiary, the local man, and Leonard, who was responsible for the investigations. Achiary immediately went out of the room, leaving us alone. After the preliminary questions concerning my name, age, address and occupation, the more important ones followed:

'How do you know Dr Marion Gallois (codename GYNAECOLOGIST)?'

'I've just heard the name for the first time and have never met him.'

The Commissaire interrupted, 'I am sorry, Monsieur, but you are not telling the truth. He visited you at your hotel and gave us your address.'

Opening my arms wide, I answered, 'I don't know French names very well, and this name is unknown to me. If you could show me his photograph then I could tell you whether I know him.'

The Commissaire produced a photograph. After scrutinising it, I replied,

Oh yes, I do know him. We dined at the same table at the Gabrinius Restaurant in Marseilles for quite some time. We talked about my country and about the political situation. I considered him a clever chap. I didn't see him for some time after that as I moved to Algiers. The next time we met was here, at the Café Etoile, and I was very pleased to have met someone I knew. We dined together, and I told him that my son had pleurisy and was at the hotel. Being a stranger, I had no idea where to find a good doctor in Algiers. He said that he was a doctor and would be pleased to take a look at him. We went to my hotel where he was kind enough to confirm my son's illness and to reassure me that the worst was over. Obviously, I was very grateful to him. But that was the only time I saw him here.

The Commissaire gave me a long look. 'Yes, that's all very innocent, but he named you as head of a British Intelligence network and said that you sent him to Commissaire Marcel Dubois with a letter of recommendation. I want you to know that I have just returned from seeing Dubois in Rabat.'

I laughed heartily.

I am surprised at you, Commissaire; fancy believing such stories! I am an economist and a business man, they're the only things I know about. I lost everything in the war. Now I've organised a factory making oatmeal products in Algiers, and our product reaches the French P.O.W.s in Germany. I have too much to lose by getting involved with people like Gallois. As far as Marcel Dubois is concerned, he is my friend, he knows me well and as you've just seen him, I'm sure that he confirmed what I've just said. Incidentally, I'm not in the habit of recommending people I hardly know to my friends!

Leonard put his final question. 'Do you know Lieutenant Engineer Jekiel of the Polish Navy and what is your connection with him?'

My reply followed faithfully DOKTOR's own testimony. I added with surprise that as far as I knew he was a sailor and not an engineer.

Thus finished my interrogation by Leonard. On my return to the detainees' room, DOKTOR was eager to know the outcome. It was clear that they had nothing on him from his work here, only something that came after him from Nice. I asked whether there was a chance that he had been betrayed by someone French. He did not reply.

I spent the first night on a mattress on the floor of the common room and stayed awake for a long time. My arrest, meeting DOKTOR, and the interrogation had affected my nerves. Had

Sophie managed to dispose of the cipher books and the Intelligence documents, reports and maps waiting to be despatched to London, or had they found them all? In moments like this one tried hard to remind oneself of similar experiences from the past, and to guess where the new danger might arise. I was lucky so far; let's hope it stayed that way. Sleep, however, was still not forthcoming, and the heavy snoring of the others did not help.

In the morning the security man who arrested me was the first to arrive at the office. The others came shortly before 8am. One of them brought the coffee and rolls for breakfast. They discussed the hardening of life in Algeria, and complained of being tricked – all the food was going to Germany. Another brought the military information from the monitoring station. Today they actually asked me for my commentary. To my delight, my yesterday's prediction had become an overnight reality. One happily remarked, 'You've more sense than our Staff Officers who believe in Hitler's victory!' They again invited me to forecast the next moves of the Russian offensive. Their naive optimism made me feel very uneasy.

From the time Hitler attacked the USSR, a kind of anxiety, akin to fear, developed inside me. Russia had become an ally and Stalin was not to be trusted. I could not efface the memory of the Red Army invading Poland in 1939. I always had to be on my guard when talking to friendly French people in North Africa, and not disclose my fears for the future. It was clear that neither the French nor anyone else had any idea of the political implications. The USSR, by becoming our ally, was also looked upon as a friend. One could detect that feeling even in Algiers.

I took a different view. Having greater industrial potential and a far greater population than Germany, we would secure the final victory. But, in the event of a great Soviet victory and the defeat of Nazi Germany, who would push the Red Army out of their newly acquired lands? My Polish experiences of 1939/40 increased my fears and presentiments.

My deliberations were interrupted by loud French voices. The distant future matters very little when one is under arrest. They were engaged in an animated discussion about the pro-German

Commissaire Leonard, who was supposed to have returned to Marseilles, leaving the investigations in the hands of the local police. With Leonard out of the way, the moment was opportune to 'introduce' myself to Achiary. His deputy, Commissaire Lofredo, passed by, and I asked him whether I could speak to his chief. Meanwhile, stuck in the office until midday, I observed the comings and goings of the security men and was now certain that I could recognise them again in town. At noon Commissaire Achiary invited me into his office.

He was of medium height, stocky, with dark blond hair, a pleasant face, and in his thirties. After the usual greetings, I asked him outright, 'Monsieur le Commissaire, do you know the following password, "I come from room number five from the Hotel Albert the First"?'

'Yes, I am aware of it!' He looked at me with a mixture of anxiety and astonishment. Looking him straight in the eyes, speaking quietly and slowly, I said, '*Je suis le Chef des Services de Renseignements Alliés sur le territoire d'Afrique du Nord*.' His amazement increased, and he seemed unable to control his voice.

'Why didn't you say so at first?'

'I had no reason to. I'm telling you now.'

We shook hands.

'Right,' said Achiary. 'Commissaire Lofredo will write the report on your interrogation, with your assistance. As far as you're concerned, Leonard has nothing on you, there's no proof. It's far worse for Jekiel. I'm not sure whether I'll be able to keep him in Algiers.'

After this I helped Commissaire Lofredo to compose the report on my interrogation. The rest of the day was spent in DOKTOR's company. I gave him a roll of a few thousand francs which I always carried on me; we discussed my chat with Achiary, and his precarious position in Algiers. DOKTOR was assured that we would do everything possible to set him free. The night was again spent on the mattress on the floor. This time I slept well.

On the morning of the 28th Commissaire Achiary ordered a 'search' of my hotel room, and I went there with two inspectors. While they were going through the motions of a search, I swapped information with George, who was bedridden. Apparently, Sophie was at the Governor General's office attempting to secure my release; George would tell her that I should be back home tomorrow.

Returning to the Office of Public Security, I was in time for my third commentary on the Eastern Front. Even for me, I was extraordinarily lucky: the Red Army offensive had almost followed my predictions, and my prestige with the security men was at its highest. They seemed quite sorry to see me go when I was released and they made me make a solemn promise to pay them another visit. We parted on a jovial note and there was loud laughter at my final riposte, '. . . and I shall come to see you myself, so there's no need to send anyone to collect me!'

At 2pm I was home. Sophie and Mme Aliette had searched for me at all the police stations in Algiers. Prior to that, Sophie had hidden all the papers in MUSTAFA's room and informed BANULS and RENÉ of my arrest. When their search proved fruitless, Sophie telephoned Marcel. He told her that, after receiving a visit from a gentleman from Marseilles, such a turn of events was expected. Marcel advised her to see the person he had mentioned when she was in Rabat. Sophie saw him during my short trip to the hotel and was told that there was nothing to worry about. She had kept everyone in the Agency informed of the developments.

I expressed my warm appreciation to both the ladies. MUSTAFA would inform BANULS and RENÉ of my provisional release, and our work would continue. London was immediately notified of my arrest and release, and that, as far as the Agency's work was concerned, nothing had changed.

During November 1941 we radioed fifty-seven messages and received forty-eight. Among the more important information sent to London was:

November 1941

Military
Further German transports at the airfield of El-Aouina (41/206); French military garrisons in Casablanca, Rabat and Marrakesh

(41/247); transfer of fighter aircraft group from Maison Blanche in Algiers to Sfax in southern Tunisia (41/248); defence of Metline, guns calibre 340mm (41/210).

Naval
List of French naval units in Casablanca port 29/10/41 to 10/11/41 (41/220); military hydroplane base at Arzev to be increased by one wing twelve hydroplanes (41/223); Oran ship movements (41/224); Oran list of ships in port (41/225); oil tanker SS *Le Tarn* reported by message 41/172 on 23/10/41 to sail from Oran via Bizerta to Tripoli was torpedoed by British submarines and is being repaired in port of Algiers (41/213 and 41/238); German transporters in Tunisian territorial waters (41/201); sinking of transporter carrying German Afrika Korps unit 135 (41/198).

Various
Transfer of interned British airmen to the camp at Laghouat (41/212); transport of flour from Tunisia to Libya (41/200); increase of 'German tourists' in Algeria and opening of 'German centres' to be known as consulates in Casablanca, Algiers and Tunis (41/234).

As a routine precaution, Central Office required confirmation of many of our previous messages, also additional information regarding Bizerta port and Tunis airfield, which appeared to be of very special concern to them.

13

DECEMBER 1941: A NEW ALLY, THE USA

Central Office were now sending us the names of individuals suspected of collaborating with the Germans, with instructions to inform them of those people's activities. This was a typical counter-espionage task requiring special agents (which we did not have), and was a specialised activity requiring time, resources and the co-operation of the police. How was it possible to organise such a service when we ourselves were subjected to the activities of local counter-espionage? London regarded it as another mere bagatelle. Nevertheless, I would have to give it serious consideration.

WICHER's message regarding Agency Africa's financial problem stated that they could offer us 100,000 francs, and that only in December. Compared to our ever-increasing expenses, it amounted to a drop in the ocean. By 1 December our balance had fallen alarmingly. I was almost at the end of our resources and would have to organise some sort of loan for the Agency. Fortunately, thanks to my reputation as an industrialist and my relations with influential French people, I could borrow certain sums until my 'Swiss capital' arrived. This would ameliorate the situation temporarily but it could not be regarded as a permanent solution. If we were left very much longer without adequate funds it would prove disastrous. I had been afraid of such a possibility even before embarking for North Africa. Now it had become a reality.

I was irritated by Central Office's messages informing us of the transfer of funds through Lisbon and requesting an estimate of our 1942 budget when we had insufficient to last out the month.

I replied that there was no change in our budget; we required funds immediately. I also asked what had happened to my proposal regarding Shell.

Our message 41/229 to Central Office appeared to have caused a great upheaval, judging by their nervous radio despatches concerning the arrests of DOKTOR and myself. In DOKTOR's case, it was already old news, yet on 9 December they were still warning us that the French Police were looking for him. I answered them in one despatch on the 15th, stating that DOKTOR was in prison in Algiers and might be transferred to France and that I was carrying on my work.

From information received through WICHER, I learned that November had been a fatal month for Polish intelligence. Czerniawski was arrested in Paris after only a year's work, betrayed, out of jealousy, by his closest female agent, Mathilde Carré, known as 'La Chatte'. The network was dismantled by the Germans, and TUDOR had to go into hiding in Marseilles. We were very fortunate that our agency was basically unaffected.

The DOKTOR affair had, however, produced an added problem. RENÉ was now known to the police, and had to be evacuated immediately from Africa. His old contacts from our evacuation work could help him reach Tangiers and, with the help of 'friends', he could then travel to Lisbon and London. A large quantity of important documents substantiating our radio messages had accumulated. I asked him to take our pouch to Tangiers and deliver it to the British Consulate with a request for it to be transferred to the Polish General Staff in London. If he were to be stopped by the police, he would have to dispose of them quickly, especially as they were in French. RENÉ readily agreed and, after receiving the necessary papers, disappeared from Algiers and soon arrived safely in England.

Having lost the services of two of our Intelligence Officers, I turned to Central Office for help. Their reply advised us that, since sending replacements from London would be very difficult, I should select them from the officers whom I had earlier sent to Africa (6652). To a desk officer in London this would, of course, appear the easiest way out. Unfortunately, their advice contained the inherently dangerous suggestion that one should get round one problem by creating another that was even bigger. At the moment all our officers were being kept behind barbed wire by the French authorities as a result of an abortive escape attempt. They were all known to the authorities and would help to unmask our Agency and destroy the network so painfully built up.

One should not, however, underestimate the difficulties facing Central Office in trying to find volunteers willing to swap a desk job for an uncertain future in Africa. It convinced me that I could rely only on BANULS, MUSTAFA and myself, and that it would be extremely foolish to depend on any outside help.

My friendship with MACIEJ had become extremely close. He continually reported that his French superiors had noticed his ever-increasing radio traffic with WICHER, to which they were not privy. It all boiled down to the necessity of having our own radio station. There was only one way of getting a radio, and that was by having it sent from Lisbon to a given address in Algiers. It was a risk we had to take. There was a slight chance that French customs would not inspect the parcel, as the latest Polish model (made in a specialised Polish radio factory in Britain) was fairly small.

At last, BANULS found a suitable room for my office – with the Aboukaya family in a big house on the Rue Isly. They were Jewish, deprived of the right to work by Vichy's latest racial laws, and were anti-German. All my papers were soon transferred there and I could now work free of the anxiety that Commissaire Leonard's men would suddenly materialise at our hotel.

December 1941 saw the formation of our third Intelligence outpost, in the district and town of Constantine. Three new agents were admitted (nos. 1850–52) and Paul Schmitt (agent 1850) became its commander, with BANULS initiating him into his duties. A post box was set up at Algiers for our new outpost. A further expansion of our Oran network took place that month, when new agent 1817 was accepted.

Central Office in London were becoming increasingly interested in the activities of German and Italian agents (primarily counter-espionage matters), and I would have to check on possible co-operation with my new acquaintance, Commissaire Achiary. The opportunity arose sooner than planned. Achiary contacted me at the hotel in connection with DOKTOR's arrest. He had been ordered to transfer him to the military prison in Algiers from where he would eventually be shipped to Marseilles. As conditions in the jail were very austere, I suggested that Achiary should use his influence to allow DOKTOR to receive decent meals from restaurants in Algiers. This was risky as Leonard's faction could investigate all those who appeared interested in him but we decided to waive the safety rules in order to ameliorate his position.

I confided to Achiary London's demands concerning Axis agents and their associates. While I supposed that he was very interested in this subject, obviously he would not have been allocated funds for anti-German activities. I therefore proposed a deal. I would provide him with a monthly budget for his counter-intelligence work, in return for his reports on the activities of the Axis consulates, the Armistice Commission and German and Italian agents and their spies. Achiary was very enthusiastic, adding that the reports would be delivered either by Commissaire Lofredo or himself. I was very pleased with the way that this tricky problem had been solved and hoped that it would soon bring good results. On a personal level, one of its offshoots was that a close friendship rapidly developed between Achiary, Lofredo and myself, which soon extended to our families.

The French community in North Africa vented their national pride in a bellicose attitude towards Great Britain. The British attack on the French Fleet at Mers-el-Kébir, the Dakar Incident and the open hostilities in Syria and the Lebanon had left a profound impression on the Frenchmen working in our agency. Not surprisingly, therefore, our agents demanded assurances that they were working for de Gaulle and not the British. The fact that we were all Allies working for a common cause had no effect. They demanded confirmation by having their catchwords inserted in BBC transmissions in the French-language service from London, and many, in fact, contained such phrases.

Personally, I was convinced that relations between the Free French and the Poles in London were friendly, but this proved not to be the case. It was not my responsibility – others, much more highly placed, were responsible for Franco-Polish relations. But this state of affairs made me conscious of the fact that the British would never have been able to organise a network like ours in French North Africa. Feelings had been aroused too strongly against them.

During December 1941 eighty-four messages were despatched and forty-eight were received. This time, however, our radio messages contained only a summary of the documents to be transferred to Central Office in our clandestine pouch. Since sending our last pouch through RENÉ, the accumulated material had grown beyond all proportions and included maps, plans, descriptions and reports, and my elaboration of the French defensive system in North Africa with the disposition of their troops. Its size compelled me to search for a way of sending it without endangering either the courier or our precious pouch. Fortunately, as will be seen, two completely unexpected events helped me to solve this problem. Meanwhile, the messages radioed to London give some idea of the contents and the amount of documentary material, which was later sent there in our next secret pouch:

December 1941

Military

The coastal defences of the port of Sfax with descriptions of positions and calibre of guns (41/253); use of Cocouville airfield, south of Sfax, by the Luftwaffe on their way to Tripoli (41/252); airfield of El Aouina constantly used by 100 German planes in a night shuttle service to Tripoli (41/312 and 41/255); constant flow through Gabès of transport from Tunisia to Tripoli of food, petrol and munitions (41/254); inspection of the Mareth defence line by German and French officers (41/315); information on strength of military garrisons in Spanish Morocco (41/267, 41/268, 41/269, 41/270); information on military garrisons defending Constantine and Philippeville (41/320); list of targets for aerial bombardment in Algiers and Oran (41/300); strength of forces in the defence of Oran is 16,000 men (41/258).

Naval

Movement and no. of ships in Algiers and Oran (41/261); movement of ships in port of Oran (December) (41/262); sailing line Oran–Marseilles, Casablanca–Marseilles (41/258); ditto Marseilles–Dakar (41/259); ditto Marseilles–Côte d'Ivoire (41/260); Yugoslav cargo SS Serafino Topic now transformed into Italian SS Cosalo loading various mineral ores in Algiers destined for Italy (41/279); Italian cargo ships sailing from Sfax on 9 December (41/283); an escorted convoy of thirty-eight French cargo ships carrying munitions and supplies to Rommel's Afrika Korps has entered port of Sfax (41/311).

Various

Pétain has agreed that the Germans can use ports of Bizerta, Bône, Philippeville and Mers-el-Kébir (41/277); number of sailors in the French Navy will be increased from 60,000 to 80,000 (41/324); eight British airmen rescued from the sea off Algiers (41/284); list of members of the Italian Armistice Commission in the ports of Bizerta and Tunis (41/325).

Central Office, for their part, requested details of the Franco-German agreement facilitating the use of French North African ports and airfields by the Axis forces, reports on petrol reaching Libya, and rubber latex from Dakar. Also, the composition of the Armistice Commission's personnel and of the Axis consulates.

Meanwhile Weygand, recalled to Vichy in November 1941, was dismissed as Governor General of Algeria. On Hitler's orders he was not allowed to return to Algiers, and was banished to Antibes. A stronger German pressure could now be expected. Yves Châtel, a civil servant, was nominated as his successor. Weak and obedient to the Marshal, he was reputed to have said, 'I have nothing to lose and this appears to be my last good job'. General Juin was appointed Commander of the French forces in North Africa.

Châtel's nomination, in fact, resulted in an increasing pressure for collaboration, and the strengthening of the Légion, the SOL (*Service d'ordre légionnaire*, the Special Service of the Légion, known as the French SS), and the Chantiers de la Jeunesse (the Vichy youth movement). Huge amounts of Vichy propaganda were broadcast day and night, preceded by the Pétainist hymn '*Maréchal, nous voilà*'. Stiff penalties were incurred by those caught listening to the forbidden BBC.

Châtel informed Hutten-Czapski, the Polish Government's delegate, that the Polish Consulate had ceased to exist, and that only semi-official Polish offices would be allowed, as had occurred in Metropolitan France. Purges of known Gaullists took place in Government offices. The Gestapo acted as advisers but in reality became overlords. Our confidential information was that the Vichy regime intended to send to Algiers its Minister of the Interior (Pucheu), whose mission was to intensify the purges, strengthen the anti-Gaullist forces and, simultaneously, glorify collaborationists.

There were even more sinister changes in the air. The Germans did not have much faith in Châtel's abilities and favoured his replacement by another Frenchman, Sabatier, a protégé of the Gestapo. As a consequence of these events, and not wishing to subject PIERRE to repressive measures, I abandoned our post box at the Prefecture.

As is usual, pressure in one direction results in a reaction in another. The opposition was fragmented but Vichy's adversaries included republicans, radicals, socialists and communists, also Gaullist supporters in Algiers and Oran, which could not yet be described as an organisation.

In Algiers the illegal Gaullist paper *Combat* appeared irregularly. Associated with it were René Capitant, Guy Menant, Cost-Fleuret and Dr Morali. André Achiary also played an important role because of the key post he held. In Oran, on the other hand, the anti-collaborationist movement united totally opposing political factions, among them Henri d'Astier de la Vigerie, a Royalist; Carcassonne, a socialist; and Father Cordier, Jean Rigault and Lemaigre-Dubreuil, extreme right-wingers.

The greatest hostility towards the Vichy regime and its policies came from the Jewish community. The introduction of Nazi racial laws limited them in their professional occupations and trades. Not surprisingly, therefore, many Jewish doctors and lawyers sympathised with the Gaullist movement. Prominent among them were Dr Raphael Aboulker and René Moatti, the Chairman of the League of Human Rights. We had information on all these groups. I carefully observed all these trends and attitudes, without, however, consenting to enrol any of them directly into our work.

The local French community was divided. Some, prompted by events in Syria and the Lebanon, wholeheartedly supported Pétain's policies. Others supported de Gaulle without voicing their views openly because of the purges taking place. All the French settlers were, however, united in one thing – their hostility towards Britain.

The economic situation deteriorated still further. North Africa was threatened by a serious coal crisis. Stocks in Algiers and Oran for public consumption were almost exhausted. There was a shortage in the Merchant Navy. Only the army had stocks, but it had begun using them, and nobody knew how long they would last.

As a result of the coal shortage, the authorities issued new railway timetables on the Tunis–Algiers–Oran–Casablanca run. Train services were restricted, with arrivals and departures from Algiers only twice a week. Keeping in touch with our Intelligence outposts became a great problem. A courier bringing reports from the outposts would have to wait in Algiers two or three days for his return train, inevitably increasing our expenses. There were also certain passenger restrictions and special permission was required to travel by train. Checks were anticipated on passengers at railway stations.

Buses were also restricted and, as with private cars, would be adapted to run on gasogene, distilled from wood. New laws to reduce the private consumption of electricity and gas were introduced. Overstepping of norms (which were low) would not only be punished by fines but those guilty were to be denied its use in the future.

With the increase in food exports, supplies to Algiers deteriorated and the produce of the *bled* (the interior of the country) was exploited by the black market run by local Arabs. Wine production dropped as alcohol was demanded by the Germans for various purposes including fuel. Menus in restaurants shrank to a few items. Notwithstanding the pressures and propaganda of the Vichy authorities, anti-German feeling inevitably increased.

On 7 December 1941, the world was shaken by the news of the Japanese attack on the American fleet at Pearl Harbor. History had repeated itself. The Russo-Japanese War had begun with a surprise Japanese attack on the Czarist fleet at Port Arthur in 1904. After the sudden Nazi attack on Poland in September 1939 (not to mention the Soviet stab in the back on 17 September), and their invasion of the USSR in June 1941, this method of declaring war should no longer have come as a surprise.

As a result of Pearl Harbor and Hitler's declaration of war on the United States on 11 December, America now became an ally in the common struggle against the Axis powers. Their losses would induce a psychological reaction, and a strong desire for revenge. In consequence, our situation also changed and we could enter into relations with their Consulate in Algiers. I decided, however, to mark time. BANULS would insinuate to Mrs Tuyl during his next visit that some kind of Polish Intelligence service was operating here in Algiers. We would then see how Mr Knox reacted to this 'leak'.

Since Châtel's accession, German pressure had had its effect and relations with the American Consulate and its Vice-Consuls had deteriorated. Their freedom of movement, hitherto unrestricted, now became greatly limited, and their Algiers office was surrounded by German agents. Every visit to their Consulate (occupying an entire floor of an eight-storey building on the Rue Michelet) was hazardous and needed an explanation.

The discreet amount of information leaked by BANULS had its effect. Mr Knox was present at BANULS's next English lesson. Greatly interested, he asked for details and whether its chief could contact the American Consulate. During BANULS's subsequent English lesson, Knox was informed that I agreed and they settled on the time and an exchange of passwords.

Entering the American Embassy discreetly, I met John Boyd and

John Knox, to whom I introduced myself as 'Monsieur Roger'. Both appeared sympathetic and made a good impression. The discussion began with general political and military matters and soon moved to topics of common interest. I asked whether they had any contacts or information from the Algerian area. They answered affirmatively. My next question was directed at discovering the extent of their knowledge of the port of Sfax and the Mareth Defence Line. They knew nothing about either. I asked about other ports in various locations. Their answers were the same; they had no information whatsoever.

I passed my latest information concerning those areas on to them. They were surprised and their interest increased when I led them to understand that my Intelligence network covered the whole of French North Africa. On hearing all of this, Mr Boyd said that it would be very useful for the Allied cause if we could maintain permanent contact, and asked what sort of help the Consulate could give me. I replied that of course we should maintain contact, and that the only help my organisation needed was to have our Intelligence documents transferred to London. This could be done by sending them in the American diplomatic bag to the British Consulate in Tangiers. My suggestion was greeted with enthusiasm and they informed me that their bag was sent there every week. I thanked them for their co-operation, adding that my first pouch would be delivered to them on 2 January 1942. Before parting, we established a method of keeping in contact. On 28 December 1941, message no. 332 was radioed to Central Office: 'Intelligence documents will be sent to British Consulate in Tangiers thru' American diplomatic bag on 2 January. Reply if received.'

During a meeting with Achiary, I brought up the subject of the anti-Vichy resistance movements in Algiers and Oran, which were devoid of any real organisation or leadership. I cited the example of the Polish underground movement, the only one on Polish territory that was then unified and under one command. He agreed to my suggestion that something similar should be attempted in French North Africa, and was keen on my idea of a conference with representatives from Oran.

BANULS was, therefore, sent there to contact its leaders via Robert Ragache, the Oran commander. In the event of their agreement, he would fix the dates of their arrival in Algiers for the first unifying conference. Returning from Oran on 18 December, BANULS reported that Henri d'Astier de la Vigerie would arrive in Algiers on the 22nd, accompanied by another delegate. D'Astier was then informed that a meeting was set for 23 December at Achiary's private apartment.

I arrived early to discuss the agenda. Achiary felt it would be appropriate if I made the opening speech, especially as I was not a Frenchman and would be acting as a neutral party. At about 8pm André led me into his study and I was introduced to d'Astier, whom I had heard about from my Oran reports. He was of medium height, with brown hair, and about forty-five. His erect stature and slow distinctive movements were meant to convey the impression of a man of the world, in a nutshell an aristocrat. I knew that he was deputy to Colonel van Hecke, the leader of the Chantiers de la Jeunesse, the Algerian Youth Movement. His position was a very interesting one as far as our work was concerned.

His companion from Oran was a young man of about twenty-five named Carcassonne. His description tallied exactly with that given by BANULS – a young man of slender build and medium height with black hair and passionate dark eyes. The Algiers resistance movement was represented by Achiary and Captain L'Hostis from the local infantry regiment, to whom André had introduced me previously.

At first we engaged in a general discussion. I learned that d'Astier came to Oran with his family in 1940, after the fall of France, following his unsuccessful attempt to reach Britain from St Jean-de-Luz at the same time as I was there. Our host then proposed that, as the initiator of the proposed unification of the African resistance, I should chair the meeting.

I presented the case for unifying the existing movements into one resistance organisation directed by a single leadership, unified under one command, and gave the Polish example with its underground government and Home Army with a commanding officer and a general staff. After some discussion, they unanimously agreed to unite under the leadership of General de Gaulle. The newly formed resistance organisation would embrace youth (d'Astier's responsibility), the army (L'Hostis), the police (Achiary) and the civilian population (Carcassonne). The two candidates for the post of chief of the 'Résistance Africaine' were General de Lattre de Tassigny, the commander of the troops in Tunisia, and Colonel Van Hecke.

As far as my own position was concerned, I explained that I could not take an active part in their new organisation. The struggle against Vichy and the preparation of the French Forces for a future armed conflict were internal French matters. It was up to them to work out the principles of their organisation, working methods and future plans. My duties in French North Africa were of a special military character aimed exclusively at the Axis military forces. Obviously, as far as it was within my power, I would help them with their contacts with London and financially (though I was offering them funds without having any myself). In return, I asked only for their co-operation in the performance of my duties. London would be made aware of today's conference and Robert Murphy would be asked to send a similar message to Washington.

I was warmly thanked for my initiative, 'which contributed to a unified resistance movement in Algeria', and also for my offer of further help. D'Astier stated that he might be moved to Algiers shortly and it was agreed that my contact should be maintained through him, and through Achiary. It was d'Astier who raised the question that inevitably divided the feuding French political factions – how to reconcile the different political opinions of individuals united in a single organisation. My view was that these matters should be left until the final victory, when the entire nation would have an opportunity to reach a decision democratically. I guessed that he wanted to subjugate the resistance to his own royalist views. He was in close contact with the Comte de Paris, the Pretender to the French throne, who was now living in Morocco.

Sensing that we had reached a common understanding, and not wishing the meeting to degenerate into political wrangling, I raised a new issue, counter-propaganda against Vichy. We should show the populace that a unified resistance was at work by painting counter-slogans everywhere in red paint. For example, Pétain's phrase '*Famille, Travail, Patrie*' should be replaced by '*Patrie et Victoire*'. This sort of thing was being done all over Poland with positive results. In fact, after a time, many such slogans did appear all over French North Africa, which helped to keep up the morale of the French. Strangely enough, the police were not in a hurry to dispose of them. Only SOL seemed eager to remove them.

Thus ended our meeting, which for security reasons lasted only about an hour. London was notified on 24 December: '23rd Inst., conference unifying resistances of Algiers and Oran. Murphy received their plan for Washington. Action based on army, police, youth and others. We give help and decisions' (41/326).

In the evening I gave Mr Boyd at the American Embassy the same information to be delivered to Minister Murphy. On the 28th, after discussions with d'Astier, London was informed that a plan of the new resistance organisation was included in my Intelligence pouch sent through the Americans, also their request for a representative to be sent from London to establish contact with them, for which I suggested a rendezvous some five kilometres west of Algiers (41/330 and 41/331).

I was well aware that the new organisation would be no bed of roses. It would give us extra work, and the perpetually quarrelling French factions would undoubtedly cause problems. On the other hand, its existence was necessary to counter the ever-increasing pro-German propaganda of the Vichy authorities, and it would be extremely useful in Agency Africa's Intelligence work for the Allies.

Towards the end of the year, and in accordance with my agreement with Mr Boyd, I was busy preparing our first Intelligence pouch to be sent through the Americans, which would be impressively heavy. Sorting out all the documents and plans – which included data on the deployment of French forces, on the German economic exploitation of North Africa, and on the important role played by the French merchant navy in supplying the German military machine with essential resources – needed careful elaboration in a clear and presentable form. Every piece of paper had to have the correct number of its corresponding message as previously radioed to London. This was our first opportunity to get rid of all the material that had accumulated since the beginning of our work. The bag previously despatched through DOKTOR and RENÉ had contained only the most important information and, for security reasons, could not have been very bulky.

As mentioned previously, most of this material was kept at our hotel room and George, who was frequently confined to bed, occasionally acted as a watchdog over it. I was very pleased with our achievements, which were due to the efforts of our Intelligence Officers, outpost commanders and their agents. BANULS warranted the most credit because of his unusual intelligence and total dedication to duty, while two of our outpost commanders – Robert Ragache (agent 1812) in Oran, and Roquemaure (agent 1820) in Tunis – led our French colleagues' accomplishments. Our basic principle was maintained. The Vice-Consuls and the heads of the Resistance knew me only as 'M. Roger', while the Chairman and Floc-Av personnel knew me as 'Stawikowski'. Only a few people in our network knew the identity of its chief, and secrecy was maintained.

Despite our desperate shortage of funds, our overall situation was improving. Paradoxically, however, because of increasing Gestapo involvement in one's everyday life, our individual situations were becoming more difficult. In short, to complete the task for which I had originally been sent to French North Africa, only Morocco and Dakar needed to be organised. Unfortunately, the latter would be a very tough nut to crack.

I pondered on the obstacles strewn along our path, including my detention on the ship and my arrest by Leonard. Looking closely at all these events, I was struck that the same pattern should emerge again. Events that at the time seemed ominous appeared in retrospect to be positively beneficial. For example, it was George's unfortunate illness that allowed me to stay permanently in Algiers: it provided me with a legitimate excuse and made the explanation of my connection with GYNAECOLOGIST very plausible.

Nobody knows what fate has in store for them. Nobody can tell what will be good, and what may turn up even better. I was ending the old year in an optimistic mood and continuing to trust in my luck.

14

JANUARY AND FEBRUARY 1942

I went to Chairman Godziszewski's New Year's Eve party with Sophie in a buoyant mood. There, I was introduced to many prominent local French people including their leading judge, who was also head of the Court of Appeal and the Tribunal for Special Jurisdiction, under whose competence all espionage cases came. 'Something just right for me,' I thought.

The Chairman continually introduced me as his associate and, to my obvious reluctance, as a former diplomat specialising in Soviet affairs. After exhausting the topic closest to their hearts, which was the food shortage, they moved on to a discussion of the military and political situation. Naturally, everyone regarded themselves as an expert. The most heated discussion concerned the Eastern Front, and whether Hitler would defeat Stalin.

Opinions were divided. Vichy supporters, succumbing to the myth of the invincible German Army, were certain that the Nazis would win. Others, presumably secret supporters of de Gaulle, drew a comparison between Hitler's attack on Russia and Napoleon's retreat from Moscow. During the heated exchanges that followed, the two parties, prompted by Godziszewski, finally asked me for my opinion. Obviously I was not very keen on revealing my own views to the local bigwigs, and especially to the judge. I glanced at our host, who raised his eyebrows and gazed at me expectantly. He hushed the others and beckoned to me to proceed.

Not having much choice, I told them that Hitler could have achieved total victory over Stalin and destroyed the communist system in the first few months of the war. The insurmountable obstacle was the Nazi racialist ideology. If, when the Wehrmacht entered the USSR, he had announced a return to private ownership, and adopted the old Leninist slogan 'Freedom to the oppressed nations and their religious liberty', the Soviet empire would have collapsed.

By rejecting this policy for ideological reasons, and by introducing even greater exploitation, terror and misery than Stalin, Hitler would be defeated. Disillusioned by the Nazi terror, all those in the vast Soviet empire, who had hitherto regarded any potential invader as a liberator, would be bound to rise up in defence of Mother Russia as had the Russian serfs during Napoleon's invasion in 1812. Stalin would benefit from the situation; Nazi Germany would sustain enormous losses, which would hasten its final collapse. Here lay another great risk. The Red Army could become an immensely powerful victor, thus facilitating Soviet plans for world domination, which could prove as dangerous to democracy as German National Socialism.

I noticed that my interpretation of events did not quite come up to Vichyite expectations, and that the judge gave me a long, searching look. Shortly afterwards, having excused ourselves, we left for a party of our own at the Isly Restaurant. As New Year's Day was also the name day of the chief of Agency Africa, I invited my two Intelligence Officers and their wives to my little banquet, which, as expected, turned out to be more lively than the Chairman's effort.

The next evening, 2 January, I took our Intelligence pouch to the American Consulate where Messrs Boyd and Knox awaited me as arranged. They were very bewildered at such a substantial package and I unpacked it to show them that it contained nothing dangerous. As they ransacked the plans and reports, which were in French, they became increasingly amazed. After satisfying their curiosity, they agreed that we were doing a great job and that our material was invaluable. The package was repacked and sealed in my presence. In the ensuing conversation, both assured me of their unlimited assistance, and that my pouches would be despatched to Tangiers every Friday. I was grateful for their co-operation, and would maintain personal contact with them. The next pouch would be delivered on 9 January.

Establishing a regular flow of Intelligence pouches to London greatly simplified my work and that of Central Office. Henceforth only urgent messages requiring coding needed to be sent by radio. The vast majority could be despatched by pouch, thus saving time on coding and decoding. This would enable me to maintain more efficient control over our activities and find ways of improving our work. At the moment our Agency was left with only two Intelligence Officers and the outside work was divided between them. BANULS was now responsible for contacts with the outposts in Oran, Tunis and Constantine through our post boxes. MUSTAFA had taken over the outposts in Algiers abandoned by RENÉ and the port of Algiers from DOKTOR, who had been arrested. Consequently, my own daily routine remained unaltered.

Judging by the number of messages received, it appeared that my message 41/326 on the organisation of the resistance movement must have created a stir in London. They wanted detailed information on its character, its strength, importance and composition whether help was required and a representative from London was considered necessary. My reply (42/001 and 006) and my written report (Ref. 42/1/tj) would be despatched in our second pouch through the Americans.

Central Office asked whether the money and the hurdy-gurdy sent on 27 December from Agency Lisbon had been received (6850 and 6952). I despatched a laconic reply (42/002): 'No money, no radio, my total for 1/1/1942 amounts to only 15,802 francs.'

BANULS's Intelligence material from the Oran outpost contained information from the ports of Arzev, Mers-el-Kébir and Oran, which would be despatched in our second pouch on 9 January. I had no idea why we were not receiving any reports from the Tunis outpost or why its post box was always empty.

On 9 January, while handing over our second Intelligence pouch to the Americans, Mr Boyd communicated to me their State Department's instructions that our pouch should be delivered open and unsealed. I was obviously dissatisfied by this unexpected turn of events and remarked somewhat sharply: 'But by giving you my work in an open bag, it will mean that all my Agency's secrets will be read and be known to everyone while they are in transit. How do you intend to send them now, and to whom?'

Boyd was taken aback by my attitude and quickly reassured me: 'The pouch will be sealed after it reaches the United States Military Attaché at our Consulate in Tangiers. We can do nothing about it,' he added, 'although I know that it may seem rather unusual to you.'

Having no alternative, I was compelled to agree. I well realised that, by handing the Vice-Consuls our unsealed pouch, we would enable them to exploit the fruits of our labour by copying our information and sending it directly to Washington. I resigned myself to writing it off as a payment to the Americans for the service they were more than willing to perform for us. Information gathering was our primary task; in reality it was unimportant whether London or Washington obtained it first.

There was another matter of considerable importance wherein I had to rely on their help. I notified Boyd about the parcel supposedly on its way to me via the US Consulate in Lisbon, which should contain US $12,000 and a radio transmitter. We established a code word to be telephoned to me at the hotel as soon as it arrived.

On 6 January Central Office, responding to my information sent in October 1941 concerning British airmen interned in Tunisia, sought to discover whether Flight-Lieutenant Charles Lamb was among them. My message of the 11th confirmed that he and others were now interned at the Laghouat camp a few hundred kilometres south of Algiers (42/011). Achiary (now codenamed SREBNY, 'silver' in Polish) confirmed our previous report from the commander of the Tunis outpost regarding the Mareth defence line. The town of Gabès would be the centre of the Defence Command, with two subdivisions – North and South. The cement had already been prepared for the construction of the fortifications.

At last Mr Boyd informed me that the radio transmitter had arrived but there was no sign of the money. Sophie and Mme Aliette were sent to collect the parcel on the assumption that a woman with a shopping bag would attract less attention. We now had our own hurdy-gurdy (about the size of a large portable radio), and, to our enormous satisfaction, it was Polish-made. It was moved to my office that evening. All we needed now was a radio operator to go with it.

Our new social standing in Algiers and increasing circle of influential friends meant that we urgently required a suitable apartment to arrange soirées. There was a housing shortage, due mainly to the influx of European refugees, and finding such a place would not be easy. It also had to provide the possibility of a speedy exit in case of emergency.

BANULS's reports from the Oran and Constantine post boxes continued to flow but there was still nothing from Tunis, and their silence was causing me considerable anxiety. Among the reports from the outposts, the following dealt with the Mareth line and supplies to the Germans:

General Juin's marching orders to the Algiers and Oran divisions for readiness to mount the Mareth Line defences (42/014); rubber latex being shipped from Philippeville port (42/015); stores of petrol and diesel oil in German metal containers stored at the railway station of Ouled-Rahman are being prepared for despatch to the port of Gabès (42/018).

On 16 January pouch no. 3 containing our latest Intelligence information and my report on radio linkage was delivered to the Americans. The problem of radio communication with London was extremely difficult. We had to have an operator and a suitable place for installing the station and the aerial. Its location had to be safe and also fulfil the technical requirements of clear reception and transmission.

Until now MACIEJ had been our medium of communication and we did not know the most elementary data necessary to connect us with London: the wavelength, the radio calls or the fixed times for transmitting and receiving messages. He himself had never been in direct contact with London, only with WICHER in the south of France, and did not know either.

Turning to WICHER and TUDOR for help, I requested them to find me an operator from among our men in France (42/020). They were unable to find anyone. Worse still, WICHER could maintain contact with us only until the end of March, as he was calling his Polish radio Intelligence team in Algiers back to France. The situation looked potentially disastrous. I passed the buck to London, requesting a radio operator and explaining why we would otherwise have to cease contact with them as from March (42/023). Let them worry for a change.

Another message from London about the money. The Americans had received it in Lisbon and the American Consul, Mr Cole, would hand it over to me within four days. The four days passed and there was still no sign of the cash. The problem could not be solved by my continual borrowing, as I was already far too much in debt with the banks and the money-lenders. They would begin to suspect that my 'Swiss capital' was a load of bullshit.

I wrote several reports acquainting Central Office with some very important matters. An outline of Agency Africa with its problems and proposals for its future development was presented (42/5/tj) which constituted a reply to their five previous messages, also an additional explanation regarding our work in Tunisia (42/9/tj) and radio linkage with London (42/13/tj).

I also sent them a description of Admiral Darlan's visit to Algiers and Tunis, which produced changes in the command of the French Forces in Tunisia. It was a complete mystery to us why General de Lattre de Tassigny should suddenly have been sacked and removed to France. Also despatched was Roquemaure's information on the Tunisian Arab political party Destour, which wanted full independence and national sovereignty; they were a progressive, anti-communist party and wanted to co-operate with the West.

All this material was incorporated into pouch no. 4, which I handed over to Mr Knox on 23 January. He, in turn, gave me an envelope, which I hoped would contain US $12,000. He asked me to check its contents in his presence. To our great surprise there were no dollars – only 75,000 Portuguese escudos.

I was speechless. Knox was equally amazed. We stared at each other in silence. Portuguese escudos were the one currency that was unwanted on the black market, and therefore unconvertible into anything else. If one tried to exchange such a large amount of unpopular foreign currency in French North Africa, one ran the grave risk of unmasking oneself and jeopardising the Agency. This I was not prepared to do. Knox was very willing to help me out by agreeing to my proposition to have the exchange done by the American Consulate in Tangiers. Central Office were informed immediately that escudos instead of dollars were received, and of the dangers we ran by any potential exchange, not to mention the Agency's financial loss for having to pay out such a large commission (42/027).

I'd had enough. Having had no support whatsoever from London, encountering nothing but difficulties from them which could only damage our work, and not wishing to be made a scapegoat for the collapse of our agency, I asked to be relieved from my post. There was an immediate reply (42/626), explaining that the error in Lisbon with the escudos was being investigated and that the money should be returned to the senders for exchange. Regarding my resignation, at the moment this was totally unacceptable. I was then informed that a solution had been found for the money, which was being put into effect. It was the one that I had already discussed with Knox.

BANULS's reports from the Intelligence outposts continued their weekly flow and their commanders adapted themselves to an established routine. MUSTAFA brought me his reports: Oran, Algiers and Constantine were functioning well. Only those from the Tunisian post box were still missing, and my anxiety was increasing. As things stood, we already had sufficient material for pouch no. 5, which included report no 42/14/tj showing the latest political and general changes. Knox received it on 29 January.

During January 1942, Central Office were informed that new agents nos. 1818 and 1876–8 had been accepted. They radioed forty-eight messages during the month and received forty-three from us. There was still no confirmation from London of the receipt of our Intelligence pouch no. 1 sent via the Americans – who were definitely hanging on to it for far too long.

During this time, despite (or perhaps because of) our close

friendship, MACIEJ began causing me some concern. He became very suspicious about being left behind in Algiers while his team was gradually recalled to France and our own radio station was almost operational. I tried to calm him down. Unfortunately, he only became convinced that there was no conspiracy against him when, after a tragic accident, he realised that being left behind had saved his life.

Part of MACIEJ's team, four Polish officers and their 'guardian' (a French captain), embarked on the SS *Lamoricière* bound for Marseilles in January 1942. The ship was a shallow vessel intended for coastal traffic only. On the Mediterranean, near the Balearic Islands, amid a violent storm, the ship suffered a disaster. Having most probably struck a reef, and after only partly effective salvage operations by several other vessels, the ship sank. Three of the four Polish officers and the French captain who accompanied them were killed. The total toll of victims was dreadful: 222 out of 272 passengers and fifty-seven of the 100-man crew perished.

When the news was reported, terrible scenes took place outside the shipping office on the Boulevard Carnot where lists of the missing passengers had been posted. MACIEJ, who read the names of the three officers of his team, was crushed. Sophie and I had to put considerable effort into restoring his mental stability. This tragedy, unusual for the Mediterranean, passed comparatively unnoticed at the time. It still remains among my most painful memories of the Second World War.

The long-awaited message (382) addressed to M. Jean Lacaze, the Director of the Société Shell in Algiers, arrived on 22 January. It was in English, advising him to 'pay 600,000 French Francs to the bearer' of the document, and signed by the Chairman of the Shell Co. in London.

At last we would have adequate funds. Only the plan of action remained to be worked out. I would wait a few days to ensure that M. Lacaze himself had received a similar message from them. Obviously, he would never pay out such a large sum simply on the strength of a piece of paper with the Chairman's name on it; such a document could easily be fabricated by any self-respecting confidence trickster.

The consequences also had to be considered. Despite his reputed anti-collaborationism, and even with confirmation from London, we could not be absolutely certain of his reaction. Perhaps he would be afraid of losing his post or suspect German or Vichy provocation. On the other hand, he could decide to take a gamble and co-operate with us. The most doubtful aspect was – how would he behave towards our messenger?

The operation needed a special touch. We had to send a woman who, in Lacaze's mind, would not present a direct personal threat, as might be the case if he were dealing with a man. Whom could we send? It could not be a Frenchwoman since quite obviously the Germans and Vichyites would use one. It must be a foreigner. As such, there was no other choice – it could only be my wife.

Despite the dangers involved, Sophie agreed to go. Everything would depend upon her judgement, intuition and astuteness. After being granted a personal interview with Lacaze, she would hand him the message and say, 'I was sent by my chief, Mr Roger, involved in special work in Algiers. He wants to know whether you would be willing to follow the instructions on the message and pay out the sum of money stated.' No other explanation should be given. If he agreed, an appointment would be fixed for me to meet him. If he refused or issued threats, then she would warn him that her visit must remain secret, otherwise both he and her chief might find themselves in great danger. This would be intended as a not particularly subtle threat.

On the afternoon of the 27th Sophie went to the Compagnie Française de Shell. While she was away, I suddenly felt guilty for sending her on such a dangerous task. Was our information about his reliability genuine? I tried to reassure myself. Surely the Paymaster at Central Office would not be so naive as to order someone to pay out £3,000 on the strength of a scrap of paper? Would he have done so himself? He, for whom every penny required different orders, assignations, confirmations and receipts? No, of course he wouldn't. Lacaze's notification must have occurred some time ago. I was worrying for nothing.

Anyway, the game had already begun and it was too late to

stop it. I was certain that Sophie would be perfectly able to play her allotted role. Her charm, self-confidence and intelligence would see her through. When, after two and a half hours, I heard her voice in the hotel lobby, my heart began beating faster. Her mission must have been successful, as she had come back safely. Soon she gave me a detailed account:

I entered the Shell building unnoticed. I told the receptionist that I wished to speak to the General Director, M. Lacaze, about a personal matter. After waiting about five minutes, I took the lift to the first floor and was ushered into the director's office. M. Lacaze was middle-aged, elegant, quite good-looking and seemed pleasant. He rose to greet me, asked me to sit down, and inquired what he could do for me.

I replied that I was sent by my chief to ask whether he was familiar with the message which I handed to him. He took it with curiosity, read it, and said, 'Yes, I know the name of the man who signed it, but I have no other information, and do not know anything about this matter.'

Obviously, such an answer made a deep impression on me. I was practically speechless and had no idea how to reply. It must have looked like a blackmail or fraud attempt. He was watching me attentively and, after a moment, softened.

'Who is your chief and what does he do?'

I told him that M. Roger was my chief and that I was not qualified to give any further information. I added that he could meet him when this matter was settled.

He asked me a further question. 'You are obviously not French, What nationality are you?'

'I am Polish,' I answered.

'My wife is also Polish.'

'Yes, we know. Miss Halina Domanska worked in the Polish Embassy in Paris as secretary to General Kleeburg, the Military Attaché.'

My comment surprised him. He was even more astonished at our detailed knowledge of his private life, which emerged as the conversation touched on other subjects. At the end of my visit, he expressed his readiness to pay out the money providing he received a direct message from London. I told him that it would arrive very soon. He was extremely polite throughout, and as we parted he said that he hoped to see me again soon.

I had no doubt that it was only thanks to Sophie that we had avoided a total catastrophe. It also painfully revealed the extremely inefficient way in which Central Office functioned. It was supposed to be the duty of those at HQ to facilitate the work of agents in the field who continually risked their lives in situations of danger. The kindest thing one could say was the total lack of realism on the part of the officer dealing with the money. He should have been aware that the chairman of a commercial enterprise could not be expected to pay out a large sum of money (even to his best friend) without proper cover for his company and himself. It would have been simple to have sent confirmation to Lacaze directly through Lisbon or Tangiers or even through the American Consulate.

We should have had the money in our coffers by now and there should have been no need for me to be worrying about the agents. Most importantly, the Agency would not be in danger of imminent collapse. At the moment (1 February) all we had was 3,858 francs, a debt of 170,000 francs, and constant anxiety about obtaining new loans to be able to continue our work for the Allies.

I radioed a message (42/031) on the same day, expressing my surprise at the way the matter was being dealt with and requesting immediate notification to Lacaze through the American Consulate. However, this took a much longer radio conversation than necessary. For two whole weeks it hung in the balance. Finally, losing patience, I sent another message on 18 February demanding that they speed up their reply, as Lacaze's co-operation was needed urgently (42/084).

On 24 February I finally received a positive reply – a copy of message 1295 in English sent directly to M. Lacaze. The matter was settled at last. Now, with a clear conscience, I sent Sophie to Shell on the 26th to arrange my meeting with its director.

On arrival, she was quickly ushered to Lacaze's office. He was smiling and said that he was expecting such a visit. After reading our copy of the message he said that everything was now in order and that he would pay us the money, but in instalments as the sum was rather large, and it would require an entry in the company's books. Sophie thought that this would be acceptable to her chief. Lacaze wanted to meet him, and asked whether 'Mr Roger' was in contact with London and, if so, whether he could send his reply through our channel. He then gave her a short message (42/105), which was passed to the addressee that evening.

The risk paid dividends. We would receive 600,000 francs, which would secure our work for some time, and it enabled me to contact M. Lacaze, whose position would be very useful to us. As other very urgent matters had cropped up in the meantime, this would only be possible on 7 March.

On the day of our appointment I was received by the General Director at his office. His description was already known to me from Sophie. He struck me as having great strength of character, his personality radiated energy, and his informal manner indicated that he had acquired certain American characteristics. I began with an apology and emphasised that I was compelled to choose this method of receiving subsidies from London because it was of the utmost importance to our work. If there was any misunderstanding, it was London's fault. He was put in a difficult situation and so was I. However, our information about him had proved correct and I thanked him in the name of our common struggle to liberate our respective countries.

Lacaze confessed that he had had a great number of reservations but that the lady who visited him had inspired him with confidence and he had decided to take the risk. He was very happy that his judgement had been vindicated. We chatted as if we were old friends. I told him that London wanted detailed information on the reserves of motor fuel in French North Africa and that his data on such matters would be of vital importance to the Allies. In reply, he provided me with very precise information. We decided that in future we would only meet personally.

Returning home satisfied, I immediately sent three messages to London giving the stocks of military and civilian fuels and heavy oil and their state of production (42/119, 42/120, 42/121). I also gave M. Lacaze the codename SMUTNY.

15

FURTHER ADVERSITY

In the meantime the 'other urgent matters' alluded to previously that had prevented me from meeting Lacaze immediately had exploded on us on 1 February 1942. BANULS, knowing how impatiently I was awaiting news from our Tunis outpost, retrieved the reports from the post box and brought them to my hotel while I was at the oatmeal factory. On my return from Floc-Av, Sophie handed me a small, thin envelope. A terrible presentiment gripped me. It should have been the usual thick bundle full of reports and plans.

My forebodings were justified. One of the surviving agents of the Tunisian network reported the arrest of Maxime de Roquemaure, the commander of the outpost (agent 1820), together with agents 1821 and 1822 on 5 January. The Tunisian police were directing their inquiries towards Algiers, supposedly the centre of the espionage ring.

I immediately ordered a total cessation of our activities in Tunisia. It had happened at last. Agency Africa had finally caved in. The most urgent question was, what did Roquemaure know about BANULS, and what did the police find at his flat? According to my orders, BANULS's original briefing with him contained strict instructions not to keep any names, addresses or notes. Had he disregarded them?

I took Sophie to lunch in a sombre mood, while my brain was working overtime. The arrests had occurred four weeks ago and as yet there was no visible sign of a police investigation. Possibly they had no proof and could get nothing out of Roquemaure.

Alternatively, it could be a trap sprung for our courier from Algiers in the hope that he would lead them to our headquarters. One way or another, I had to see Achiary that evening to discover whether he had any further information from Tunis.

The afternoon was spent working in my clandestine office on the Rue Isly. It was difficult to concentrate with Tunisia on my mind. At 5pm I was back at the hotel. BANULS came at 6pm. He had heard a rumour that two men had questioned the hotel porter some three hours ago about a person whose name was unknown to them but whose description fitted himself. Fortunately he was out of town with his wife at the time. After hearing this news, I gave him an urgent order: 'You must leave your hotel immediately! Tell them you're leaving Algiers. Move into my office at the Aboukayas at once. Stay there and wait for me. Agent 1820 has been arrested in Tunis.' BANULS, extremely disconcerted, returned immediately to his hotel and within half an hour he and his wife had settled into their new home.

Late that evening, at 10pm, I called at Achiary's flat and luckily found him in. I told him about the arrest and that I was worried about the others. Had he received any special information from Tunisia? Achiary disclosed that only today two inspectors had arrived from Tunis with orders to arrest someone staying at the hotel on Briand Square. They were unaware of his real or his assumed name. From the hotel porter's description they concluded that he must be a certain Henry Łubieński, a Pole. They telephoned Tunis and obtained an order to arrest him and take him back there immediately. Achiary assured me that they did not connect it with DOKTOR's arrest. Leonard had returned to France convinced that the Algiers spy ring had been broken, while the Tunisian authorities were positive that Łubieński (BANULS) was the head of another organisation.

As to the affair in Tunis itself, Achiary knew that the agent was a certain Roquemaure, who was arrested after a search of his flat had revealed incriminating material. The police had found detailed descriptions of the port defences of Sfax, Sousse and Bizerta. Worse still, they had discovered his close contact with General de Lattre de Tassigny. This had necessitated Admiral Darlan's special visit to Algiers and Tunis – an indication of its importance, since he was the second most important person in the Vichy regime, subservient only to Marshal Pétain himself. Darlan had immediately relieved Tassigny of his post as commander of the French army in Tunisia and he was transferred back to France. General Barré would be taking over the Tunisian command on 12 February.

French security in Tunisia began their investigations after the police at Sousse had noticed Roquemaure's continual visits there and his frequent inspections of the coast. They followed him back to Tunis to discover his place of residence. After his next appearance in Sousse, however, and a thorough surveillance of his movements, they searched his flat. It was likely that, if they had found nothing, they would have left him alone. His carelessness and disregard of orders had brought us to this pass. I was very grateful to Achiary for his information.

I felt much more relaxed on my journey home. The cave-in may not have been as bad as we thought; BANULS was certainly secure at his new abode. Carelessness and over-keenness produced mishaps. Roquemaure failed to comply with our instructions not to keep any incriminating material. After all, the purpose of the post boxes was to move the reports quickly. We were witnessing the results of not adhering to orders.

Although it was fairly late, I dropped in on the Łubieńskis. They were put in the picture and told to stay there until the Tunisian inspectors stopped lurking about in Algiers. Nevertheless, under cover of darkness, we both went out to see what had happened to the Tunisian post box. The streets were still crowded. The house where the post box resided in the doctor's surgery on the first floor was strongly illuminated, and there was a police guard outside the building. They were searching the doctor's apartment. BANULS could now see for himself why caution was so necessary.

When I returned to the hotel in the early hours of the morning Sophie was waiting up for me. I lay in bed thinking about the initial mishap and the sequence of events. If I hadn't received the Tunisian report, I could quite easily have belittled BANULS's story about the inquiries at his hotel, in which case he most certainly would have been arrested. Achiary told me in the morning (2 February) that the Tunisian inspectors went to Łubieński's hotel at 6am to arrest him. Our post box operator, Dr Charles Stora, was arrested even though they had found nothing incriminating at his flat. His name had appeared in Roquemaure's confiscated notes and apparently that was sufficient.

The Tunisian business had created a dangerous situation but the Agency's work had to continue. Mr Knox telephoned a codeword indicating that my parcel from Tangiers (with the exchanged Portuguese escudos) was ready for collection. I had no idea how many dollars or francs they represented but it would give me a chance to repay part of my mounting debts. I intended to visit the Consulate in the evening. MUSTAFA was given new instructions about the post boxes during BANULS's temporary unemployment. It was essential that messages should be collected as soon as they arrived. This would make for greater security, both for the Agency and for everyone involved in it.

The railway timetables revealed the possible movements of our couriers to and from Algiers. Normally their first steps were always directed towards depositing their reports in the post box. BANULS and his wife used to collect them at their convenience. Now it would be MUSTAFA's task to find suitable collectors, one for each post box. They were mostly operated by medical practitioners (less likely to attract attention) except for the one at the Prefecture, which we had closed down. Although one had been arrested (Dr Stora), we still had another two operating in Algiers.

The collector of the reports, simulating a sick patient, would attend the doctor during his surgery hours. He would stay in the waiting room until the last moment to ensure that the courier carrying the package had deposited it with the doctor. The collector and the courier would not know each other; frequently they could be sitting side by side in the waiting room. The depositing and collecting of packages was performed after an exchange of simple passwords. The courier handed it to the doctor, saying, 'The letter for Mr John.' The collector would reply, 'A letter from Mr Michael.' Once the reports were collected they would be handed over to MUSTAFA and then delivered to me.

Before his return journey each courier had to revisit the post box to obtain instructions for the commander of his outpost. It was always in the form of a letter, which he received from the medical practitioner after an exchange of simple passwords.

MUSTAFA was informed of the Tunisian mishap, and that the police had identified his friend Łubieński. He was now responsible for organising his own network of collectors for the Oran and Constantine post boxes from among very reliable Frenchmen. The instructions for the outpost commanders, on which I was now working, would have to be delivered to them shortly via the post boxes. He was also advised to inquire among his agents for a radio ham who could operate our station. Any hope of obtaining one through WICHER or TUDOR had been abandoned.

Later in the evening Mr Boyd handed me a packet containing the money from the exchange of escudos, which amounted to 517,500 francs. My debts, totalling 230,000 francs, would be repaid, thus confirming the existence of my 'Swiss capital' and improving my chances for further credit. This, together with the funds I hoped to receive from Lacaze, would tide us over for a considerable period.

In their reply to our earlier message, London informed us that Hutten-Czapski, the Polish Government delegate in Algiers (codename DELEGATE), had been notified that we should co-operate. This was the green light for me to contact him and I visited him at the Hotel Georges a few days later. We worked out a scheme to try to help our soldiers imprisoned at the Mecharia Camp. They were due to be transported further south to Colomb-Bechar, prior to being used as forced labour on the 'Alger–Niger' (the Trans-Saharan railway). DOKTOR was still incarcerated in the military prison in Algiers and the authorities had not yet decided his fate. We were still providing him with meals and paying for them, but they were delivered as if ordered by DELEGATE through the Polish Consulate.

MUSTAFA now delivered his first reports from Oran and Constantine. Apart from the usual descriptions of the coastal defences, they also contained information on

SS *Cap Falcone* leaving Algiers, destination Tunis, with a shipment of motor fuel; south of Tunisian border with Algeria and Libya, a concentration of large French military units at Fort Saint is imminent; a British bomber plunged into the sea near the port of Mostaganem (42/45, 42/46, 42/51, 42/53).

London required further details on this last item, which the Oran commander was able to provide, and it was despatched in our pouch no. 6. The plane was a Wellington bomber; there were three dead and three wounded airmen who were being treated in hospital in Oran (42/77).

Pouch no. 6 was in fact delivered to Boyd on 6 February. Felix Cole, the Consul, and the big chief, Robert Murphy, the Minister, wanted to meet me. Presumably this was the result of their thorough scrutiny of our Intelligence pouch. Mr Cole was an elderly gentleman who was almost preposterously polite. We discussed the African situation and the position of the Allies. He expressed his appreciation of my work in North Africa and told me that if I ever found myself in difficulties I should turn immediately to him.

Robert Murphy was friendly and sympathetic. He had a simple and unaffected manner and was the best type of American. After greeting me warmly, Murphy said that he already knew something of my work. He expressed his pleasure at my co-operation with his Vice-Consuls, who were under his orders, and hoped that we would continue to work closely together in the future.

I protested that he was praising me too much; I had an Intelligence network behind me to which I owed my success and would always be pleased to pass on information and news. After all, we were Allies and working for the same cause. As he must be well aware, I was giving his Vice-Consuls the fruits of our Intelligence labours in an unsealed pouch and they could draw on an unlimited supply of information as required by Washington. I had no objection to that, provided that they were informed that their source was Intelligence Service Agency Africa of the Polish Army in North Africa. The Minister gave an enigmatic smile and said, 'Naturally it is understood that this is part of our gentlemen's agreement.' We parted on excellent terms.

As yet there was no confirmation from London that any of our five pouches sent through the Americans had arrived. Officially I did not know what had happened to them. Unofficially it was not difficult to surmise that the delay was due to the 'close co-operation', that Murphy had mentioned. I decided to discontinue sending them until confirmation had been received. Central Office were notified of my decision that pouch no. 6 would be the last until the others had been found (42/55/tj).

London's messages began to show a far greater interest in our work and their replies were much speedier. There were additional and more precise tasks covering the coastal and anti-aircraft defences, naval armaments, stocks and quantities of motor oil and the transport by sea of metal ores to France.

At last Central Office acknowledged receipt of pouches no. 3 and 4 but the first two had still not arrived and they asked me to reclaim them from the Americans (931). They wanted a detailed description of their contents and informed us that the British Consulate in Tangiers had not received them either (1108). I was really anxious. The first pouch contained information of inestimable value from Tunisia and we would suffer irreparable damage if it had been lost.

I intervened with Boyd, who appeared disconcerted. He promised a thorough investigation and would notify me of the result. His concern was sufficiently reassuring for me to decide to resume forwarding our pouches through the Americans. However, I had to wait a considerable time for the outcome of the search. News came towards the end of February that the two pouches were being kept at the American Embassy in Lisbon, and London was informed of this on 27 February (42/108). It took considerably longer for them actually to reach their final destination.

Achiary informed me through his Inspector Schmitt, who was also on our payroll, that after hunting for BANULS and his wife for several days the Tunisian Inspectors had given up and returned home. I went to see BANULS with the happy news that he was now released from his temporary 'arrest'. He was very depressed at what had happened to Roquemaure (agent 1820) and his wife, an elderly couple, who were now confined in an old Turkish prison. He was yearning to get back and resume the contact with his men that had suddenly been broken off. He was forbidden to discuss the arrests as it could dampen their zeal.

Achiary (via Schmitt) invited me to see him on the evening of the 9th. One had to be careful of the Vichy agents who stood ostentatiously outside his flat and whom he pointed out to me through the window. As a suspected Allied sympathiser he was being watched but he was not quite certain by whom. He told me that the Vichy Interior Minister, Pucheu, would be flying to Algiers around 21 February and that his arrival would herald a hardening of policy. The resistance movement wanted London to take some action – in other words, to shoot down his plane. They wanted headquarters to be informed and I promised to do my best. That same evening I pushed coded messages 42/61, 42/62 and 42/63 under MACIEJ's door.

The Pucheu affair was a nuisance and gave us a great deal of work. At first London described the information as 'very interesting' and requested full details of the Minister's flight (1084), which we provided. Meanwhile, Pucheu's aeroplane landed safely at Maison Blanche airfield. Obviously no action had been taken. My efforts came to nothing and the Resistance were very disillusioned. They cursed the British while I had the unpleasant task of trying to explain the possible reasons for London's inaction as if it was my fault.

Matters worsened when the authorities in Algiers welcomed the Minister with parades of the Légion and other similar entertainments. The anti-Vichyites became more unfriendly towards the Allies, while everyone anticipated great changes for the worse. The most nervous, obviously, were those of Jewish descent. Our apprehensions soon became a reality. London had missed out on their welcome for M. Pucheu, and I was in total agreement with the Resistance that the deteriorating situation was directly connected with his arrival. There was nothing much I could do about it. The Algerian newspapers, which were full of his visit, were forwarded to London in our next pouch.

After receiving the contents of the post box on the 12th, several important messages were sent to London:

Air France ordered to work out how long it would take them to adapt their aeroplanes for the transport of war materials (42/064); SS *Kroumir*, Co. Busk, black funnel, lettering B-4000, entered Algiers on its way to Marseilles with a cargo of rubber latex destined for Germany (42/040); a recruiting campaign has begun for volunteers to the Army in Syria (42/065); a prospective change in command of the cruiser *Dunkerque*, Captain Tanguy recalled, his successor as yet unknown (42/066); four troop transports and a French destroyer carrying survivors of a sunken ship arrived in Tunis on 4 February (42/073); Governor Châtel supplied 500,000 tons of wheat to Rommel, 18,000 tons to Vichy, approx. 18 February, 800 tons of fuel oil for Rommel from American sources (42/076); SS *Lucille* left Bône 16 February with cargo of 4,000 tons rubber latex for Germany via Marseilles (42/082); the Italians searching for airfields in Dept of Constantine (42/069).

Our pouch no. 7 was despatched on 13 February. Some days later our post boxes produced more interesting reports:

Movement of ships in and out of ports Bougie, Bône and Oran; warships sailing from Oran to Toulon bearing the marks X-53, X-54 and X-93 (42/089); requisitioning of cars running on alcohol in Dept of Constantine and their despatch to Tunis (42/091); recruitment of volunteer drivers for Tunis at a daily wage of 116 francs (42/092); sailing of SS *Sudest* from Bône on 20 February to Tunis with a cargo of 600 tons alcohol required for cars on the Tunis–Tripoli route (42/93).

Pouch no. 8 was delivered to the Americans on the 19th; the next one should be ready for 26 February.

On 10 February London asked us whether we could meet some Free French officers from Gibraltar on the North African coast and deliver them safely to Algiers (1045). We needed time to find a suitable landing spot, a hiding place and transportation. Our tentative reply was that this was possible but that we would provide the landing place later on (42/083). This was eventually forwarded to them in pouch no. 10 with a written report (42/26/tj) recommending Colombi Island near Tenes, and a map of the district was also enclosed.

London was always interested in the movements of French ships and we gave it priority. They urgently demanded immediate information on the cruiser *Dunkerque* (1241). As from the 15th its new commander was Captain Anniel (42/088). We also reported on the 20th that, together with two destroyers and five submarines, it had left Mers-el-Kébir at 5am that day, probable destination Toulon (42/094). In the ensuing radio correspondence Central Office asked for the source of the information (1266). We replied that 'the source was our own Intelligence network – outpost Oran' (42/097).

The expansion of our network, the increase in the scope of its tasks, plus the greatly improved and detailed reports from the outpost commanders, meant an augmented flow of considerably longer messages – invaluable information but requiring an enormous increase in coding and decoding. I was overloaded with work, toiling from early morning until well past midnight. The hot weather, which lasted for almost nine months of the year, added to my exhaustion and fatigue.

The Intelligence tasks were mushrooming fast. Everything had to be written in clear and concise language for the commanders of the outposts. Frequently their agents, who came from different strata of society, would not be able to understand military jargon or brief definitions.

The post boxes supplied a daily average of a hundred reports all edited in French by our outpost commanders or their agents. All this information passed through my hands. It was my duty to read them all carefully and assess their importance. All the urgent ones requiring immediate radio transmission to London were translated into Polish, coded and prepared for MACIEJ. Generally, this was information concerning the movement of enemy aircraft or ships and the arrival and departure of Axis officers and military units. The movement of French merchant marine and navy, important changes in the military garrisons and in the economic and political life of French North Africa also had priority.

These messages to London also indicated that the important information would be included in our next Intelligence pouch together with detailed descriptions and plans. The remaining 90 per cent of our reports consisted of routine descriptions of the coastal defences, military garrisons, airfields, ports and railways and information on goods carried by rail and road. Economic data was also extremely important, particularly the production figures for local industry, especially mining. London frequently asked us about the transportation of ores to Germany, and for a detailed estimation of its metal content, which we had to have chemically analysed.

All these reports had to be studied and my own comments and observations appended to them. Frequently they were insufficiently precise and the outpost commanders had to be asked for further details. Often they were queried by London and had to be explained separately. Each report was then numbered, ready for inclusion in the next pouch.

Apart from Agency Africa, there was also my other role as Commercial Manager of the Floc-Av Company. The increased production and exports of the oatmeal factory (which even reached the French POW camps in Germany) required me to spend more time at the office. Keeping registers of sales and accounts – separately from my account books for Agency Africa, of course – devoured any spare time that might have been at my disposal. Having only one cipher book and one set of cipher tables, I was still doing the coding and decoding myself, occasionally assisted by my wife. Sophie, by the way, became quite an expert, even to the extent of being able to spot printer's errors in the ciphers.

I continued to work in my hotel room as BANULS was still forbidden to move from my clandestine office. The intensity of the work gradually forced me to make changes in our routine. Envisaging the setting up of our own radio station, MUSTAFA became responsible for our technical section and also for military information. He was released from his duties as Intelligence Officer for Algiers and it was turned into an outpost with Maurice Escoute (agent 1847) as its commander. BANULS, who had already been initiated into the Agency's office routine, took over our economic section and naval and political affairs. Meanwhile, during February 1942, we received fifty-two radio messages from London and sent sixty-nine.

16

A SHORT TRIP TO MOROCCO

Central Office increased their pressure for information on Morocco. On 26 February, while thanking us for our reports, they again stressed the urgency of obtaining detailed data on the coastal defences of Tunisia, Morocco and Dakar (1290). Descriptions and plans of the Tunisian coastal fortifications had been despatched in our first Intelligence pouch via the Americans and I was beginning to weave Morocco into our network. Dakar, however, would be far more difficult than London could ever have imagined.

I had several matters to settle in Morocco – the arrest of two Polish officers by Marcel Dubois, collecting an assortment of information that Central Office were prodding me to obtain and, last but not least, the need to prolong our visas for our stay in Algiers. In the meantime Marcel had written about certain commercial propositions that I might find interesting but that required my personal inspection. As almost all the outstanding matters in Algiers had been settled, I was free to go there for a short trip.

I booked a sleeping berth on the night express for the 26th and would travel directly to Casablanca, arriving there on the afternoon of the 27th, without stopping off at Rabat. As well as not wishing to abuse Marcel's hospitality, I felt that my presence there might prove inconvenient to his work. Sophie would inform Marcel and the others of my departure. Trying to work out some kind of timetable for the trip, the rhythm of the train soon put me to sleep.

Early in the morning, at Oujda, passport controls were effected quickly and I went to the restaurant car for breakfast. The train was now back to its top speed, cutting through the empty wastelands of the desert. The scenery flashed by, framed by the window of the wagon, like back projection in a film. Returning to my compartment, I became engrossed in the map of Morocco. I began to study all the previously marked places of interest about which London were so curious, adding new symbols specifying the type of information required.

The most difficult task would be the inspection of the southern coast of Morocco and its small ports of Mazagan, Mogador (now known as El Jadida and Essaouria respectively) and Agadir. During my previous visit there with Marcel his presence had unwittingly reduced my chances for real Intelligence. Now, the only way to get there would be by car or coach as there was no railway link. Travelling by coach would be very inconvenient as it tied one down to a timetable and a set route with very little freedom of movement. Restrictions of this kind would jeopardise my plans.

As we pulled into Rabat station, I spotted Marcel, who, learning from Sophie about my trip, had come to greet me. I told him that I'd be staying at the Excelsior Hotel on the Place de France. He said he'd visit me there in the morning. An hour later I was in Casablanca.

After settling into the hotel, I paid a surprise visit to Mrs Goworowska at her pharmacy. Leaving her assistant to look after the shop, she invited me into her flat. We discussed the Moroccan situation, which was similar to that in Algiers. Pro-Nazi propaganda and Légion activities had also increased. The indigenous population had recently become very hostile towards the French authorities. The nationalist movement's demand for a total separation from Metropolitan France was a leading topic of conversation. As a Polish woman, Mrs Goworowska enjoyed the confidence of the local Berbers and Arabs and obtained much interesting information from them, which resembled our reports from Tunisia on the Destour party and my own private observations in Algeria.

The subordination of the French authorities to German and Italian forces in North Africa had fatally undermined the myth of French power with which France was once credited by the native populations of her overseas empire. What was puzzling was that the deterioration in French prestige was more advanced in Morocco than anywhere else in North Africa, prompting the obvious suspicion that her position was gradually being undermined, by certain foreign interests. It was dangerous to France and her future relations with her North African possessions. What was surprising was that this aspect was ignored by my French acquaintances whenever the topic was discussed. My own personal view, as a Pole reared in the nineteenth-century tradition, was that I entirely supported the spread of freedom and self-determination to all nations, providing it did not lead them into enslavement by their own political opportunists.

Mrs Goworowska gave her observations on the arrest of Birkenmeier and some of his companions – the affair that Central Office had asked me to investigate. It appeared that they were released because of lack of evidence. In the evening, visits to bistros in the port area gave me some idea of which naval units were stationed in Casablanca – the information was embroidered on the sailor's caps.

On the morning of the 28th Marcel came to see me at the hotel. We went to the Café de Paris and began by discussing my arrest in November and that of Dr Gullois. Marcel described his conversation with Commissaire Leonard from Marseilles, who had obtained evidence against Gullois from the latter's jilted mistress, adding that his boss, Colonel Herviot, paid no attention to Leonard. However, Marcel hinted to me that he had to be more careful as he had many personal enemies in the local police who would like to see the back of him. Also, General Nogues had intensified the purges of suspected Gaullist sympathisers. I had suspected such a development, which is why I had bypassed Rabat and travelled directly to Casablanca. Hearing of my departure from Sophie, he had guessed what had happened. Marcel then put me in the picture about the Birkenmeier affair.

I knew Birkenmeier before the war as a Polish security officer in the northern district of Vilna. I had no idea that he was in Morocco. Marcel had been tipped off that some Poles had a radio transmitter. Not wishing the affair to be exaggerated by other French security people, he had stepped in quickly to handle it himself and, following rumours and denunciations, he had arrested Birkenmeier and Majewski, another Polish officer. The information reached London via France, i.e. TUDOR, who was warned in a note from Morocco. They, in turn, notified me: 'TUDOR reported Dubois liquidated Casablanca, Majewski arrested, report the details' (32/4467).

Once he had the two arrested Poles in his custody, Marcel had directed the investigation in such a manner that there was no real evidence of guilt – only presumptive evidence based on hearsay. The matter was settled but Marcel felt that it would be in everyone's interest if they were removed quickly from North Africa. It was clear to me that Birkenmeier, wishing to play his part in Polish Intelligence activities, had befriended Major Wysoczański, whom I had originally authorised to proceed to North Africa. They had ordered Captain Tonn to cease his activities and hand over the radio transmitter he had received from TUDOR; Polish gossip had done the rest. Undoubtedly Marcel Dubois had saved us all from disaster.

Concerning the business he had in mind for me, unfortunately this would require my continual personal supervision, which completely missed its *raison d'être*. My situation required me to stay permanently in Algiers. I needed a business in Morocco, run by my representative, only as an excuse to travel around the country. I was unable to explain it to Marcel so openly. Instead I told him that the oatmeal business was doing very well and demanded my constant supervision in Algiers. The Moroccan business was more of an investment, with someone else doing the donkey work. After a moment, he agreed to look for something suitable for me. He then suggested I accompany him to the police station to meet Commissaire Canon, who might prove useful to me in the future.

I invited them both to the nearest bistro where, over brandy, our conversation would be less inhibited than at the police station. Commissaire Canon related some very ribald anecdotes about the German Consul, Auer, whose 'specialist interests' were well known to the local police (the Commissaire gave us a huge wink), and for the pursuance of which he frequently visited Marrakesh.

Later, before Marcel's return to Rabat, we went for a snack at the Café de Paris, where we met his acquaintance Saoul Laskar, a local businessman, to whom he'd always intended to introduce me. He seemed a pleasant and friendly sort of chap who said he knew that I was Marcel's close friend, and he'd 'heard a lot about me'. We arranged to meet the next morning at the same place.

While taking Marcel to the railway station, we stopped at some shops to buy toys for my godson and presents for his mother, Lucienne. Chatting to Marcel through the open window of the train, I promised to see his family in Rabat 'around 4 March' before my departure home, and reminded him about our visas. 'Don't worry – everything will be done!' shouted a grinning and waving Marcel as the train moved off.

In Casablanca I took a cab from the railway station to see the town, have a good look at the army barracks and check whether any changes had occurred in the local garrison. The disposition of the army unit and detachments remained unchanged. The horse trotted slowly along pulling the cab lazily towards the port. Once there, I decided to take a stroll and to check the naval vessels, which were clearly visible from the boulevard. The evidence discovered in the bistros was undoubtedly anchored at sea. It was impossible not to admire the low-slung silhouette of the *Jean Bart*, the most modern French battleship, with its long heavy guns mounted in their armoured turrets. Judging by their size, their calibre must have been more than 340mm. I made a mental note of the lettering and signs painted on the submarines and destroyers. The commercial docks were busy unloading cargoes of ores, large crates and steel drums. At about 4pm I returned by cab to the hotel.

After a refreshing shower and realising that there was ample time before dinner, I remembered Marcel's stories about a part of Casablanca that was unique. Outside the hotel I told the Moroccan cabman, 'Bousbir!' No need to repeat it – he'd heard that one before.

Bousbir was a town within a town. It was surrounded by a very high wall with only one big gate, guarded by sentries from the various armed services by rotation, and also a mixed Franco-Moroccan police unit. This little Moorish town was situated next to the newly built Arab medina. The Pasha of Casablanca was its sole master and derived a very substantial income from it.

It was also of great interest from the Intelligence point of view. Hanging above the sentries' office was a list of units of the local military, naval and air force garrisons with the dates on which members of the forces were allowed to visit the town. The actual composition of the garrisons defending the Casablanca district could be determined from it. Civilians, on the other hand, had free access to Bousbir at any time.

According to Marcel, Bousbir was inhabited only by women – between 5,000 and 6,000 of them. They were of almost every colour, ethnic group and nationality, young and old, representing almost the entire spectrum of the human race. They were all 'volunteers' who had joined the community of their own free will. Each received the Pasha's permission to work inside Bousbir, and was provided with accommodation and primitive furnishings. They repaid a certain sum, agreed in advance, by instalments according to local tradition. Once having entered Bousbir, a woman could leave only after having repaid her 'mortgage'.

The cab took me right outside the gate. The sentry was from the battleship *Jean Bart* – it was navy day. I carefully studied the names and numbers on the board, which agreed with our information. Through a large gate, groups of women could be seen standing on the streets or shuffling slowly around. Once inside, I found myself on the main street and was immediately surrounded by noisy, gesticulating clusters of women, white, black and brown, all attempting to woo their clients in the same customary manner. It was a real tower of Babel with separate snatches of languages, some familiar, others totally obscure. I had to push the bold ones forcibly aside, while others, realising that here was someone oblivious to their charms, simply ignored me.

As it was hot, some wore only scanty clothes, and others dispensed with them altogether. On both sides of the streets there were shops, cafés and bistros packed to capacity with these ladies and their admirers. Some gentlemen of rather advanced age sat quietly sipping their aperitifs, surrounded by jostling female flesh, singers and bursts of uninhibited laughter. They appeared resigned to their remembrance of things past.

All this was on the main road. The shadowy streets that branched off contained the living quarters of the belles of Bousbir. Further down the main road, the number of women diminished. For obvious reasons, they preferred to hunt their prey near the gateway. They were of all ages, from those destroyed by life to those who were practically children, from fat sickly ones with sagging flesh to walking twigs of skin and bone. As in the casbahs and souks of North Africa, there was an all-pervading odour of sweet Eastern scent mingled with perspiration. A modern Sodom and Gomorrah in one.

I had had enough of it and returned to the cab that was waiting for me. The women were not interested in those who were leaving; they knew that their efforts would be in vain. So I walked uninterrupted as a novice spectator to scenes out of Dante's *Inferno*. The cab drove me back to the hotel. From Marcel's remarks, it appeared that Bousbir would be the best place in the world to hide, better than jungles or forests where one went in fear of hunger and wild animals. Here, a different law prevailed – the law of the knife, *dintoira*. How many people had perished within its walls nobody could tell. The local police never combed, let alone patrolled, Bousbir; it would have been pointless. Frequently, however, under the high walls of the town, headless bodies were found, which were buried quietly and without the usual inquiries.

After an excellent dinner, I retired early. Tomorrow I planned to inspect the Atlantic coast and, if it proved possible, the positions of the fortifications.

I met Laskar at 11am on 1 March at the Café de Paris. He was extremely knowledgeable about the situation in Morocco. He was an intelligent man with an expressive face, lively eyes and a humorous disposition; I liked the look of him and decided to trust him. During our chat, he asked how he could be of assistance to me. As he was aware, I wasn't French, I had salvaged a bit of money and I wanted to invest it profitably. I was involved in a partnership in Algeria, which was going quite well, and would also like to find something in Morocco. A small factory or industrial workshop would be OK – not necessarily in Casablanca; in fact, somewhere on the south coast would be preferable.

Laskar thought this was a wise choice. If he came across something appropriate he would certainly let me know via Marcel. He suggested we lunch at a small restaurant known for its specialist cuisine, something of a gourmet's paradise, and I didn't contradict him. En route, he told me something about himself. During the German invasion he and his family, who were Jewish, had to flee from Paris and he had to abandon his business. In Morocco he had set up a small fish factory at Agadir and was exporting fish to France – salted, dried and specially prepared. He was leaving for his factory, where he employed two of his sons and some Arabs, the next day – a lucky coincidence.

The waiter suggested a menu, which Laskar agreed to. He apologised, explaining that, as an habitué, he was always offered the best dishes, which is why he had chosen without consulting me. The cuisine and the wine were marvellous. After a few glasses, I steered the conversation towards his trip to Agadir. I had never been there and presumed that it was a very interesting part of the world. His response was immediate: 'Come with me! I'm travelling alone by car and it would be a great pleasure to have your company!'

I had succeeded in making the arrangements that had given me so much anxiety. What a bit of luck! Laskar wanted me to meet his acquaintance, the publisher and editor of the local daily *Vigie Marocaine*, whom he had just spotted. Invited to join us, he amused us with local gossip and even some from Paris. The time passed quickly before he had to leave for his office and the restaurant became deserted. While taking our leave, it was now my turn to be invited for supper by my guest. Laskar added: 'We'll choose the route for our trip. I feel as if we are old friends!' I thanked him for his invitation and reciprocated with similar warmth.

Having a few hours to spare, I took a cab and asked to be driven to the coast in the direction of Anfa and Ain Diab. On the way, I took a good look at the coastal defence positions at Anfa, which had a heavy 240mm battery. There were no similar emplacements until we reached Ain Diab, which also had a heavy artillery battery of the same calibre. I stopped at a café on the beach. It was empty; everything was peaceful. The sun was beautifully warm and one could hear the roar of the Atlantic waves from far off. Hitler, Stalin and the war seemed a million miles away. On the return journey, I took a second look at the batteries.

Back at the hotel, refreshed by the sea air, I again studied the map of Morocco. The southern coastlines didn't appear to be worth defending. Whoever held Casablanca and its surroundings could gradually take over the rest of Morocco. I therefore presumed that there were no fortifications along this coast. The road ran alongside the Atlantic and it would be easy for me to see for myself. Laskar could choose the actual route.

We met at the Café de Paris in the evening. Laskar was a pleasant and cheerful companion with a fund of amusing stories; he reminded me of Bernard Libermann. Apropos the journey, he would collect me at the hotel at 6am, we would drive to Mazagan for breakfast, then Mogador with lobster for lunch, arriving in Agadir in the evening for supper, which he left unspecified. We would have covered over 600km. I admired the way he combined business with pleasure and made it sound like a gourmet's grand tour. He explained that from Agadir I could take a bus to Marrakesh and return to Casablanca by train. I returned to the hotel for an early night, pleased with the way my short-term objectives – a trip to the south and potentially useful contacts – had been fulfilled.

At exactly 6am Laskar arrived outside the hotel in his small, comfortable Nash truck, and we were immediately on our way. Once outside the town, we belted along the asphalt road at some speed. The scenery was picturesque with camel caravans and small Berber settlements dotting the route.

At 9am we drove into Mazagan, a Portuguese town with an old port dating from the sixteenth century. Its defensive walls and citadel bastions were still intact, a witness to the 250-year Portuguese reign. The old town was now a Mellah, inhabited by Moroccan Jews. Their houses could be recognised from afar. The windows and doors were painted blue; the walls were white. The town itself was very charming. The small old port, well protected on its Atlantic side, was used mainly for transporting agricultural produce. There were two army camps, constituting a small garrison, on the outskirts of town.

My companion was greeted like an old friend. After a hearty breakfast, we were off again, driving along a highway leading inland. The landscape changed as we headed south – deciduous woods and large areas overgrown with agave, used to manufacture good-quality paper. At 2pm we were tucking into the promised lobsters at Mogador, washed down by an excellent wine, then we took a quick look at the town. Mogador was an unimportant port until the eighteenth century, when it served as a military base for the Sultans of Morocco and as a fortress assisting them to suppress the warring southern tribes. Some of its old defensive walls still survived; it also contained a small military garrison.

We left at 4pm with another 175km still to go, mostly in the mountains where the High Atlas reaches the Atlantic. Laskar, who knew the route well, assured me we'd arrive in Agadir before 8pm. He was concentrating now, and only occasionally pointing out the Berber settlements. The road, snaking through the mountains at the edge of the ocean, provided a spectacular view. Here, in the vicinity of Agadir, sardines were plentiful and attracted fishermen from as far away as Portugal and Brittany.

We reached the Hotel Excelsior in Agadir before 8pm. The bus station for Marrakesh was next door. I immediately booked a ticket for the following morning, while Laskar managed to obtain rooms at the hotel. Encountering officers from the local garrisons in the hotel restaurant, I was able to verify that their regimental and unit numbers had not changed since my previous trip with Marcel. I liked Laskar very much. We had hit it off very well during our day-long trip together. There was already a close affinity between us, difficult to define, which would make him an extremely good colleague. After supper, we parted on the warmest of terms.

On the morning of 3 March I was on the bus to Marrakesh. Crossing the High Atlas mountains was tiring. The mountain ranges, interspersed with valleys, were devoid of vegetation – wild, with bare rocks of different shapes and colours. Very occasionally in the distance one could discern human settlements clinging precariously to the rocks, surrounded by what appeared to be cultivated fields. It was a relief to descend to the flatlands and to arrive at the town by nightfall.

I found a room at the Mamounia, a luxury hotel with magnificent drawing-rooms and beautiful gardens inhabited by what would now be known as the international jet set, and rested. Germans, members of the Armistice Committee and of the Gestapo, lived at the hotel. All I wanted was to verify whether any changes in the composition of the local garrison had taken place since my last trip. Two hours tomorrow would be sufficient to see everything. I could leave around noon and be in Rabat by evening.

There were very few people in the dining-room. Two tables were occupied by Germans, (not difficult to spot) whom I had not seen a few months earlier. Obviously their units had changed. There were also several high-ranking French officers from regiments that I had recorded last time. There were no changes in the garrison: a relief, as I would not have to prowl around the barracks tomorrow.

The following morning (4 March), en route to Casablanca in an empty compartment and having browsed through the newspapers, I dozed off. We pulled into the station at 4pm. The Rabat train left an hour later and arrived there at 6pm. I took a room at the Hotel Balima and went straight to see Marcel.

I told him about my trip and my conversation with Laskar. Marcel said that he was very reliable and that I could trust him. Our visas would be ready the following morning, so my departure would not be too delayed. In the meantime two police officers from Dakar were coming to dine with him that evening. He wanted to introduce me to them, which could be extremely useful if I ever decided to go there. Naturally, this suited me fine. Dakar was undoubtedly the Agency's most problematic and sensitive area. That evening I met the two gentlemen concerned and, thanks to the friendly atmosphere, they actually invited me there.

I lunched with the Dubois family at noon the following day. Lucienne Dubois, always an accomplished *cuisinière*, really surpassed herself. We were joined by Marcel's mother, his son by a previous marriage, and his niece, whose husband was one of his junior commissaires. After lunch, before I even had a chance to thank them or apologise for my early departure, Marcel took me to one side and said, 'You've still got plenty of time to catch the train. There's something I want to ask you.'

As it was I who always asked him for everything, I was surprised and somewhat apprehensive, and had no idea how to interpret this sudden request. Returning our passports with the visas, he asked, 'Mietek, have you any contacts with the Americans?' Greatly surprised, I immediately replied, 'Yes, I met them in Algiers through a woman who gives English lessons.' He looked at me, and nodded his head.

'I don't like the way they're poking their noses into our affairs or the way our Royalists are helping them. It's none of their business. I'm a Frenchman and I'll never consent to France or any of her possessions being destroyed!'

It was imperative to reply honestly. Apart from the fact that we were close friends, any false answer would imply that I was playing a double game, which, in the context of his remarks, was certainly not true. Looking him straight in the eyes, I said, 'From my contact with them, I'm positive they're all real novices – at least, those that I know in Algeria. I can assure you that it's not yet in their capacity to be able to hurt France. Besides, they're like us – they're anti-German.'

He didn't pursue the conversation. Instead, he called his family and said, 'Mietek is leaving!' Within half an hour, I was sitting in the express train hurtling towards Algiers.

Marcel's confidences had given me an unexpected insight into French fears in North Africa. Faced with an increasingly insubordinate Arab population influenced and encouraged by the decline in French prestige and power, German and Italian propaganda, and now an American incursion, it was not surprising that they were anxious for the future of their colonies.

While satisfied with my trip, which had also served as a much-needed break, I was even more pleased to be back. The following day, 6 March, I resumed my duties and was intensely curious to discover what news awaited me. Central Office, for their part, would receive plenty of interesting reports on Morocco, and a new Intelligence outpost in Casablanca could probably be organised by the end of the month.

17

IMPORTANT ASPECTS OF AGENCY AFRICA

Before returning to a chronological account of the history of Agency Africa, a description of some of the important aspects underpinning its development is relevant. They include the development of the Floc-Av Company; the machinery of the Agency, which can be described more simply as the network in action; and the beginnings and evolution of our own radio station.

The Floc-Av Company

The Floc-Av Company, the first factory to manufacture oatmeal in North Africa, played a role in Agency Africa's success that cannot be overestimated. Its product, popularly known as Floc-Av, was sold only at chemists' shops, safeguarding it from the restrictions on the sale of food introduced by the Vichy authorities, which Chairman Godziszewski had anticipated. In fact our oatmeal became the only food product that could be purchased without restrictions. It was exported to France, and even sent to the French POW camps in Germany. Not surprisingly, therefore, demand exceeded supply.

The sales organisation in the department and town of Algiers was the responsibility of the Chairman's wife. However, we experienced some difficulty in finding a suitable salesman for Oran, which, as Commercial Manager, was my headache. Because of the lack of professional salesmen in French North Africa at the time, I decided to employ my outpost commanders. After all, they could do the job as well as anyone else and, with a little coaching, they could even pass the scrutiny of our Chairman.

This would, of course, greatly facilitate the agency's work, especially as road and rail travel had been further curtailed by the authorities. As representatives of the firm, they would inevitably receive priority for unrestricted use of transport. Moreover, as salesmen of oatmeal they would have fairly easy access to military units, airfields, naval bases, ports and even warships and cargo boats. Only my two Intelligence Officers would know about my plan. Our agents, as well as the Chairman and M. Delfau, would not be allowed even to suspect that I was favouring any particular person for the job.

I asked BANULS to advise our Oran commander, Robert Ragache, to apply for the post of representative for Floc-Av in Oran. He was to tell him that he knew of a vacancy with that firm and it would greatly assist him in his Intelligence work. Ragache duly applied for the post, I interviewed him and he was accepted by Floc-Av. It also gave me the opportunity to acquaint myself with the commander of the Oran Intelligence outpost without him being aware of it.

Ragache proved to be an excellent salesman. His job helped him enormously as cover for his Intelligence work, and his Oran outpost produced excellent results. The experiment was so successful that it prompted me to employ Paul Schmitt (agent 1850) as Floc-Av's commercial representative for the Constantine district.

After a time, the Chairman tried, as was to be expected, to enlist my support for an expansion of the business. Such a venture demanded further finance, to which I was utterly opposed. There was no point in investing any further capital, which the Agency needed and which stood a good chance of being lost if the enterprise foundered. Also, I couldn't tell my associates that, in the event of French North Africa coming into the Allied orbit, our factory would cease production. After many tactical manoeuvres on my part, it was decided that the business should continue at full production but in an unexpanded form.

The 1942 harvest failed to produce the estimated amount of grain and the authorities decided to reduce the amount of barley for public consumption. This was the official explanation, which my two partners accepted. It was obvious, from my reports, that the reduction in grain supply to the Algerian market coincided with its increased demand by the Germans. Their exploitation increased to such an extent that our factory lost its barley allocation altogether. We continued production by drawing on our reserves, which, in turn, helped to cover our barley purchases from the Arabs on the black market. This was dangerous as the penalties for black marketeering were very severe. Nevertheless, we managed to keep going for some time, but in November 1942, immediately before the Allied landings, the restrictions forced us to close down.

During the spring of 1942, in Floc-Av's heyday, our Chairman became excessively over-confident and revealed despotic tendencies. He frequently adopted a dogmatic and high-handed attitude and there were heated discussions with strong language being used on both sides. As far as I was aware, these rows were limited to business policy, and our personal relationship managed to survive intact. I knew that he was in a hurry to make a fortune and that the poor old devil realised that it was his last chance.

He expounded breathtaking schemes of truly astonishing ingenuity to make us all a vast fortune, every one of which I turned down. As far as I was concerned, I had obtained more than sufficient cover and security for my real work. My activities at Floc-Av were already taking up too much of my time, forcing me to work on my Intelligence reports late into the night.

The Chairman refused to give up. One of his latest brainwaves was to start a pig farm and, since it was closely connected with Floc-Av, it was difficult to dismiss out of hand. The general idea was to rear pigs on the leftovers from the produce of the oatmeal factory. The more I tried to escape from this project, the more he would suspect that I had other vested interests. After all, Floc-Av would do good business by selling the oatmeal by-product, which otherwise we had to pay to get rid of.

After careful consideration it was clear that, as there would be a meat shortage in North Africa, my new investment would be safe. Once again, the Chairman's persistence had got him his own way. I didn't want to be tied down to the new enterprise, as it would curtail my time even further. I therefore proposed to him that, although I would be investing my own capital, my wife would be his prospective partner. The Chairman's friends in the General Governorship helped obtain a substantial allocation of cement, wood and bricks to build the new pigsties. The new company purchased a plot of land on the perimeter of Maison Blanche airfield and the construction of the necessary buildings was soon under way. The initial and floating capital amounted to 50,000 francs per partner.

Soon it became apparent that neither the Chairman nor Sophie knew anything about rearing swine. Luckily for us all, my youthful studies in Warsaw had included economics and commerce, and animal husbandry had been part of the course. Hitherto, I had had no need to draw on my rusty – or rather rustic – memories of these particular studies. If anyone had ever told me that one day I would have to rear swine in Algeria for the benefit of an Intelligence agency, it would have seemed absolutely ridiculous.

Our Intelligence reports noted an increased presence of German and Italian warplanes at the airport. Standing high up on a pig bunker with my binoculars gave me a good observation post. The farm had its uses after all. The business thrived. The Chairman was rubbing his hands and forecasting huge profits from the Christmas sales.

In July, my business partner surprised me. He had received some good offers from local businessmen who wanted to buy Floc-Av. They offered him two million francs. 'Why didn't you tell me about it?' I retorted. 'We could have sold it and made an excellent profit!' He gave his habitually cunning smile and replied, 'Because I asked for three million, and they didn't come back.' There was no doubt about it: his business sense was being blinded by his intrinsic greed. Another incident took place on 20 September 1942, after my return from my third visit to Morocco. Sophie learned that the Chairman had sold both their shares in the farm to their third partner, Delfau, without her knowledge or agreement. Although he had absolutely nothing to offer in his own defence, he behaved as if he were the injured party. After this, our relationship went into cold storage.

It was only due to our regard for Delfau, who was unaware of the Chairman's high-handed action, that Sophie finally agreed to her shares being sold. In fact, they were sold to Delfau at a profit. Nevertheless, the motives behind the Chairman's action remained a mystery. After Operation Torch, the Americans, needing to extend Maison Blanche airfield and to build large depots there, purchased Delfau's pigsties for a very substantial sum.

The first Floc-Av balance sheet was produced in October 1942. It showed that, in the ten months of its existence, the company made 120,000 francs net profit after tax – a very good return on the capital invested (150,000 francs). The partners received their share according to the contract: Delfau and myself 30 per cent each and the Chairman 40 per cent. The cash balance of Agency Africa was enriched by 36,000 francs.

When, due to the barley shortage, the company finally closed down on 8 November 1942, I proposed that the Chairman should take over my shares. My explanation was that I had to abandon our partnership because of my recall to the Polish Army. He readily agreed, especially as I asked for only 100,000 francs, which amounted to the return of the original capital I had invested. I didn't ask for more because the future did not look very bright for him and, anyway, I had no desire to emulate his example.

The Floc-Av Company, which, by a strange coincidence, lasted only as long as Agency Africa needed to remain secret, had fulfilled its purpose. The company provided an excellent cover both for the Intelligence outposts and for myself. It made a profit, returned the capital originally invested to the Agency and, during its lifetime, provided the directors with a monthly salary of 8,000 francs, which, in my case, was passed on each month to the Agency. The Chairman never learned what a great service he had unwittingly contributed to the Allied cause as he died shortly afterwards. Both he and M. Delfau could have been greatly affected if the Vichy authorities had stumbled on my real activity. Fortunately for all of us, this never happened.

I mentioned that my share of the yearly profits (36,000 francs) was paid into the coffers of Agency Africa. As far as I am aware, an Intelligence agency operating successfully in wartime and managing to make a financial profit must have been unique in the annals of the Secret Service. Major Frank Ptak, head of the Finance Department of the Second Bureau of the Polish General Staff in London, took a different view and simply deducted it from the Agency's next allocation of funds. Furthermore, he presented the November 1942 accounts in such a way as to make it appear that there was no connection between the head of Agency Africa and the Floc-Av Company. There was nothing about our funds being invested as capital and interest having been received.

In his final liquidating assessment of 9 November 1943 (under file no. Ldz 43/6452/Fin.), he stated: 'The expenditure of the Agency for this month has been reduced by 36,000 francs, treating this as a partial repayment of their allocation.' This was obviously a distortion of the facts. Later, after the end of my service in North Africa, when I discussed it with him, he told me frankly, 'The Secret Service cannot make a profit; it can only produce expenditure!' His interpretation made any further discussion pointless.

The network in action

Frequently Central Office requested immediate information on the military, industrial, economic and political aspects of French North Africa. For example, in January 1942, London demanded immediate notification of all shipments of rubber latex from North Africa to France with details of quantities, types, ports, sailing times and the estimated route, since counteraction was expected (42/525). How could one fulfil such an assignment? The territory covered ran into thousands of square miles without any radio or telephone links; road and rail communications were few and far between and there was constant danger of police and army surveillance. Additionally, the information was required immediately.

The machinery was set in motion when London radioed the original assignment to WICHER in the south of France. He then secretly transmitted it to MACIEJ in Algiers, who delivered the message to the chief of Agency Africa at 10pm. From then onwards it was our responsibility.

The Chief deciphered the assignment, studied it and prepared detailed instructions for the commanders of his Intelligence outposts. In this particular case they covered ports, important road and rail junctions and large depots. They contained detailed orders for the particular agents working for the outpost commander, consisting of the following questions: name of port of loading; name of ship, tonnage and description; quality and quantity of rubber latex loaded; date when the cargo was ready for sailing; date of sailing and the port of destination in France.

These orders were then placed in our post boxes in Algiers (each of which served a particular Intelligence outpost), to be collected by the courier agents from the outposts shortly before their departure from Algiers, and handed over to their commanders. The commander's duty was to select the right agents for the particular tasks, copy the required number of assignments and ensure that they received them.

After receipt of their orders, agents contacted their own informants, who would most likely be employees of the depots, port officials, dockers or sailors. The information flowed back to the outpost commanders, who, in turn, sent them through their courier agents to the post boxes in Algiers. The Chief studied their reports and elaborated on them. They were then coded into messages and passed on to MACIEJ. He transmitted them by radio to WICHER who transmitted them to London.

How long would it take for such an assignment to be completed? It was virtually impossible to say. Generally, detailed elaboration in concise language was required for each order. Our agents were not specialists; they were ordinary individuals who required special coaching for this type of work. Obviously, with experience their work became more efficient, faster and safer. A serious drawback was that we were dealing with written material, which always provides the best lead for a security service to eliminate an Intelligence network. In the event of an agent being arrested, they knew that they were dealing with only the tip of an iceberg. We continually tried to improve our method of transferring information but, for the moment, it remained rudimentary.

The beginnings of our own broadcasting station

Transmitting back secret information promptly, especially in wartime, is obviously of the utmost importance. Normally the method is organised by the central office of the particular Intelligence network involved. In our case we had to make our own arrangements with the assistance of WICHER and MACIEJ. This worked sufficiently well, but, as the workload increased and the territory covered by our Agency expanded, it became inadequate.

As our radio correspondence increased, MACIEJ had additional problems with his French patrons. The Polish Enigma team's interception results plus the other official work they were carrying out for the French in no way justified the increased volume of radio traffic between WICHER and MACIEJ. Their patrons were becoming uneasy; personally, I was surprised that we had managed to get away with it for such a long time.

Our current method also had a further disadvantage – it could be used only once a day. In the case of urgent information, the delay could nullify its value. TUDOR and WICHER could not help me solve this problem. The only assistance Central Office offered was the hurdy-gurdy sent through the American Consulate.

As I hope has been made clear, we owed everything to MACIEJ, who was playing a superb double game with the French. WICHER's message informing us of the recall of the Polish Enigma team from Algiers came, therefore, as a great shock, and threatened the very existence of the Agency. Fortunately WICHER, who was in an extraordinarily difficult position, managed to work out a compromise between his orders from the French and London's insistent demands. The team was to return to France in January 1942, but MACIEJ himself could remain in Algiers until mid-April. We would have some breathing space to organise our own transmitting station. After a considerable search, we found an operator among our agents – Joseph Briatte (no. 1845), a Frenchman like all the others. Internal changes were made. MUSTAFA became responsible for making the transmitter operational and then supervising its work.

Organising reliable radio communication with London was extremely difficult. We had to find a place that would satisfy both technical and security requirements. I planned that we should be on the air at least twice a day, morning and evening, for information to be transmitted to London as speedily as possible. As Briatte was a radio technician by profession, my plan was to open a shop selling radio equipment, which would also house our hurdy-gurdy. This would provide excellent cover. Before leaving for Morocco, I had instructed MUSTAFA to find suitable premises and set up a shop, selling and repairing radio equipment, in conjunction with Briatte.

Our new radio operator was very enthusiastic about his work. As a specialist, he received permission to repair the transmitters of merchant ships, and to put up a special aerial necessary for carrying out transmission tests – which was very useful. MUSTAFA found appropriate premises on the Rue Sadi Carnot, in the Arab quarter, near the commercial port. A shop with a workshop attached was quickly arranged for less than 25,000 francs. Now for our testing for sound with London.

All the necessary technical data were sent to them in our telegram no. 109, and tests were carried out on 4 and 5 March 1942. Our hurdy-gurdy transmitted signals but did not receive any in return from London. They were asked to send us the results. WICHER reported that he could hear our signals; London, on the other hand, had not heard them.

Central Office suggested new tests on the 10th and 11th which were carried out several times with increasingly improved results. Our aerial setting had to be changed and other technical adjustments made. Finally, we obtained very good results and decided that from now on only our own radio would be used. Central Office were informed that, as from 12 April 1942, the Agency's station would be in regular operation, morning and evening, and call signs and transmission times would also be arranged (42/196).

Briatte installed the hurdy-gurdy in an ingenious way. He placed it inside an empty radio casing, which stood on a shelf together with other equipment for sale. At the appointed time, he simply connected an aerial to it and we were on the air.

Mieczysław Słowikowski (RYGOR) after graduating from Warsaw's Higher Military Academy.

Słowikowski as a young soldier after the Polish–Russian war of 1919–20.

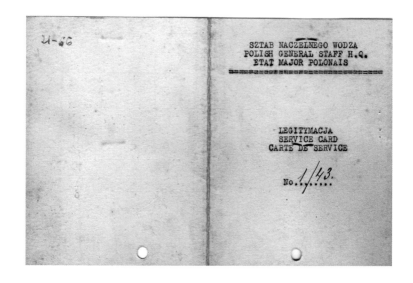

Słowikowski's service card issued on his trip to Britain
a few months after the successful TORCH landings.

SZTAGU NACZELNEGO WODZA

Mieczysław Słowikowski
Stwierdzam, że wyż.wym..wła-
ściciel paszportu służbowego
Seria...B........ Nr 853/34/43
...............jest oficerem
Armii Polskiej w stopniu......
..Majora.
I certify hereby that the
above-mentioned,bearer of the
service passport Series..B...
No.853/34/43...is an Officer
of the Polish Army in the rank
of..Majo.
Je certifie que le porteur du
passport de service, Serie.B..
No..853/34/43....est Officier
de l'Armee Polonaise, dans le
grade de..commandeur............

Podpis właściciela legitymacji.
Signature of the owner of the
Service Card.
Signature du porteur de la
Carte de Service.

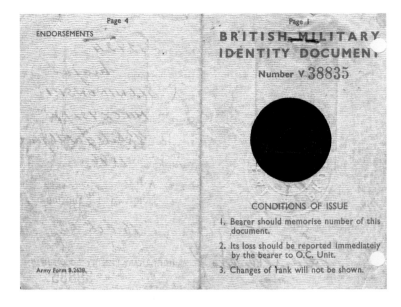

Service card issued after Słowikowski and the Agency
were admitted to CSDIC.

Słowikowski as a staff officer, 1930s.

US troops arriving in Algiers, November 1942. (Getty Images)

Słowikowski, now with the rank of Major General, at an official function in London in the 1970s.

Major Wincenty Zarembski (TUDOR) and his wife,
London, 1943.

Słowikowski's
wife, Sophie,
in the 1920s.

Słowikowski with the family during their last holiday together in
the Carpathian Mountains of southern Poland, 1939.

Słowikowski on a family outing, summer 1966.

Słowikowski with his dog Skipper.

Operations of this nature could hardly expect to escape the attention of the Germans, particularly the Armistice Commission. Their mobile direction finders, equipped to track down illegal transmitters, operated all over French North Africa, and were in evidence until the Allied landings. Frequently, while we were transmitting, our lookouts warned us of an approaching monitoring truck, but our operator never interrupted his work; MUSTAFA was always present at the shop during these times.

In the event of our being unearthed, we planned an armed response. The German vehicle's personnel never comprised more than three or four. We always had a couple of armed lookouts in the street who, moving ahead of the approaching vehicle, would stop in front of the shop to ascertain the German response. Moreover, inside the shop, in the second workroom, MUSTAFA and the operator would be waiting with weapons at the ready. In other words, if the Germans wanted to arrest us, our strengths being equal, and with our advantage of surprise and determination, they would have had a formidable fight on their hands. Escape would be easy as this was the Arab quarter, which favoured such activities. Moreover, it was virtually impossible to recapture a fugitive in the Casbah. Fortunately, we had extremely good luck: the Germans never unearthed us, and this situation never arose. Our station was in continuous operation up to the time that the Agency was wound up.

Regarding Joseph Briatte, for his 'contribution, exceptional work, devotion and courage' he received the Polish Silver Cross of Merit, as well as the shop and workshop where our hurdy-gurdy had sung its songs so well. It is a platitude that Intelligence work attracts more than its fair share of eccentrics, colourful or otherwise unusual characters. I must record that our operator was exceptionally myopic – in fact he was almost blind – and that a special pair of glasses had to be sent from London for him. Additionally, he was hard of hearing – yet, according to our Central radio station, he was the best and fastest radio operator they knew and everyone was keen to work with him.

My last memory of Briatte was very touching. He admitted,

after receiving his well-deserved decoration, that during the ceremony he could see only my hands and the cross. He asked for permission to take a very close look at the face of his unknown Chief. Permission was granted.

18

A MEDLEY OF SURPRISES. . .
INCLUDING COMMISSIONER BEGUE

On my return from Morocco on 6 March, I visited BANULS at his flat (alias my old secret office) on Rue Isly. He reported on his work during my absence and on his collaboration with the new commander of the important Algiers outpost, Maurice Escoute (agent 1847), who was extremely enthusiastic. Remembering the fate of Roquemaure, I hoped that this would not rebound on us. In fact, Escoute was very efficient and had managed to plant informers in the commercial port and a new agent at the Maison Blanche airport. As I was leaving, Miss Aboukaya, whose assistance I had previously sought in finding me a flat, told me that a very nice apartment would be available in early April. Unfortunately her cousin, Dr Akoun, had to give up his medical practice, in conformity with Vichy's latest anti-semitic decrees, and was returning to Tunis with his family. The flat could be viewed by arrangement with her.

In the afternoon I went to Floc-Av as usual. The Chairman greeted me particularly warmly and offered his congratulations on my choice of our new Oran representative. Apparently, after only a month, the orders had doubled. The situation became extremely amusing. I would chat to Ragache every month about the firm's sales, while he had no idea whatsoever that I was the chief of his Intelligence network.

That evening I saw Hutten-Czapski to sort out the Birkenmeier affair, and to get them sent to Portugal as soon as possible. Our Casablanca Consulate should arrange everything; the Agency would cover the costs but my role in it would remain secret. Unfortunately, there would be some delay due to a change of personnel at the 'Polish Office' in Casablanca involving the dismissal of a member of the staff. Lieutenant Edward Przesmycki, a Polish Foreign Office official who happened to be in Algiers, had been designated as his successor and would settle the matter.

Returning to the hotel, I suddenly remembered that Przesmycki had co-operated with our clandestine headquarters in Marseilles in the search for escape and evacuation routes. He could be invaluable. As he was still in the army he could be used in our Intelligence work; as an official, authenticated by the 'Polish Office', he had perfect cover and freedom of movement. BANULS was instructed to make an approach.

Preparing our tenth consecutive pouch for the Americans, after some hesitation I decided to send Central Office a copy of the Agency's cash book as well as the balance sheet. As mentioned earlier, I had hung on to it, despite security precautions, in order to avoid any future unpleasantness. In the event, Mr Knox accepted a rather bulkier pouch than usual. Intense surveillance was making visits to the American Consulate increasingly difficult. The danger point was entering, usually with a pouch full of goodies; leaving, on the other hand, presented few problems.

In reply to London's urgent request, we were able to inform them immediately that 240 tons of rubber were ready to leave Algiers port on the *Charles Lebourge*, destination Marseilles, on 7 March. Further urgent information on Algiers port was sent to them on the 8th:

> The arrival of Annamite troops on the Djabel-Nador (42/122); departure of the *Kroumir* armed with 75mm guns and of the *Procida* with a cargo of ammunition (42/123); landing at Maison Blanche airport (at 1pm, 8 March) of six Italian bombers (42/124).

Confirmation of the last item was sent on the 9th and we reported their departure for Rio de Oro on the 11th (42/128). It was difficult for our informant to supply us with the markings and numerals of the aeroplanes. However, he was able to tell us that Italian airmen were involved and they were in a part of the airport that was guarded and inaccessible. London's reply in April pointed out the obvious, that the markings and numbers should always be stated. There was no suggestion, of course, as to exactly how this should be done.

Having obtained his consent (via BANULS) to join the Agency, I met Przesmycki (now codenamed VINCENT) on 12 March to discuss his work as head of the Casablanca Intelligence outpost. He was leaving Algiers shortly to take up his new duties at the 'Polish Office' and the Intelligence outpost would become operational as soon as he arrived there. Obviously his extramural activities would be kept secret from DELEGATE.

VINCENT's territory was French (and if possible Spanish) Morocco, specialising in military and naval matters. General political and economic affairs would be of only secondary importance. Particular attention would be paid to Tangiers, partly because of its neutral status and also because of the presence there of Allied, Axis and Neutral consulates and various Intelligence networks. Many of the immigrants were Jewish and would be very helpful to us.

On the morning of the 13th I went with Sophie to meet Miss Aboukaya at 4 Rue Chanzy. Her cousin's flat, on the third floor of a large four-storey building, consisted of six rooms, a kitchen and a bathroom. It was comfortably furnished and fully equipped, as he was only taking his family's personal effects to Tunis. The layout was excellent. The flat was completely surrounded by a long balcony connecting all the rooms, providing a convenient and concealed method of communicating between them. The monthly rent, 4,000 francs, was not excessive for conditions prevailing at the time.

Regarding our neighbours: the concierge lived on the first floor with her Yugoslav husband and son; there was a ladies' tailoring establishment on the second floor and a solicitor's office on the fourth. The constant stream of visitors to the building would help to cover the visits of my associates.

Sophie returned to the hotel in high spirits while I lingered to orientate myself with its topography. The house was on the corner of

Rue Chanzy and Rue Isly. The former was very short and connected the junction of two main streets. Arrival and departure could be facilitated from different directions – it was ideal for Intelligence activities. At last I would be able to work without hiding my papers every time there was a knock on the door. The telephone, in the doctor's name, was also very useful. Finally, we would be able to receive people who were important to us, and resume our soirées.

My pleasure was short-lived. A note from André Achiary awaited me at the hotel. He wanted to see me urgently that evening. There were still no reports from the outposts – perhaps there had been arrests. I would have to wait patiently to find out what had happened.

Achiary awaited me impassively – the news was sombre. He had been notified that morning that Commissioner Begue would be arriving in Algiers in a few days' time. Begue, a specialist in counter-espionage, was being sent by the Vichy authorities to wind up the spy network operating in French North Africa.

André presumed that this was the result of the Tunis affair and BANULS's disappearance. He also detected a lack of confidence in himself as a reputed anglophile and a suspected Gaullist. Although Begue was bringing his own agents with him, he was a stranger in Algiers and would be compelled to co-operate with Achiary. André was therefore assigning Inspector Schmitt to him. He was highly trusted, and could be relied upon to inform him of Begue's actions and to give advance warning of any danger.

This was a great relief since I also knew Schmitt quite well – in fact, he was now on the Agency's payroll. He was one of those Frenchmen who hated the Germans with an unbelievably ferocious intensity. I knew something of his tragic background. He came from Alsace, where the Germans had forced his young wife to work in a Wehrmacht brothel. His obsession was hardly surprising.

I asked about DOKTOR, who was still in prison.

'There's already a decision to move him to France before the end of the month. I'll let you have his departure date at the appropriate time.'

Fortunately, they hadn't connected the two cases. I then asked whether there was anything from Tunis about Dr Stora and Roquemaure (agent 1820).

'Agent 1820 remains silent for the time being. As for Dr Stora, he's being kept under arrest until Commissioner Begue's arrival.'

I returned to the hotel well after midnight and found it impossible to sleep. It was imperative to protect BANULS and his wife; they could easily be spotted in Algiers, where Europeans were virtually concentrated into a few streets. We didn't have any safe houses. Oran would be the best place. Ragache would have to arrange them as soon as possible. I wasn't going to tell BANULS just yet.

On the morning of the 14th I went to meet my informant near the Basilica. I was very fond of this peaceful place at the highest point in Algiers with its panoramic view of the coast and the town below. The Basilica, famous throughout North Africa as 'the place of miracles', was always full of worshippers, including many Arab women – a strange yet moving sight. Its immensity and its simplicity were impressive. One could meet here and merge imperceptibly with the crowds.

Arriving early, I sat in a pew and feasted my eyes on the beautiful statue of the Black Madonna above the altar. A feeling of calm and serenity seeped through me. My reverie was interrupted by someone sitting down beside me. It was my informer. We left, then sat on a bench outside and discussed our current business. He departed first; I remained a while longer.

Then I had a brainwave, which was ridiculously simple. BANULS must disappear from Algiers and a totally different person would emerge instead. Before his transformation he must be hidden, possibly in an isolated villa. I asked Sophie to find out from her hairdresser (but without arousing his suspicion) where it would be possible to buy a man's wig in Algiers. It was needed to transform BANULS from a balding, fair-haired Slav into a dark-haired Spaniard.

That evening I told BANULS about Commissioner Begue and my plan; the idea amused him. First we must find somewhere for him to hide while awaiting the wig, then set him up in a private flat. Achiary would prepare all the necessary documents in a new name.

During this time he and Marta would remain at my old place on the Rue Isly without appearing in town. Marta would also have to change her appearance, which, after all, shouldn't be too difficult for a woman. BANULS would stop contacting agents (I would take over contact with the Algiers commander myself), and he would be told when to 'disappear'.

At the same time our agent from the black market was directed to find a place for us in the Moustafa Superior quarter. A villa was rented, which was relatively easy at this time of the year, on a little-used road. After a few relatively peaceful days I was notified that Commissioner Begue had arrived in Algiers. Late that evening BANULS and his wife, together with adequate food supplies, were installed in the villa, where they remained in isolation for some weeks, being supplied with provisions, newspapers and information twice a week. Meanwhile, Commissioner Begue and his men were hunting the streets of Algiers for them.

The wig idea was not as simple as it appeared. For one thing, wigs were not made in Algiers but in a part of occupied France near the Belgian frontier. Moreover, the hairdresser had to have the exact head measurements and insisted that the client should come to see him personally. Obviously, this was impossible with BANULS holed up and Begue wreaking havoc in the town.

Sophie, therefore, spun a yarn about a young married couple in which the husband, having been ill with typhus, had lost all his hair and was ashamed to show himself in public. She asked the hairdresser how to take the measurements and whether it would be sufficient if she did it herself. He was sympathetic and commiserated with the young husband's feelings. He showed her how it should be done, but added that he would not take the responsibility for the wig fitting badly.

The hairdresser was supplied with the measurements; it was to be made for a brown-haired man, the estimate was for 800 francs and the order was sent. We had to wait a considerable time. Meanwhile BANULS, under 'house arrest', dyed his moustache and eyebrows brown and was going crazy with boredom.

I paid Lacaze another visit, picking up 200,000 francs and

information on petrol supplies to the Axis forces in Libya, which was forwarded to London urgently (42/137).

After taking over the Algiers outpost from BANULS, I always met the commander at his home. He knew neither my address nor my real name. Security had to be tightened; it was imperative to work out a new system of delivering reports and messages. I asked for the addresses of people to whom our agents could send postcards and letters in an arranged form consisting of harmless greetings. They would immediately be delivered to him and then passed on again. I also asked for a few trustworthy individuals who would allow us to use their letter boxes, normally found in the entrance gate of the building, the keys to which would be delivered to me. The Algiers commander promised to arrange everything before our next meeting.

Before departing for Casablanca, VINCENT was provided with personal contacts, including a letter to Marcel and a method of contacting me through the good offices of Mr King at the American Consulate in Casablanca. He would address his correspondence to 'Mr Roger', and mine would be to 'Mr Johnson'. He was given funds to cover travel expenses and wished good luck.

I had to make a special trip to the American Consulate to discuss contact by post with the new Casablanca outpost. Opposite the building, I noticed someone conspicuous by the way he was dressed, doubtless one of Begue's agents. Having no incriminating material on me, and being dressed, as usual, *a la mode*, I entered confidently and he ignored me. Mr Boyd sorted everything out. Jotting down the pseudonyms that would be used, he asked me on behalf of London whether I had received the money from M. Lacaze. I told him the matter had been settled.

It was not until 26 March that, much to my relief, MUSTAFA handed me a backlog of three weeks' reports from Oran and Constantine. Apparently the delay was due to difficulties in obtaining permits for travel by rail. The mailbag contained a wealth of material, which took three days to sort out and elaborate. It was only on the 29th that I was able to hand over pouch no. 11 and Boyd gave me VINCENT's Casablanca mailbag in return.

On 31 March Central Office's assessment of the Agency's work for 1941 arrived, which they described as 'excellent'; we were congratulated on our success (2300). This encouraging news was passed on to the heads of our outposts.

I had been communicating with London for some time, urging their assistance in obtaining safe cover or even passports, if possible, for our Intelligence Officers. This would safeguard them from arrest, in the event of betrayal, and assure them exit visas as a kind of insurance policy. Their replies indicated that we could not rely on their help. The exception was their telegram at the end of April recommending that we apply for passports for the 'BANULS family' to go to the United States (3099). Everything, therefore, continued to move along the same old track and we were still left to our own devices. The same applied to Agency Africa's financial allocation, which, for the second quarter, I asked to be sent via the American Consulate.

During March 1942, we received sixty-two messages and sent sixty-seven to London including the following items:

March 1942

Military
Ammunition supplies in Constantine marked on plan of town encl. in pouch no. 1 (42/136); Bône and Philippeville ports used by Italians and patrolled by their fighter planes (42/168); stocks of aircraft petrol in Bône equal 200,000 litres (42/178).

Naval
Cargo ship *Rabelais* sails 14th from Algiers with ammunition for Tunis (42/134); cruiser *Dunkerque*'s ammunition for her 330mm guns transported to France from Mers-el-Kébir (42/139).

Economic
Port of Bougie is centre for delivery of North African phosphates to France (42/141); transport from Maison Carrée to Rommel in Libya of 90,000 litres of petrol (42/174).

DOKTOR's long spell in an army prison, the problem of supplying him with food and the recent decision to extradite him to France all worried me. Central Office, informed of the new situation on 13 March, asked us to 'supply name of ship, date of departure and the route'. I had wanted to organise his escape for some time but London's orders were 'organise escape only if it does not compromise anyone, since we plan to remove him from the ship'.

We reported on the 21st that he would be conveyed to France on a passenger ship, further details were sent on the 25th, and on the 27th the departure date, name of the ship, route and time of departure from Algiers were supplied (42/170 and 42/171). On the 31st DOKTOR was brought from prison and placed on board while Sophie and Marta bade him farewell from a discreet distance. London was immediately notified that the ship had sailed from Algiers.

Once he was en route, I had no means of ascertaining his fate. It was not until early April that we were informed that he had not been removed from the ship and that the British were proposing some sort of exchange with the Vichy French. This was a very disagreeable piece of news. Reading between the lines, it meant that the Agency could not depend on any help. Nevertheless, we pressed on with our work and kept our observations to ourselves.

I paid Miss Aboukaya's cousin, Dr Akoun, six months' rent in advance for the flat at Rue Chanzy. The hotel owner was genuinely upset that we were leaving; I also felt a twinge of melancholy. It held many memories and we were literally moving into the unknown. We would certainly miss Felix, the hotel cat, and the way it waited patiently for our bits of food. He was also very clever – the only cat I ever knew who went to the toilet like a human being; the only thing he couldn't do was flush it! Our friends only believed us when they witnessed it for themselves. As compensation we later acquired a dog, an equally extraordinary character whose exploits could easily fill another volume.

In the event, we moved on 2 April. Sophie had to be very careful with the Arab cleaning lady inherited from Dr Akoun as her gossip could finish us all off. Consequently she was never allowed to open the front door; this partially shielded my colleagues from her curiosity. Although guests usually came in the evening, sudden and unexpected visits could never be ruled out.

I commandeered the doctor's surgery and arranged it as truly befitted the Commercial Director of Floc-Av, replete with samples of our products. Inserted in the glass-topped desk was a map of North Africa on which our Intelligence outposts and observation posts were clearly marked, which, in any unfortunate eventuality, could easily be explained away as the places where our products were sold. This map, showing Agency Africa's network at a glance, was invaluable when sorting out Intelligence reports and determining where pressure should be exerted to recruit more agents.

As a result of nine months of organisation, all the ports and administrative and military centres were covered. Only the inland networks – the larger towns, railway junctions, mining centres etc. – needed to be organised. I already had about a hundred principal agents, who in turn had their collaborators, who had their collaborators and so on almost *ad infinitum*, constituting a vast and complex human pyramid. One never really knew how many there were, since only the most important ones had agency numbers. I felt like an enormous spider enveloping ever larger spans of territory in its web. The only problem was that this spider lacked mobility. It had to stay in one place constantly guarding its web, otherwise it would be yanked down and destroyed.

Sophie ruled over the rest of the flat and, with Commissioner Begue around, we stopped paying frequent visits to town. The black market supplied us with sufficient food, which was delivered directly to our house. The problem was that our consumption of electricity and gas exceeded the limits laid down by the authorities. This was not difficult in a large place, with frequent soirées, and my habit of working at night with the blinds drawn. Sophie dealt with these crises in the traditional way by slipping an appropriate financial contribution to the official, the excess balance being carried over to the next period, which was then repeated, and so on.

I also took advantage of the black market to keep a generous supply of all-important booze, without which hardly anything could be settled. Many a tongue was loosened by a few glasses, especially as the supply of wine and spirits was officially restricted. In short, we soon began to feel completely at home and reasonably secure, and visitors could now be received without the nagging fear of betrayal.

The addresses needed for my correspondence with the Algiers commander were now available. The delivery system could be speeded up and our security increased. I devised a code to be used for postcards and short notes relating to the transportation of ore and munitions, the movement of Axis ships, etc. These communications were intended to be short and concise, where every word had its own special meaning. The Oran and Constantine commanders received the code, directions and an allocation of addresses for the ports. It was now sufficient for an agent who wanted to communicate urgent information concerning a particular transport to send a short missive. It was emphasised that this method was only intended for important and urgent items.

I also devised a new system for delivering reports inside Algiers itself, to be effected immediately. Every recipient of reports from a 'direct' post box – one where the courier from the Intelligence outpost had left reports – received an address that was as close as possible. There an intermediate box was to be found where he would post the reports he had just collected from the 'direct' box. Previously the system had entailed handing the mail to MUSTAFA or someone else. The new system was a great improvement – the entire operation was impersonal and the recipient rid himself of the material quickly. The intermediate boxes were then emptied by MUSTAFA, BANULS, myself or, occasionally, our wives. Happily, nobody was ever caught in the process.

As mentioned previously, we began using our radio exclusively from 12 April. MACIEJ's visits now became more infrequent and he was awaiting orders to embark for France. From the moment his team left for France until our own radio became operational, we had to reduce the amount of radio messages to London significantly, otherwise it would have compromised him with the French authorities. After that we could send as many as we liked.

Their number continually grew and our hurdy-gurdy operated twice a day, at 8am and 6.30pm. MUSTAFA collected my messages before going to the radio station and placed those from Central Office in the letter box of my house.

The actual technical work, the coding and decoding of telegrams and the editing and extracting of vital information, continued to take up a great deal of my time. The mailbags from the Intelligence outposts contained the commander's reports and those from the agents. The latter were signed with their cryptonyms. I inserted the agent's number when it reached me in order to avoid the impression, should the outpost be exposed, that a powerful organisation with a widespread spy network was operating in French North Africa. Sophie continued to help me enormously as volunteer cipher clerk. I left her the telegrams to be encoded for our evening transmission before going to my afternoon job at Floc-Av.

Our social circle was increasing and we organised our first big get-together during the Easter holidays. Considerable diplomatic skill was needed to avoid friction between certain French people. These soirées greatly helped our Intelligence work and I asked Sophie to keep the accounts for these gatherings, which were only partly covered by me. In 1944, this account book had the honour of being examined by the Ministerial Council of the Polish Government in London. The head of Central Office was questioned about these expenses; 'Stanislas' (alias Colonel Gano) told me that he found them difficult to explain. I responded daily: 'In my opinion, this is the best proof that the money was being spent on Intelligence work, the results of which were excellent. I am surprised that you were unable to explain it properly!'

The new system worked well and my letterbox was soon crammed with mail from the outposts. New agents (1848–9 and 1853–7) were recruited, as a result of which Central Office had to be approached for certain prearranged broadcasts in French to be made from London, reassuring them that they were working for the Free French. This was especially significant as agent 1856 (Monsieur Abeille) became the commander of our newest outpost at Tlemcen.

Our financial report, the April balance amounting to 517,000 francs, was also forwarded to them. It was difficult to forget the experience of being short of funds and, for many reasons, I could no longer borrow. To run short now would be disastrous. With the increasing number of agents and new Intelligence outposts, our expenses continued to grow rapidly.

In reply to my March message regarding our allowance for the second quarter, Central Office informed us that it had been sent on 18 March 'via the Americans for RYGOR'. After waiting patiently for news from the American Consulate, I asked them on 8 April, 'When and where was the allowance sent?' Instead of explaining, they asked me whether the allowance for the second quarter had been collected.

The exchange of messages continued throughout May and it was only on 15 June that we received our allocation for the second quarter (US $12,000). So an allowance that should have been received at the beginning of the period arrived only towards its end. This is a good example of how the transmission of money through safe and official channels for vital work can actually become, for no apparent reason, a lengthy and difficult process.

Even when the money was finally received, my problems were still far from over. It then became necessary to change it at a good rate and not to lose on it. One had to be a financial wizard and familiar with foreign exchange rates on the black market. Again, this was not very safe with large sums involved and various hostile elements snooping around. It caused me many sleepless nights.

Money, especially if it comes too easily, leads to avarice. It is the best medium for collecting Intelligence, confirmed in biblical times. Somewhere there ought to be a Chinese proverb to the effect that 'An ounce of gold can save a barrel of soldier's blood.' At the same time, money becomes dangerous if too easily obtainable and too easy to spend. Many spy networks were unravelled as a result of dubious financial transactions. The disposal of money in the Secret Service must therefore be effected very carefully and with great skill. This is a cardinal point.

On 11 April, while I was handing over pouch no. 13 at the American Consulate, Mr Boyd gave me one from London in return. This was a real surprise – the first mail from Central Office. However, it contained nothing of importance; neither did their subsequent ones, which we received infrequently. They preferred to order Intelligence tasks by radio, which they considered a more secure method.

When I handed over pouch no. 14, the Consul General, Mr Cole, asked me for reliable information on an 'individual of Czech origin' who had been employed by the Consulate. He feared that a German agent might have been planted and automatically assumed that I would have little difficulty in finding out. In the event, I was able to reassure him on 24 April that the Czech was completely trustworthy and that my information was based on reliable sources.

On 25 April there was a very interesting report from the Algiers commander. A small ship, capacity approximately 200 tons, had loaded diesel oil and food in Algiers port, left on the night of 23/24 April and returned in the morning without its cargo. The diesel oil had been supplied by the French Government and, according to rumours rife at the port, the fuel and provisions were for German submarines at sea.

This was our first information of this type – similar to that which TUDOR and I had obtained in Marseilles in 1941, to the effect that ships were sailing down the Rhone at night and that the police had sealed off the bridges and the river while they were in transit. We had concluded at that time that they might have been German pocket U-boats en route to the Mediterranean. I had no idea whether TUDOR forwarded the information to London. This new data concerning the supply ship tended to confirm our earlier information from Marseilles and was sent to Central Office (42/218).

On the 24th we were informed that two similar supply ships were loading diesel oil and were due to sail that night under a Spanish flag (42/224). Our agent could only provide a general description – steel ships with varying capacities, maximum 200 tons. The diesel fuel was received from the port authorities and the food from civilian suppliers. They usually left the port at night and returned in the morning.

Information was sent on the 29th that a fourth supply ship,

approximately 400 tons, with one funnel and a black stripe, left the port on the night of 29/30 April. The battle for Egypt was also being waged at sea. The Allied convoys had suffered severe losses from air and U-boat attacks. At least the German submarine supply base could now be roughly pinpointed as being east of Algiers.

In late April a go-between reported that a four-room fully furnished flat in a side street off the Rue Michelet was for sale. The owner was leaving Algiers; he wanted 80,000 francs and it was available immediately. I told the go-between, 'I'll give 70,000 francs – go and bargain!' A few days later he reported the owner's agreement. The papers were drawn up in the name of 'Monsieur Maureau'; I made a down payment and agreed to pay the balance at the end of the month. The good news was conveyed to BANULS's wife. New French documents were drawn up for 'M. and Mme Maureau' with Achiary's indirect help; only the photographs, dependent on the legendary wig, were missing.

In late April Henri d'Astier de la Vigerie paid me an unexpected visit. Oran had notified me that he was actively involved in the resistance movement there. He had now been transferred to the headquarters of the Chantiers de la Jeunesse; our contacts would therefore be more frequent. D'Astier provided details of their position and readiness and requested me to contact London for them to send a representative to Tangiers to meet their delegate between 5 and 10 May. I promised that their reply would be conveyed to him immediately. Meanwhile, he liked my suggestion that he should bring his wife next time in order to give the impression that our meetings were purely social.

The next surprise was on 30 April when Sophie returned from her hairdresser with the wig and a bill for 800 francs. It was delivered in the afternoon to Marta, who told us that it fitted BANULS perfectly and that she was 'delighted to now have a husband with hair!' Their move was now imminent, so I gave her the keys to their new place and expected him to come and see me. Naturally, the appearance of the new BANULS was awaited with some impatience. In the meantime, Miss Aboukaya told me that they had moved; the room at her house was again at my disposal.

April's tally of telegrams was fifty-seven from Head Office and fifty-five sent to London. Among some of the more interesting were:

April 1942

Military
Coastal defences of Cap Falcone – two 75mm guns (42/193); effectiveness of manoeuvres of Moroccan Army (42/197); Arab reserve NCOs have received call-up papers to be ready for mobilisation (42/219); Salines airfield outside Bône, three new Italian Hunter aircraft in service (42/221); German Colonel Boehm, member of the Armistice Commission from Wiesbaden, not satisfied with his inspection of coastal defences of Morocco, possible use of Wehrmacht (42/232).

Naval
SS *Djebel Amour* leaves port Philippeville via Bône, sails to Marseilles with cargo 20 tons of rubber (42/198); tanker SS *Norrait* Algiers–Tunis with 500 tons alcohol (42/216); the battleship *Jean Bart* is ready for action, has received ammunition for all guns, while in port surrounded by protective steel nets (42/228).

Economic
Shipment of cobalt from Nemours to France on 19th (42/217); German U-boats supplied with 600 tons diesel oil on 22 April in ports of Algiers, Arzev and Philippeville (42/218); railway connection between Tenes–Orleansville in Algiers being dismantled, rails will be transported to Kennasa (42/230).

19

COUNTER-ESPIONAGE – 'TREASON IN PARIS!'

London continued to send us an increasing number of counter-intelligence tasks, a highly specialised activity, which I could not realistically expect my agents to undertake. Other ways of solving this tricky problem had to be found. Among such orders were to observe and provide information on German spies working in North Africa.

Initially, in order to bind Achiary closer to us, I had offered him financial assistance in return for counter-intelligence and an exchange of information. Agency Africa could now extend our agreement. One evening I explained the situation to Achiary, emphasising that it was extremely difficult, especially with Commissioner Begue on my back. André said that Begue was irritated at being unable to pick up the trail, and that he himself was obviously very interested in the German agents, as it fell within his domain. I asked him whether he could assign one of his most trusted inspectors to keep in touch with me over these matters. He suggested his assistant, Inspector Lofredo, which was ideal as I had first met him while under arrest and had grown to trust him.

Lofredo came to see me the following day, delighted at having been made our contact. Faced with such enthusiasm, I immediately confided that I would like him to become head of my counter-intelligence outpost in Algeria and Tunisia. He would be provided with data about German agents which he could also use for his own work. In return, he would provide detailed information on all Axis agents and their contacts, and lists of the members of the Armistice Commission and the German and Italian Consulates. He readily agreed and was given the cryptonym FREDO. As head of our counter-intelligence he would receive an allowance, and our method of communication was fixed. As far as Morocco and Tangiers were concerned, I was optimistic that VINCENT was capable of sorting it out with Marcel as I had done with Achiary. I'd send him a note in our next mailbag.

I had no doubt that our hurdy-gurdy's messages were being monitored by the French and the Germans and that they were attempting to decipher them. MACIEJ explained that there was no such thing as an unbreakable code. It was only a question of time, and obviously the more messages were sent, the easier it became to break. Certain words and phrases are inevitably repeated, greatly facilitating deciphering. For example, we always repeated the names of ships, ports, airports, towns etc. How was it possible to avoid it?

The Oran outpost sent me a list of French merchant and requisitioned ships where the word *Saint* appeared before their proper names. I numbered them consecutively and, using numbers instead of real names, initiated a double code. Furthermore, a number was far easier to encode than a name, and also facilitated decoding. Pouch no. 14 was prepared from the next batch of outpost reports, with a complete list of French merchant ships to be encoded, an explanatory report, and the date when it should be effected (42/38/tj).

In reality Central Office should have issued us with additional special codes. Since this was not forthcoming we devised our own. With MUSTAFA's help and MACIEJ's specialised knowledge, we worked out a new codebook in case we needed to send messages in a foreign language. In the event, it soon came in useful. Its principles were enclosed in pouch no. 15, and consisted of our report (42/41/tj) and an obscure French novel in two volumes.

May 1942 began well. BANULS appeared to be safe; Begue's progress had been blocked and Commissaire Lofredo, who visited me regularly, and Achiary kept me informed of his movements.

One evening someone rang my door bell and an unknown man asked, 'Does Dr Akoun live here?' I only recognised BANULS by his voice. The wig was a perfect fit, and he was unrecognisable; with dark glasses, he could easily pass in the street as a Frenchman, a Spaniard or even an Algerian.

I ushered him straight to my office. We discussed the current situation and he was allotted new Intelligence tasks for the outpost commanders. His previous work would continue, i.e. contacts with those agents he knew personally, with the exception of the Algiers commander, which I would retain myself. I gave him the keys to the intermediate letterboxes to extract the mail and put them in my letterbox. After advising him not to appear too frequently with Marta in town and to contact me in the evenings, I thought we needed some light relief.

I led him to the drawing room and told Sophie that I wanted to introduce our new visitor. BANULS disguised his voice and it took her some time to recognise him. His disguise was a success. As a token of his gratitude he handed her his 'Ode to a Wig', which he had composed in hiding. Unfortunately, in the course of our interminable moves, this witty poem was lost. In the midst of our revelries, we received a surprise visit from a lady who knew BANULS quite well. He left shortly afterwards and she was curious to know the identity of the gentleman. Sophie told her (with considerable truth) that he was Monsieur Maureau. The diversions were not only amusing but also very reassuring.

Our hurdy-gurdy was playing very well. As a novelty we were now receiving WICHER's messages for MACIEJ and sending his replies by the same route. MACIEJ, in fact, remained in Algiers for quite some time. Once he arrived agitated, because he had been stopped in the street by plain-clothes police during a round-up, presumably on Begue's orders. It was only thanks to Achiary, who happened to be present, that he was not arrested.

Messages concerning military matters now being received from London gave the distinct impression that something there had changed for the better. Their replies to our communications were speedier and more concise. It seemed that, at long last, someone was studying our reports and taking an interest in us. I wasn't certain who, but the mere fact that we now knew that our information was needed had a profound psychological effect. Some of their messages gave us new, interesting tasks, which continually extended the scope of our activities.

Our Intelligence reports showed that the aim of the German–Italian Armistice Commission, which had branches in large army garrisons, was to weaken French military strength by limiting their arms, munitions and numbers. The French North African Army Command, on the other hand, tried to increase their military strength – a situation, which, ironically, resembled the illegal rearmament of Germany after the Treaty of Versailles. Hitler may have considered invading French North Africa. If, however, the Allies decided to occupy it first, the Armistice Commission's actions would undoubtedly benefit them.

The attitudes of the *pieds-noirs* (the French settlers), moulded by Vichy propaganda, were anti-British yet increasingly anti-German. Anglophobia was particularly noticeable among French naval officers, who were almost entirely under Admiral Darlan's influence. The French *colons* regarded themselves as French Algerians, exploited by the metropolis despite the fact that many had subsequently made huge fortunes. The majority were extreme right-wing nationalists with decidedly reactionary views who, on the whole, supported Vichy's collaborationist policies, which they also found financially rewarding.

The majority of the population, however, tended to be pro-American. Radicals, socialists and communists were to be found among the urban working classes, which, since mining and industry only really developed in the twentieth century, included more recent immigrants. Towns with a strong working class and an intelligentsia tended to be against collaborationism and Vichy's policy of over-exporting food products. The exceptions were the higher officials, who constituted a mandarin class.

Listening at home to the BBC evening broadcasts, I felt the situation was grave. In Libya Rommel's Afrika Korps was moving towards Egypt and the British Army appeared unable to hold them. On the Eastern front the Wehrmacht was on the outskirts of Stalingrad and the Germans were occupying the northern Caucasus. The Royal Navy had suffered great losses in the North and South Atlantic and in the Mediterranean, where it was unable to sail beyond Malta. In the war with Japan, the United States seemed to suffer continual setbacks.

In the circumstances it was hardly surprising that the Vichy regime yielded to the ever-increasing German pressure for more supplies of raw materials, food, military equipment and transport. Vichy's radio and press propaganda urged people to join the Légion and the PPF (Parti Populaire Français). With Governor General Châtel in Algiers, General Nogues in Morocco and Admiral Esteva in Tunisia all supporting Pétain policies, the repercussions were enormous. Pressure against those opposing collaborationism and supporting de Gaulle was now increasing. Lists of names were prepared, to suppress any opposition.

I desperately tried to maintain a surplus in the Agency's cashbox in case of an emergency, which could strike at any time. Consequently, when reporting our financial position as at 1 May, I asked for the third quarter's allowance to be sent as well.

As a result of increasing Axis use of the Maison Blanche airport, we organised a good observation post to monitor the passenger and goods traffic. We also sent news of the prospective arrival in Casablanca of a German admiral from the Armistice Commission to carry out a check of the naval base. German interest in the state of the Moroccan coastal defences seemed to be connected with fear of an Allied invasion, and they even allowed the French defences to be slightly strengthened.

Contact with Henri d'Astier brought me closer to the Resistance and, in any case, I still maintained contact with London on their behalf. London wanted to be informed when their delegate would arrive and given data on the structure of the group, its size and its leaders. D'Astier and I discussed these matters and on 5 May the details were sent, including the date (20 May), in three different messages. Central Office then inquired who would be the group's delegate. I had to ask d'Astier again before sending it – it would be a senior official of the General Government – and reported that the group were requesting a high-ranking officer to be sent for talks in Tangiers between 20 and 25 May (42/274). At the same time, Central Office asked for my opinion of the group and its leaders, whether they had any contact with the Vichy Government, and if they were insisting on Tangiers as a meeting place. It was not until 19 May that I could finally inform them that the meeting place had now been changed to Tipaza, which would be ideal.

Algiers was now very tense as a result of rumours that the Germans were about to take over French North Africa. German airmen were frequently to be seen on the streets of Algiers and French Army units were placed on a state of combat readiness. D'Astier spoke to me about the active campaign the Resistance intended to wage in such an eventuality. London were informed of this conversation – that, in the event of the Axis armies occupying Algiers, the Resistance planned an uprising and were requesting arms and ammunition to be delivered to a strategic redoubt west of Oran. Information regarding its location was passed on to Mr Williams, an official of the British Consulate in Tangiers.

A speedy reply was received. London asked who would hand over plans of the location to Mr Williams in Tangiers, and when and where they would do so – information that was necessary in order to ensure the security of the group and its delegate. It was not until 10 June that I was able to give them details of the handover and the name. Even on the 16th London were still asking whether new plans had been sent. I immediately replied that nothing had changed. This exchange of messages gives some indication of the amount of time I was compelled to devote to discussions with leaders of the group and also to encoding and decoding messages relating to the Resistance.

One day I received a note from one of my personal informants proposing a meeting at a well-known rendezvous on the outskirts of Algiers. As usual Sophie warned me to be careful of possible police swoops and, as usual, I dismissed her fears. My trusted and reliable informant had some very valuable material on German demands for the exploitation of North African mineral resources. Returning by tram with the secret documents in my pocket, I decided to be particularly cautious. I stayed on the platform on the back of the tram, giving me a better view of the street and enabling me to leap off and make a run for it if necessary.

As the tram was approaching the town centre and the Place du Gouvernement, a young man jumped on shouting in Arabic, which produced pandemonium among the Arab passengers, some of whom jumped off immediately. Intrigued, I gazed up the street and, in the distance, saw the Garde Mobile and the police gathered by the Square. Instinctively, I also jumped off and immediately turned into a side-street with steps leading up to the Arab quarter. I hung around the Casbah for a long time and finally returned home by a different route. If, after checking my Polish passport, they had carried out a body search, the Agency's work would have been finished. I lost count of the number of times I had to slip into alleyways or cafés to avoid having my documents checked. One had to watch out everywhere for sudden police checks.

Despite all our tricks, I was still in Algiers illegally. In order to become legal one had to apply for an appropriate identity card and I had only my old Polish passport. I asked Achiary whether he could help procure identity cards for us at the Prefecture. My Moroccan visa had almost run out and I was now unable to go there to extend it. He promised to arrange it and, sure enough, Sophie, George and I eventually received them, which was an enormous relief.

My description of the 'submarine supply ships' was sent to London:

They are Spanish ships sailing under a German flag, built and bought in Belgium. One can surmise their purpose from their size, build and camouflage, the taking of diesel in quantities far exceeding their need, and also from the gossip of the crew in port. It was difficult to pinpoint the supply zone – at sea east of Algiers and probably different in each case; the diesel being pumped into the submarine at sea. During the night of 15/16 May there was an incident on board one of these ships while in port, a heavy machine gun was fired and there were wounded amongst the crew. The

German members of the Armistice Commission intervened with the Command Post of the Port (42/256, 42/279 and 42/292).

In reply to our earlier complaints regarding our shortage of officers, London informed us on 11 May that two Intelligence Officers had been allocated to the Agency and would be arriving in Gibraltar between 21 and 22 May. We were instructed to reply by return whether we could obtain the necessary documents for them and organise a welcoming party at Ile Colombi. Fortunately Achiary visited me that evening and I was able to report to London on the 12th: 'Achiary will procure personal documents. The officers must carry demobilisation cards from the French Army. The Ile Colombi cannot be used as it has been requisitioned by the army. I will look for a suitable place. The officers are to wait for news in Gibraltar' (42/271).

Central Office replied on the 15th: 'The officers are already in Gibraltar carrying demobilisation cards; they will await further instructions there; give operational details' (3761).

In the midst of all this, as a partner in the Floc-Av Company I had to keep up appearances and, because everyone knew it was Sophie's name day, I was compelled to hold a large party at our flat on 15 May. When our guests wanted to dance, Sophie, taking her place at the piano, said half-jokingly, 'Please remove your shoes, otherwise you'll ruin our expensive carpets!' One of the first to take off his shoes and start dancing was the President of the Special Division of the Supreme Court. The party lasted almost until dawn and I could have done without it.

The next morning (the 16th), after a sleepless night, my routine was interrupted by Achiary's unexpected arrival. I had never seen him looking so nervous and tense. The first word I heard was 'Treason!'

Early that morning his men had stopped a group of two men and two women arriving from France without documents, ostensibly fleeing from Paris and from arrest. They stated that they wanted to meet 'RYGOR, who is in charge of the Allied secret service in Algiers'. This news put him on guard as it reeked of provocation by the

Gestapo, who had somehow uncovered the existence of our network. He had no idea what to do with them. They had no means of support and he did not have any funds at his disposal for such a contingency. Thank God, he had arrested them without the knowledge of the Germans or of Commissioner Begue, who, fortunately, was not on the ship. The situation was extremely serious.

I told him:

First of all, I'll immediately give you some money for their support. We'll have to keep them in hiding for the time being. The Polish Secret Service is operating within Occupied France with a main outpost in Paris. Many Frenchmen and women are employed in the network. While I was still in Marseilles, I knew some of their cryptonyms, for example 'La Chatte' [in London known to Poles and British as VICTOIRE]. I've heard nothing from London about betrayal and arrests in Paris. If these people are saying something about the Secret Service there, then they must have cryptonyms if they worked for it. You must speak to them again and find out. In the meantime, I'll ask Central Office for clarification and we'll decide what to do after London replies.

Achiary, having calmed down, and with the funds in his pocket, went to obtain the information, which he would immediately report back to me.

There were only two possibilities: first, some form of betrayal leading to arrests, the liquidation of the Paris outpost and the network, and the agents' escape. I still couldn't understand how individual agents came to know about my cryptonym and my Algerian work. How could TUDOR, the only person in France who knew my cryptonym, have passed it on to Czerniawski, and how could it have become known to the other agents? That worried me most. Secondly, perhaps the Gestapo really had picked up my trail and, since they knew of our work, had sent agents provocateurs to Algiers. In that case, I resolved to get rid of them – there was no other choice. Everything had calmed down after the DOKTOR affair. Now it had blown up again, proving that nothing could be taken for granted.

Achiary returned after about an hour with three cryptonyms: MOUSTIQUE, KENT and NOUED. I immediately sent an urgent message to London: 'Do you know of agents from Paris with cryptonyms (as above) who apparently had to flee in order to escape arrest?' Their reply came the following morning (the 17th): 'We know of these agents, please get exact information from them about what happened.' I was really angry with those individuals from France who had exposed the Agency to such grave danger. Again, it was only due to luck that we had avoided the consequences of betrayal. Living expenses for the four people still had to be covered and it was difficult to imagine that we would be reimbursed.

Achiary returned in the evening and was relieved at London's response. My plan would be to give him 5,000 francs per person for their support, while he organised a hiding place for them until they could be sent to England. This would have to be on the ship bringing my new Intelligence Officers from Gibraltar. We agreed that there was no other solution, we would temporarily break contact with each other, and he and FREDO would sort things out.

Central Office were informed of my decision. They agreed to link receiving the officers from Gibraltar with the despatch of the Paris agents to London. We would send them to Oran because I intended the operation to take place within the territory of that outpost. The Oran commander was instructed to keep them in a safe house until the day of the operation.

FREDO was worried about sending our Parisian visitors by train. A car would be safer. He would take care of it and let me know the cost of the trip. While he was discussing the Oran trip with MOUSTIQUE, she had asked him whether she could speak to me. I agreed to an immediate meeting at a seaside café in the suburb of St Eugène.

Approaching the café, I spotted a diminutive figure sitting on a bench. MOUSTIQUE's cryptonym really was appropriate – she was small and slightly built. We sat on the terrace by the sea and she began by apologising for being a nuisance. I said that I knew about their work in France and had known her boss personally – circumstances had not allowed us to meet earlier. Unfortunately conditions were completely different in North Africa and they could not be used here. They were being sent to England but would first travel to Oran and await my orders.

MOUSTIQUE mentioned the fourth member of the group, who had not yet been given a codename. This was a young girl, full of life, who, having met some young people in Algiers, was very difficult to restrain. MOUSTIQUE was afraid that she could betray us and asked what her orders were, as she and KENT could easily get rid of her – 'just a little boat trip at sea and the problem would be solved!'

I told her that any 'wet job' was out of the question. She should not mention to anyone, least of all the girl, that they were going to Oran in a few days' time. If she had found a boyfriend, then so much the better. Nothing should be put in her way if she wanted to go to him. MOUSTIQUE should give her 1,000 francs for the journey, which I'd cover. The moment they left, all connections would be severed and the matter would be closed.

MOUSTIQUE, whom I remembered from talks with TUDOR about Czerniawski's work in Paris, was a nice person, intelligent and energetic. It was amazing how much energy and willpower could be concentrated into such a small frame. I asked her what happened in Paris, who was arrested, and how she knew of my cryptonym and my work in Algiers. She recounted her story.

In November 1940, Czerniawski, who used the code name WALENTY for TUDOR in Marseilles and ARMAND as head of the Paris network, arrived in Paris from Toulouse. He was accompanied by his girlfriend, Mathilde Carré, who was a nurse in an army hospital. They lived together in Paris; she was his first agent and his personal secretary. Then she became the leading figure in his organisation, recruiting new agents and maintaining contacts. Her code name was VICTOIRE. I remembered how TUDOR in Marseilles had praised her reports from Paris.

MOUSTIQUE continued. The Intelligence network was expanded, as was the scope of their work. There were numerous female agents in the network and some in the staff office that ARMAND had established in Paris. She knew him personally. He was always very pleasant and well-mannered with women, which aroused 'La Chatte''s jealousy. In the summer of 1941 ARMAND received a hurdy-gurdy from Marseilles, which started playing directly to London. During his stay in Marseilles, he had found out about the Intelligence network in Algiers and about RYGOR, who was its chief.

The Gestapo were carrying out normal round-ups and routine arrests in Paris and an agent from the network could have been caught. Perhaps he revealed something under interrogation or reports were found on him, because they began arresting people from the Paris network including 'La Chatte'. In November 1941 ARMAND was arrested and they found the radio station and all the Intelligence material. MOUSTIQUE and the others who had managed to escape went into hiding for some time, then fled to Marseilles and thence to Algiers; ARMAND had told her about our network in North Africa. As for 'La Chatte', the head of German counter-intelligence in Paris used to take her to see suspects who had been arrested. MOUSTIQUE wasn't certain whether she was this officer's mistress or whether she had betrayed the network and was responsible for it being liquidated.

I didn't ask any further questions and our conversation ended at that point. Shortly afterwards all three left for Oran, but it was not until September 1942 that they left for England in our specially staged Operation Zebra. I met MOUSTIQUE (and Czerniawski) again in London in January 1943, but did not discuss Intelligence matters with her.

'La Chatte''s trial was a *cause célèbre* in post-liberation France. Nowhere was it revealed that from November 1940 onwards an Intelligence outpost of the Polish Secret Service operated in Paris under the auspices of the TUDOR network in Marseilles. Perhaps in those heady days the implication that there was very little organised French resistance before June 1941 (and that it was begun by the Poles) would have been too painful a reminder of the true state of affairs in occupied France.

I concluded that the betrayal was the result of insufficient secrecy and the excessive number of women agents employed. Doubtless, the arrests of DOKTOR and myself were also part of its effect. The

Marseilles connection must have been uncovered, since TUDOR had to go into hiding and was finally evacuated to England in a night-time air operation. The Gestapo must also have found out about our work in Algiers, which is why their Special Commissioner, Begue, had been sent there. The fact that our North African work had been minimised was very fortunate. I had the opportunity of discussing it with TUDOR during my first visit to London in 1943.

20

NEW SURPRISES AND CHANGES

The scope of our activities expanded to such an extent that some of London's requests appeared beyond our capability and I had no idea how they could be fulfilled. For example:

What were the possibilities of the French extending the Tunis–Gabès railway to the SE of Tunis and the Italians extending the railway from Tripoli to the west in the direction of Tunis? What had they accomplished and were there any preparations for laying tracks, constructing telephone lines, etc. in this territory? (3047)

Other requests from Central Office were comparatively more straightforward and included:

Further details on the Tliananet oil well (3618); information re trade with Japan, whether there were any Japanese ships in French North African ports and what were their cargoes (3160); the current strength of the coastal defences of Bizerta base and the port of Tunis, which, according to the disarmament conditions, were supposed to have been destroyed (3271); tests were apparently being carried out on a new 46mm anti-aircraft gun in Sidi-bel-Abbès: report on the precise results of these tests (3521); information required on heavy batteries at Casablanca (3384).

We were able to report that aeroplanes belonging to the German Armistice Commission in Wiesbaden, landing at the

Maison Blanche airfield, were flying on to the Spanish colony of Rio de Oro where, supposedly, German U-boat bases were to be found (42/228).

VINCENT in Tangiers reported that his informants watching the German Consulate had noticed frequent contacts between a member of its staff and a certain official at the American Consulate. Also that it would soon be possible to change dollars into francs, and he gave the black market exchange rate. In future, therefore, he would be changing dollars in Tangiers.

On 16 May I handed pouches nos 17 and 18 to the Americans. My relationship with Messrs Boyd and Knox was now very friendly and frank, and I took it for granted that they were drawing essential information from Agency Africa's pouches for themselves. We discussed the war and the North African situation. They were depressed by it, while I was still optimistic. I told Boyd that, although London continually informed me that our funds had been sent to the American Consulate in Tangiers, they never reached me on time, whereas our pouches which were despatched by the same route reached them more or less regularly. Something was wrong somewhere. For example, they radioed that US $24,000 had been remitted for the second half of the year, but we had still not received the money sent in March. Funds were running out and without them I might have to close the shop. He took the matter to heart and promised to raise the matter immediately with those 'upstairs', adding that he could give us financial assistance if we needed it. While grateful for his offer, I preferred to avoid such a situation.

Confidentially, I asked whether he knew the personnel of his Tangiers Consulate, as one of its officials was contacting the German Consulate too frequently. Boyd was very grateful, and promised that the information would be 'put to good use'.

Among a further batch of new tasks were:

Exact data needed on quantity of iron ore exported to France (3385); state number of lorries supplied to Libya from 1 January to 1 May 1942 (3689); report on transport of valuable molybdenum – find out quantity and quality, is it ordinary or concentrated ore

(3918); data needed on quantities of transported rubber, raw as well as manufactured (3851).

How could these highly specialised tasks be accomplished? I informed Central Office that the Agency could not keep statistics nor carry out chemical tests. Such tasks would require our own laboratories and the possession of statistical information, which would be dangerous. What was I supposed to do? I eventually decided to keep the data since without it we would be unable to organise our reports. It was a risk that we had to take.

Central Office were continually pushing for information on West Africa and urging us to organise an Intelligence outpost at Dakar. I knew what lay behind it. The British Admiralty wanted information on French ships at Dakar, especially on the *Richelieu*, the most modern battleship in her class. My replies were always the same – it was being considered and would be sorted out soon. They advised me to send an agent but he would have to be given some means of communication with London or myself. This would involve a hurdy-gurdy, an operator, technical data and a method of sending and receiving mail and funds. Simply sending someone to Dakar and leaving him to his own devices would not produce any results. London seemed to have very little idea of the problems involved. However, I already held one of the keys – I had met Marcel's friends from Dakar and had received an invitation to go there. But that meant going there myself, which was very difficult. I was really stuck.

London's preoccupation with Dakar was being overshadowed by events indicating possible German preparations for a surprise invasion of French North Africa. A Spanish officer who deserted to the French side on 9 May reported a concentration of 350 Spanish tanks on the French Moroccan border with German officers in overall control. This armoured division had an air cover of ninety-eight German aeroplanes and, together with the existing 300 Spanish planes, it constituted a substantial force. This was confirmed by a new report from Tenes that twenty-nine German aeroplanes had been flown to Spanish Morocco (42/270 and 42/275). The French appeared to have issued call-up papers and placed army units on alert; anti-German conversations between French officers and men indicated the direction of the anticipated attack (42/277).

Meanwhile the German admiral, who had completed his inspection of the French air force in North Africa, began a 'British invasion' scare and announced Luftwaffe reinforcements (42/310). The latter was confirmed by the requisition of apartments in Algiers, Oran and Bône for German officers (42/296). As if this were not sufficient, FREDO brought some bad news about Achiary. Begue, who did not trust him, apparently wanted him replaced and nobody knew who his successor would be.

The Polish Intelligence Officers earmarked for the agency had already been waiting in Gibraltar since mid-May for the operation to land them in Algeria. The increase in work had created a shortage of officers and I wanted them in Algiers as soon as possible. London informed me that they would not be sent with the delegate arriving for talks with the resistance group and that I should organise a separate operation for them as soon as possible (4478).

I concluded that the best place would be the coast to the west of Oran, which was partly covered by forest, sparsely inhabited and situated near Gibraltar. Ragache, the Oran commander, was a naval man and could be relied on to organise such a landing. He would inform us of its exact location, essential in night-time operations, pick up the officers from the ship, transport them to Oran and keep them there, and then take them to BANULS's flat. We already had our own agents within the police at Oran, and procuring documents for them would be easier there. BANULS would personally convey my order to Ragache on his arrival in Algiers for Floc-Av's monthly financial meeting.

At Floc-Av, on 3 June, I discussed commercial matters with the company's representative (alias the Oran commander) and presumed that BANULS had already passed my orders on to him, which he confirmed in the evening. I reported to London that the officers must wait in Gibraltar while the operation was being prepared and that the location would be communicated to them after the landing spot had been fixed.

London was becoming impatient and instructed us to report immediately. The Oran commander carried out his task speedily, indicating his choice of a landing spot, which was then conveyed to London. I gathered that the British Admiralty refused to accept it and chose another, which I immediately reported was not suitable, in my opinion, for such an operation. However, London still ordered it for the night of 19/20 July 1942 and sent us passwords and signals. I was therefore compelled to carry out their orders. The Oran commander received appropriate instructions and the necessary information. The ship was unable to reach the coast or land the officers by boat. The operation failed.

I sent a written report explaining the reasons for the fiasco, and also a telegram (42/461). London then recommended that I should prepare another operation myself and submit a new location. In the event, this occurred at a much later date and the officers continued to wait at Gibraltar. In the meantime we had received twenty messages connected with the abortive operation and had sent fifteen ourselves.

Thanks to our Constantine outpost, we were able to notify London fairly quickly that a Gabès–Ben Gardane railway line did not exist and that no work was being undertaken to extend it in the direction of Tripoli. In reply to their other requests, I reported that:

Re lorries for Germany: 1,200 were being purchased in Vichy France and North Africa, just under 1,000 had been delivered and during April 126 had been sent from North Africa with further deliveries expected (42/278); rubber was being sent from Dakar to Casablanca then by rail to Algiers and thence shipped to French ports under the symbol 'K.Z-523' (42/300); port of Oran was closed off at night with protective nets and a submarine guarding the entrance (42/309).

London sent us the disagreeable news that the Americans had refused to issue a passport for BANULS (3868). Colonel Eddy in Tangiers was supposed to help. Thankfully, we managed to sort out the question of BANULS's security ourselves. FREDO's news was in a similar vein. Achiary had broken his leg and would be confined to bed for several weeks. I asked him to try to sneak one of our agents into the German Consulate. Later, he was able to inform me that the Consul's new chauffeur was our informant and that he spoke German quite well. This was a coup that we hoped would pay big dividends.

London wanted to know whether ships based in North Africa had stocks of ammunition and the quantity and whether there were ammunition stocks for ships based at Toulon sailing to North Africa in the event of a German Occupation of the 'free zone'. Another message inquired about the yield of the copper mine at Ouarzazate and what percentage of the metal was contained in the ore (4845). I also received a long list of Axis ships supposedly arriving from the Far East, with instructions to watch and report on them.

London now replied to my report 42/47/tj. The Agency should not keep any statistical material nor any written information; everything should be reported from memory. Their reply was a classic. All we had to do was to reequip the Agency with people capable of memorising everything concerning the vast area stretching from Tripoli to Dakar, including the names of towns, all merchant ships, airports, forts, military formations, etc., etc., as well as numerical data on the transport of various types of raw materials, munitions and, of course, all the other problems concerning this huge expanse of territory. It was clearly impossible without keeping it all in writing, otherwise our work would have ground to a halt.

After receiving Central Office's approval, as from 3 June 1942 I was able to introduce the new code which would be applied to merchant ships (42/329). Hence, they could be notified quite briefly that (say) the SS 146 laden with 400 tons of rubber was sailing from the port of Algiers to Marseilles on 4/6/42. Also, our Intelligence outposts would have numbers instead of names: Tunis became outpost no. 1, Oran no. 2, Casablanca no. 3, Algiers no. 4 and Constantine no. 5. The cryptonyms of our officers were also changed: BANULS became START, MUSTAFA became NORD and VINCENT became LECH.

FREDO now confirmed that Achiary, as a suspected Gaullist, had been relieved of his post as head of the security department and would be moved out of Algiers as soon as he was well enough.

It was still not known who would take over this important post. Governor General Châtel gave a briefing at which he warned of forthcoming purges. The PPF had already prepared a list of anti-collaborationists and supporters of de Gaulle. This ominous news was passed on to Central Office.

Another unpleasant surprise: on 12 June six French agents from TUDOR's network had been stopped on a ship arriving from France and were in FREDO's hands. This meant new worries, unnecessary expense and an increased chance of betrayal. Angry and agitated, I immediately radioed to London to order Agency France to stop their game, which threatened the very existence of Agency Africa. They quickly replied that France had not sent them: they had fled there themselves and would be sent to England through a newly organised operation (4957). So they would also be waiting, and I already had MOUSTIQUE and her colleagues on my back.

After receiving explanatory reports from Oran, Casablanca and Algiers, we were able to answer London's questions regarding ammunition stocks for French warships. Those for ships based in North Africa were on board, were very small and were being increased at Casablanca. Those based at Toulon had no stocks at all.

In June we took on fifteen new agents (nos 1862–3, 1971–5 and 1890–7) and now began to cover the interior: the railway junctions, mining centres and the state administrative offices. Among other interesting information sent to London was:

French armed forces in Philippeville (42/365); Franco-German and Franco-Italian agreements re the supply of iron ore: 64,000 tons to Germany and 15,000 tons to Italy, in return for coal and oil (42/370); 20,000 tons of phosphates per month being delivered to Germany and Italy, in return for 55 kilos of coal per ton (42/373); the despatch of 3,000 tons of grain from the port of Mostaganem on board SS 288 (42/295 and 42/332) to Tunis destined for Libya (42/358); the despatch to France on board SS 35 of 6,000 live lambs and 2,000 frozen; Algeria to supply 200,000 lambs within the next two months (42/374).

The results of the German inspection of naval bases in Morocco were sent to London in the form of an extract from a report sent to the Armistice Commission at Wiesbaden. Generally, it was unfavourable. The German admiral who carried it out did not believe that the French could defend them, and detected a lack of confidence in the younger officers (42/385). As for the air defences, the French airmen's attitudes to Germany were reported to be hostile.

Because of the increase in new agents, I requested Central Office to broadcast a special message on 20 June in the BBC's French-language service (*'les yeux se jettent dans le Rhône'*). The broadcast time was sent and the reception was excellent. They also sought confirmation of Achiary's dismissal, which, unfortunately, was final. He was moved to Sétif and appointed Police Commissioner for the town and district.

On 23 June, while I was handing over pouches 20 and 21 to Mr Boyd, he told me that my information regarding their Tangiers Consulate had proved correct and that one of its officials had now been recalled to the United States. My remarks about remitting our funds had also paid off. I was able to collect further allowances, which meant that we finally had some cash reserves. London also sent us a new quartz radio transmitter (W-370). The set arrived badly damaged with broken tubes, and I asked for new ones to be forwarded to us. However, our operator (agent 1845) proved to be an excellent radio mechanic; he repaired it and immediately started to play to London on it.

Achiary's dismissal was a very great loss to us. It was fortunate that FREDO took over his post. As head of Agency Africa's counter-intelligence, he supplied us with very valuable information on the activities of the Axis. Consul Begue had not relaxed his efforts to catch BANULS and FREDO was still watching him very carefully.

It was agreed that, after being installed as Police Commissioner in Setif, Achiary would become commander of our Intelligence outpost no. 6. His leg was mending gradually and he was hobbling about on a stick; he was ready to take up his new position in July. We spoke a great deal about his future Intelligence work. Two ports, Bougie and Djidjelli, would require special attention. Mercantile traffic, the export of mineral ores, coastal fortifications, emplacements, airports and the organisation, armament and morale of army units were particularly important.

After an enormous amount of trouble, Achiary had finally managed to obtain the release from prison of DOKTOR's agent who had been arrested in November 1941. We had given him material help and would now look after him. I made it a cardinal rule never to abandon a colleague to his fate if arrested. This fact, which the others certainly knew about, gave them a feeling of belonging and increased their work. Nevertheless, Commissioner Begue would not release Roquemaure and his wife, who would be useful in his hunt for BANULS.

There was another surprise from my informants, confirmed by Inspector Schmitt. It appears that an individual named Thomson had appeared in Algiers who was probably a British agent. He had materialised in the casino of the Hotel Aletti and had become involved with the mistress of Commissioner Begue, with whom he had also become closely acquainted. At least he was on the right track. I ordered that he should be watched closely but not contacted in any way. It looked as if Begue wanted to find out about our activities through him and bring his hunt to a successful conclusion.

Having accumulated sufficient information on Mr Thomson's activities, I asked London to remove him from North Africa immediately. He disappeared from Algiers forthwith, and only Allah knew what happened to him. Begue was left to work out another ploy. It was also fortunate that the agents who had come from Marseilles had vanished within our territory. We kept them for some time until André had procured documents for them. Then, slowly and painlessly, he got rid of them by giving them some sort of job.

Meanwhile, the Agency's work increased proportionately to the growth of the network, and the number of agents grew greater every month. I worked into the early hours, causing Sophie problems, since we were considerably exceeding normal electricity usage. I used light bulbs of the lowest wattage to try to save on electricity. This was not much help and the excess increased from month to month. The threat of having our electricity cut off was bad enough; being prosecuted by the authorities was an even greater worry. Sophie's financial bribes were the only thing that helped, and they got bigger and bigger.

As a result of the electric light bulbs, I began to get headaches after working at night, which was something new. Nevertheless, I continued reading and deciphering all the Agency's reports and prayed that, once the officers were brought over from Gibraltar, I would be less overworked. Meanwhile, somehow, the show had to go on.

21

A MEETING WITH COLONEL SOLBORG

Mr Boyd told me that Roosevelt's special envoy would be visiting Algiers on a fact-finding mission and would probably want to confer with me. Using a code, he informed me by telephone that my post from London and funds from Tangiers had arrived. Early on the morning of 15 June I went to the American Consulate to collect them. Boyd told me that the envoy, who had recently arrived from London, wanted to meet me. He left the office and some ten minutes later Robert Murphy, the Minister, appeared with a pleasant-looking man of short stature whom he introduced as Colonel Solborg.

Our conversation began in French. After the usual exchange of formalities, Solborg brought me greetings from 'Stanislas' in London with whom he had spoken about our work in French North Africa. He said he had also had the opportunity of studying our information digests at Allied Headquarters, which he said were 'very highly valued over there', which was why he wanted to meet me personally. I pointed out that credit was also due to all my colleagues and that it was only extraordinary luck that permitted us to operate in such a huge area and under such difficult conditions.

At this point Murphy, who had also expressed his regard for our work, was called away and we were left alone. Colonel Solborg caught me completely by surprise when he said in fluent Polish, 'Why should we struggle with French when it is far easier to speak in Polish?' Amazed, I asked him, 'Wherever did you learn to speak Polish so well?'

'My mother was Polish. Before 1914 my father, who was of

Finnish origin, was a Czarist general serving under Governor Skalon, one of the Russian overlords in partitioned Poland. I myself was a young Russian cavalry officer serving in a dragoon regiment in Nowy Mozowiecki near Warsaw.'

In fact he now reminded me of those cavalrymen who, leaving Russia after the Bolshevik Revolution, had settled in the United States. I was delighted that the rest of our conversation could be conducted in our native tongue.

Solborg explained that he had been gathering information from America's allies in London and wanted to hear my assessment of the war situation. He asked whether I wouldn't mind if he made some notes and looked at me attentively. Coming from one of Roosevelt's advisers, it was both flattering and amusing.

I told him that I was not qualified to give an accurate assessment, and that in any case the material at my disposal was extremely limited. I read the Axis war communiqués in the French press, listened to the BBC and the Voice of America and had access to some information obtained from a Franco-Polish radio-intelligence station. Added together, even this was insufficient. Nevertheless, Solborg pressed me for my views. Noticing a map of Africa and Southern Europe on the wall, I began: 'I don't have to remind you that the present situation is extremely grave. One thing I can't understand, the Allies do not seem to draw any conclusions from Hitler's tactics. Why don't they try to beat him at this own game?'

Solborg interrupted: 'What do you have in mind?'

'Hitler goes from victory to victory, always surprising his weaker opponents and overpowering them with the most sophisticated equipment – hence the myth of German invincibility. Why don't we do the same thing? After all, Italy is our weakest enemy, and should therefore be attacked.'

'Yes, but how do we do it?'

First occupy North Africa, and, using it as a base, attack Italy by occupying Sicily. Next, invade and free the Balkans in order to liberate Poland, which is being destroyed by the Nazis. Only then, having organised your forces, attack Germany. In my opinion,

North Africa is strategically extremely important. All the sea routes from Europe to the south and the east pass near Africa, and the air routes cross it. As far as Italy is concerned, her long coastline is indefensible – unlike Hitler's fortification of the west European coastline. This should be a surprise tactic and would give us a good chance of victory.

Solborg asked, 'How do you see the present situation in the Mediterranean and the actual occupation of North Africa?'
Pointing to the map, I said:

The Mediterranean basin can be divided into two parts: the western part, from Gibraltar to Malta, and the eastern. From Malta to Suez. The first is open to Allied convoys; in the eastern part, however, the Royal Navy is exposed to air, naval and submarine attacks and suffers heavy losses, especially when it ventures beyond Malta, which has been bombed heavily by the Luftwaffe. The road to Suez is effectively closed, which is why the British, with their limited supply of munitions, cannot stop Rommel's Afrika Korps, which is already on Egypt's doorstep. Supplies for the British forces in Egypt have to take the long route round Africa, exposing them to attacks by U-boats based in the Spanish colonies of Ifni and Rio de Oro on the west coast. The U-boats are equipped from North African ports, and arrive in the Mediterranean by being floated down the River Rhone at night.

Supposing the Germans were to occupy North Africa, the Allies would undoubtedly lose the Mediterranean. Their convoys would then be attacked along their entire route by Axis aeroplanes based there and by submarines operating from the numerous local ports. The road to Suez would be completely closed. If Hitler occupied Morocco, the convoys going to India and Australia would not be safe either; moreover, it would lead to the occupation of Dakar, which would endanger South America, especially Brazil. The entire network of aerial communications over Central Africa would also be threatened. On the other hand, an Allied occupation of North Africa, apart from destroying Rommel's forces, would ensure possession of the Mediterranean basin, protect the Suez route to the

Far East and the convoys in the South Atlantic. In my estimation, and in accordance with the information I sent to London, the Germans are becoming increasingly interested in North Africa. It is highly significant that they are offering assistance to the French to defend it.

Nevertheless, the situation is not as bad as it appears, and it could be changed to our advantage.

I saw that Colonel Solborg was listening to my discourse with great interest. He said that my assessment seemed to be to the point and was convincing. How did I envisage the occupation of North Africa?

I replied:

London possess precise details, which I sent them, of the strength of the French North African Army. They know its equipment and armaments, coastal fortifications and anti-aircraft batteries, specifications and numbers of guns, calibre and stock of ammunition, as well as the state of the French air force and the fleet. Incidentally, all this information was faithfully copied down by your two Vice-Consuls in Algiers and despatched via American Intelligence in Tangiers to Washington. The bulk of the French Army is anti-German but not pro-British. This was ascertained by members of the German Armistice Commission from Wiesbaden, and the Italian team from Turin. The German admiral in charge of the inspection concluded that all three French armed services were hostile towards Germany, with the air force being the most antagonistic. His view was that the French would not defend themselves in the event of an Allied landing, and he suggested a strong German presence in Morocco. The French population is against the Vichy regime and its collaborationist policies; the Arabs, for the moment, play no political role whatsoever.

If, therefore, the operation was carried out under the United States flag with an American general commanding the invasion forces, then, in my opinion, the French detachments would only put up a symbolic military resistance and all of French North Africa could be occupied within twenty-four hours. Landing operations should take place simultaneously on all the strategic points of the coastline. The invasion forces could consist of troops from various Allied countries, providing, I repeat, that they all went in under the American flag.

This is my assessment of the war situation on this front. I am not qualified to say anything about the others.

Turning to other matters, it was a great relief to discuss with a fellow Slav my fears regarding Stalin's intentions.

Colonel Solborg thanked me warmly for our discussion and added: 'I had a series of talks in various quarters but it is only here in Algiers that I have acquired the really essential information. I am very pleased with our discussions, and with my visit to Algiers. Have you a communications link with London, and can you send my despatch there?'

I told him that I had a radio link with London twice a day and a code by which a despatch in any language could be sent. Solborg wrote his despatch addressed to United States Headquarters in London asking for 'permission to go to Washington as a result of receiving interesting and valuable information'. Handing it to me, he asked how soon he could expect a reply.

'It depends on London. I'll send it this afternoon and a reply may arrive as early as tomorrow morning.'

We concluded our meeting by arranging that I would bring the reply personally. On arriving home, I prepared the following despatches: confirmation of receipt of our financial allowance for the second quarter and the post from Central Office (42/N353); report on my conversation with Colonel Solborg (42/N354), and the despatch of his message (encoded in special code as 42/N355). On 16 June Central Office informed me that despatch no 42/N355 had been transmitted to the appropriate address and that a reply would arrive on 18 June (42/N4907).

The following day I took our recently acquired post from the Constantine outpost with me to the Consulate. The report on the military garrison of La Calle, a small port near the Tunisian border, estimated that 50 per cent of its troops were pro-Gaullist, and gave precise details of the infantry unit and its armaments and ammunition stocks, noting that its single artillery gun had only seventy-five shells. I told Solborg that his reply would be received tomorrow and showed him the report, adding that I received similar ones on all the military garrisons, which could confirm what I had told him. He read it with great interest and, as Murphy did not have a radio link, he asked me to send his second despatch to London.

On the 18th I handed him London's reply. US Headquarters had given him permission to fly to Washington providing he reserved his own seat in Lisbon on a Yankee Clipper, which was the only civil air link with the United States. We wished each other success in our work and good luck for the future. Once again, Solborg thanked me warmly for our conversation adding, 'I am sure it will bear the fruit we desire!' Special report no. 42/54/tj describing my conversation with Colonel Solborg was sent to London in our pouch no. 21.

Contacts with the Resistance were maintained through the visits of Henri d'Astier or the Abbé Cordier, who brought information on the military and political situation in Algeria and Tunisia. During one such visit on 9 July, d'Astier handed me the guidelines for BBC propaganda broadcasts in Arabic and French compiled by the leaders of the group, which I forwarded to London.

We finally had some spare dollars in the kitty (which VINCENT could change in Tangiers), and I could stop worrying about operating on a shoestring. My plan for the outposts to have minimum reserve funds could now be put into effect. Cash amounts would be deposited with the outpost commanders, to be used only in the event of their failure to receive the Agency's monthly allowance, which would then be settled at the next meeting. This would at least insure them against broken links for about a month. It would also give the commanders who recruited the agents more freedom of action, since they would be able to reward them for excellent work, only the upper limit being set.

During July five more agents were accepted into the Agency (nos 1862, 1864 and 1833–5). Agent 1885 was a Canadian domiciled in Algiers, who later caused us some friction with Colonel Jousse of the Resistance. The network and the delivery system were functioning well; only VINCENT's Casablanca outpost was late with its post. They also appeared to be mainly concerned with Tangiers and northern Morocco, whereas I was particularly interested in the south, namely Agadir, from which one could penetrate the Spanish colonies of Ifni and Rio de Oro, where bases for U-boats operating in the South Atlantic existed. I would have to go to Morocco to ensure that we received the information we required.

London confirmed that pouch no. 19 had arrived, and were immediately notified that, as from 13 July, the names of North African towns would be encoded as proposed in my report. Three pouches (nos 22–24) had been prepared and were simultaneously handed over to the Americans on 14 July. Mr Knox was anxious.

'What happened? We haven't seen you for a long time. The Minister wants to speak to you urgently!'

'Everything's OK. It's just that I thought I'd been visiting you too often. I've got some mail to be sent, and I'll be pleased to see him.'

Mr Knox went to announce my arrival, while Mr Boyd looked through the mailbags. We had an agreement that they could all be examined at the Consulate in my presence. I had also agreed to their making copies of information they were keen on sending to Washington. Knox ushered me into Murphy's office. He greeted me warmly: 'I missed you! I have a few questions from Washington, which I'm unable to answer. Maybe you know something about them.'

The Minister read them to me. They all related to the question of North African supplies for Rommel's army in Libya.

I told him: 'Deliveries to Libya have been going on for some time, including all sorts of military material and foodstuffs, trucks and even tanks from the Maison Carrée. I've been reporting them to my London HQ since December '41.'

He jotted it down and asked, 'May I report all this to Washington?'

'Of course. It was sent to London a long time ago.'

Our conversation lasted for some time. From then onwards all my visits to the Consulate ended in Murphy's office. Our relationship became increasingly friendly. He would show me his telegrams and I would almost invariably reply, 'I've already reported it to London.' I would then provide him with military, political and economic information about North Africa.

Washington was showing an interest in military matters. Something had changed there, and I wondered whether it had anything to do with my discussion with Solborg. The wind of change seemed to be blowing not only from London but also across the Atlantic. Perhaps my ideas, which had been developing ever since I first helped send our soldiers to North Africa in November 1940, would reach fruition. Somewhat naively, therefore, I awaited London's response to my reported conversation with Solborg with impatience and curiosity. It never materialised.

Our London mailbag contained a written evaluation of our counter-intelligence material sent for the period ending 1 May 1942. It was very good and the news was passed on to FREDO and the outpost commanders. I bade farewell to André Achiary, who was leaving to take up his new post with the police in Setif and, of course, to organise our Intelligence outpost no. 6 there. He received an advance and an agency number (1830); Madame Simone, his wife, would continue to be our contact.

I was in continual postal contact with Marcel in Rabat and received much interesting information hidden between the lines. It seemed that he was not on friendly terms with VINCENT, who unfortunately, like many others from the Polish Foreign Office, tended to be snobbish and conceited. Marcel also wrote that Saoul Laskar, of whom he had a very high opinion, would be in Algiers soon and would want to visit me.

While I was handing over pouches nos 25 and 26 (42/449), Boyd told me that Colonel Eddy, who would soon be arriving from Tangiers, wanted to see me. He also said, half-jokingly, that I was his favourite spy and that my enthusiasm and work had helped his morale. Colonel Eddy arrived in Algiers towards the end of July 1942. He was a tall, corpulent American with a round, happy face who, like myself, spoke rather poor French. He introduced himself as a US Marine, a form of soldiering that was unknown in Poland. In spite of his open appearance, one sensed that he was not quite what he seemed.

We participated in a long conference in early August at Robert Murphy's special office, recently set up on the Boulevard Sidi Carnot. Eddy, who proved to have a good knowledge of our work, asked me for additional information to tie up his material. I explained that the gaps were mostly due to the fact that only our paperwork went through the Americans. All the important and urgent reports were radioed directly to London. I was willing, however, to help him with his problems, and didn't begrudge him several hours of my time, hoping that he would reciprocate by helping our men in need.

Finally, I asked him what sort of help we could expect when a 'failed' officer or agent of the Agency had to be urgently evacuated from our territory. From his reply I gathered that he could only help if they actually turned up on his doorstep in Tangiers. We discussed passwords for such an eventuality, but it was obvious that I could not depend on him very much. I met Eddy again during his next visit to Algiers but at a much later date and under very different circumstances.

Saoul Laskar arrived in late July with a letter from Marcel. Unfortunately he had not been able to find a suitable business for me in Morocco but he intended to sell his fish factory at Agadir. As I planned to visit Morocco in August, we agreed that I could look it over and give him an estimate.

Laskar described the economic and political situation in Morocco, the French community's attitude towards the Vichy regime and, particularly, the Arab and Berber attitude towards France. He then presented his own view of collaborationism, as a result of which I asked him point-blank whether he would like to work with me to help free Europe of Nazism. Surely he must be aware that, as a Pole, I was Hitler's enemy. He reciprocated immediately, that 'as a Jew' he 'could not be any less anti-Nazi' than me, and responded to my proposal with great enthusiasm. He had many close friends in Morocco who, sharing his views, wanted to do something to help the Allies but they had no leaders and did not know where to begin.

I was very keen to organise some sort of observation of the airport at Agadir, which was used by the Luftwaffe. The aeroplanes flew from Germany via North Africa to somewhere in the south, and then returned there. What passengers and materials were the planes carrying, and where were they landing? Was it possible to get from Agadir to Ifni by land or sea to try to confirm whether there were submarine bases there? Laskar promised to try to discover whether any of the fishing trawlers went in that direction and to report on his findings. I was delighted; we parted very warmly.

Another four new agents (1886–8 and 1865) were accepted into the Agency. FREDO, our head of counter-intelligence, became agent 1884. Agent 1865 was provided with funds to organise a resistance movement in the department of Constantine, which did not as yet exist.

During July 1942 we received fifty-two telegrams and sent ninety-five. Among those reflecting London's current interests were:

We urgently require Order of Battle of armies in North Africa, quantity and quality of equipment supply situation, personnel and armoury, organisation of brigades and half-brigades, mechanisation. Organisation and effective strength of anti-aircraft artillery regiments (5325); send telegrams continually and daily on movements of ships, destination, times, cargoes, arrivals, departures – these reports are very important (5362); list of army supplies for three months required, need plans for defence of North Africa, mobilisation plans, armed forces, industry, transport and passive defence (5589); check the armament of the turrets of the battleship *Jean Bart* – very important (5692); clarify Germany's demands for France to release twenty-four submarines from Toulon into the Mediterranean – very important; in Bizerta there are apparently 1,000 German officers and men from submarines (5991).

How much effort it took, at all levels of the Agency, to supply all this information as quickly as possible can be left to the reader's imagination. I can only confirm that we were able to furnish the necessary information for all the tasks we were given. Among some of the interesting items sent to London were:

July 1942

Military
Reports of constant flow of equipment, provisions and ammunition from Maison Carrée depot to Gabès and Libya; the trains are marked

with red, white and blue (42/412); battle readiness of the 19th Corps (42/428); Fort de L'Est: battery consists of 75mm field guns, not for air defence (42/444); battle readiness of the Constantine Division (42/446); information on military garrisons in Fez, Meknes and Khenifra (42/447); coastal defences of Fort Dupre: four 120mm guns; Fort 489: six 120mm guns and one battery of 37mm anti-aircraft (42/471); Italian Armistice Commission demands removal of army units from Constantine Division and their transfer to the Dept of Oran (42/476).

Naval

Tanker *Le Tarn* leaving Bizerta to supply French fleet off Alexandria (42/403); French corvette *Batailleuse* sailing in the convoys between Libya and Italy has sunk a British submarine (42/405); SS 354 transported 10,000 tons of iron ore from Nemours to Port Caroute (42/414); port of Bône (Caroute) is the principal centre for shipment of iron ore to Germany during July (42/419); convoy of French ships carrying wine, corn and metal ore to Italy from Tunis and Bizerta with protection of two destroyers and two submarines (42/421); information from Guyotville, a ship from the Société Schiaffina leaves the port every Saturday fully loaded at 6pm, returns Sunday morning empty, possibility of supplying U-boats (42/432); barges propelled by sail and motor (*Victorine* and *Vincente*) are supplying German U-boats at the heights of Tipaza (42/453).

Various

Sending of sheep to France is proceeding: 60,000 sent from Oran (42/481); at request of military organisation Combat, sending proposed BBC radio broadcasts in French for the French and Arab populations of North Africa (42/422).

The military communiqués on the French radio and in the press indicated that the German *Blitzkrieg* had ended. Heavy battles were raging at Stalingrad and on the Egyptian border. With the enormous destruction of war materials, there was increasing Axis pressure to exploit the natural resources of North Africa to the full. The Germans stepped up their demands for foodstuffs, especially cereals, lamb and wine, also mineral ores needed for the manufacture of high quality steel, and rubber.

Algeria was compelled to continue supplying military equipment for Rommel's Afrika Korps in Libya, with tanks, lorries, ammunition and fuel being sent from its own stocks. North African airports were increasingly used to refuel or repair Axis aeroplanes. Similarly, the Axis use of North African ports, particularly those situated near the straits of Sicily (Bône, Bougie, Philippeville, Bizerta and Tunis), was intensified, while Algiers and its small neighbouring ports were utilised for U-boats operating in the western Mediterranean.

Additionally, checks were carried out by the German Armistice Commission on the defence of the North African coastline. Demands that it be strengthened, particularly in Morocco, gave rise to projects involving the use of German forces. The Vichy Government, following a collaborationist policy and at Germany's mercy, was compelled to agree to their demands for supplies. It did draw the line, however, at schemes using German forces to strengthen the western coastal defences. My impression was that, if Hitler had wanted to occupy the territory, he could easily have done so; resistance from the French would not have been prolonged because of their limited war matériel.

The economic situation grew worse. There was an increasing shortage of cereals, vegetables, potatoes and fruit. There was also a shortage of fuel, necessary for irrigation, which was based on mechanical pumps extracting water from great depths. Food supplies were diverted to a fictitious metropolis and less became available for internal consumption.

The French community, used to *bonne cuisine*, were beginning to starve and inevitably became more and more disaffected. The black market, run by Arabs, flourished. As a reaction, Vichy propaganda intensified and the SOL was strengthened and received firearms and ammunition from France. Arrests and purges of Gaullists continued and Gestapo influence increased. The situation led to the growth of the resistance movement, especially among university students and young workers with radical views.

Pressure on Agency Africa appeared to have eased off. Our six outposts functioned smoothly and BANULS had eluded Commissioner Begue's clutches. However, mysterious telephone calls at all times of the day inquiring about Dr Akoun – mostly answered by Sophie – provided some anxiety. Were they normal checks as a result of Vichy's racial decrees forbidding Jews to practise their professions? Were they instigated by Commissioner Begue or even the Gestapo? Although FREDO had not reported anything suspicious, our security was strengthened. It was impossible to be too careful.

MUSTAFA was alarmed by the ever more frequent appearances of German direction-finding vans in Boulevard Sadi Carnot. I had been thinking for some time about how to safeguard our hurdy-gurdy and communications with London. In my organisational report I had mentioned the necessity for the Agency to possess a second radio station, and had even discussed buying a house or a villa with MUSTAFA where it could be installed.

We had prepared Operation Zebra and were only waiting for London to assign the date. I hoped that the arrival of the three officers meant that my workload would lessen. In this connection, I also planned to organise radio stations at our Intelligence outposts for conveying urgent information to the Agency, on the assumption that they had been taught how to operate a hurdy-gurdy at their Intelligence school.

While examining the Casablanca outpost's work, I concluded that the whole process of sending Moroccan information to Central Office should be speeded up. VINCENT, therefore, received instructions to send his Intelligence pouches direct to Central Office via the United States Consulate in Casablanca and to forward copies of his reports to me (42/448). I had, somehow, to retain the means of controlling this outpost's work for which Central Office held me responsible.

MOUSTIQUE's story of the betrayal in Paris haunted me and I could not understand why Central Office or WICHER had failed to inform us. Agency Africa had sent couriers to TUDOR in Marseilles and they could easily have been trapped. Earlier we had sent our pouches to him to be forwarded to London and, as he neither replied to nor acknowledged my communications, I stopped sending them. Communication between us broke down completely and it remained a mystery. Remembering 'La Chatte', I believe that I was right to forbid the employment of women agents. We had none and there was no unnecessary friction.

Our agents were, in fact, a motley band, recruited from divers milieux depending on the type of information we required. There were military, naval and air force men, merchant seamen, port pilots, officials and workers from the port docks, railwaymen, various classes of officials and certain influential and well-connected individuals from the political, economic and social spheres. Most of them worked out of idealism rather than for money. We all worked towards the same goal – the liberation of our countries.

As a soldier, I adhered faithfully to the treaties concluded by the Polish Government and to the historical traditions that bound us to France. Technically speaking, I had not been demobbed by the French after their collapse. I was convinced that Central Office were co-operating harmoniously with the Gaullists in London as we were doing in North Africa. Thus, in order to convince our agents that their work was known (and appreciated) by the Free French leaders in London, I frequently asked Central Office to broadcast messages in the BBC's French-language service from London. Such a message, '*La démocratie et la libéralisme sont les buts de toute civilisation*', which I had requested (42/549), was broadcast on 28 August and greatly encouraged us all.

Working with BANULS convinced me that he could be left in charge of the Agency while I went for a short trip to Morocco. Human nature being what it is, choosing him inevitably meant that MUSTAFA felt he was being neglected. The latter had the essential task of maintaining communications with Central Office, without which we would be unable to function, while BANULS would ensure that the outposts had sufficient cash and functioned normally and that the Intelligence delivery system was working smoothly. He would send all the outposts' reports to me in Casablanca (via Boyd) and I would forward them to Central Office myself.

I wrote to Marcel about my forthcoming visit and received an invitation for all the family. VINCENT was then informed that I would be arriving in mid-August for a stay of several weeks, and asked to prepare suitable accommodation.

MACIEJ was still in Algiers and continued to visit us frequently. He had calmed down after his traumatic shock at the sinking of the *Lamoricière* and the drowning of his officers. I continually advised him not to hurry his return to France, as the Allies would soon occupy French North Africa. This feeling came from telegrams, completed tasks and the interest shown by my American friends. While not inquiring too deeply, I was aware of the work carried out by Robert Murphy's office.

One day MACIEJ told me that he was going to meet General Stachiewicz at the Café de Paris the following day.

'Who?' I asked in amazement.

'General Stachiewicz, the former chief of the General Staff. He lives in Madea, his *residence forcée* allocated to him by the French Government at General Sikorski's request.'

This information took me completely by surprise. 'Why didn't you tell me this earlier?'

'I didn't know what your views were. I thought that you must have known about his presence here, and that you had special orders.'

I exploded. 'You know bloody well that my views are consistent. I'm a soldier, and never got mixed up in politics. Tomorrow we'll go and see the General together.'

I never knew General Stachiewicz personally although I knew his late brother, Julian, head of the Historical Office. I didn't give a damn about personal or political rivalries. As a staff officer, I had certain moral obligations towards the former Chief of Staff under whom I had previously served.

In the morning, we met General Stachiewicz at the café. He was surprised when I introduced myself and briefly related my story. In turn, he told me about his existence in the miserable small Arab town to which he had been exiled, on the 1,200 francs a month allowance he received from the French, completely cut off from information and from events. I discovered that Colonel Lapara, the current Chief of the Deuxième Bureau of the French North African Army, would be coming to the café to see the General. He had been French Military Attaché in Warsaw before the war and I asked the General to introduce me as 'an old friend from the eastern region' when he was commander of the Legionnaires in Wilno.

Colonel Lapara was a very pleasant and likeable chap. He had a son about George's age who was brought up in Poland and also spoke Polish. We struck up a friendship and our sons also became friends. We visited each other frequently and our relationship was never clouded by my Intelligence work since I had sufficient reliable information from other sources. His presence at our house was useful in providing us with added respectability. Unfortunately, after 8 November 1942, the circumstances of war separated us and we were compelled to carry out our different duties.

Agent 1880 provided us with an extremely important document. He had obtained a carbon copy of the protocol of an inter-ministerial meeting with delegates from the German Armistice Commission, which took place at the General Governorship of Algeria. The aim of the meeting was to increase mining and industrial production in North Africa. The document contained a precise description of all the mines operating in Tunisia, Algeria and Morocco, how much each produced and the possibilities of extending production. The protocol outlined the possibilities of utilising its mineral wealth and described the only oil well in Morocco. In short, it illustrated German attempts to drain this wealth to the utmost for their war effort.

The document, together with a covering report (72/tj), plus our usual Intelligence material, went in our pouch no. 28 on 10 August. Mr Boyd looked through it as usual, noticed the protocol and, after reading a few pages, looked at me in amazement. 'This is an unusual document. Will you let me copy it?'

'Of course, if you're interested, as long as you make sure it goes with the rest of the mail.'

Boyd took it to the Minister. Shortly afterwards Robert Murphy emerged clutching the protocol. 'This is a very interesting and valuable document. Where did you get it?'

'As you can see, it's a carbon copy of the original. They put in an extra sheet of carbon paper when they were writing it, just for me.'

Murphy instructed Boyd to copy it. When I mentioned that I'd be in Casablanca in the middle of the month, Murphy responded: 'In that case we'll probably meet there, because I'll be passing through Casablanca around the same time, on my way to Washington.'

I informed Boyd that BANULS, whom he knew, would be deputising for me, and that BANULS's mail for 'Mr Roger' should be sent to Mr King in Casablanca.

During August 1942, the Agency received fifty-nine telegrams (ten of which thanked us for providing the North African Order of Battle) and sent ninety-nine. Among the more interesting were:

August 1942

Telegrams received

How many submarines are in battle readiness at 364 and Casablanca and how many could be ready within fourteen days? (6559); which types of mines are used by the French – magnetic, acoustic or directional? How many do they have? (6849); very important: who owns the motorised sailing boats *Victorine* and *Vincente*? Give description and capacity, who supplies the diesel (6843); approx. how many motor vehicles have been sent to Libya via Gabès? (6900).

Telegrams sent to London

Vincente sailed from port of Algiers during night of 4/5 August carrying fuel and foodstuffs (42/506); 11 August at 20.00 hrs, three Junker 88s landed at Maison Blanche airport after attacking a British convoy; one plane is damaged (42/512); Axis aircraft landing at Gabès to refuel (42/526); re the bombardment of the *Vincente*, belonging to company Schiaffino, torpedoes and other equipment for submarines found on board; the Admiralty has ordered the release of three Germans (42/535); 13 August in the Keliba (Tunisia) region – two Italian pursuit boats nos 22 and 16 ran aground with British prisoners of war (42/540); boat no.

16 left, no. 22 still grounded with POWs on 18 August is to be towed (42/542); on 12 August, near 581, Savoya [Savoia], an Italian bomber crashed, crew of six were killed (42/537); from eavesdropping on Italian conversations, addendum to telegram 42/537 – the crashed aeroplane was a link with Spanish Rio de Oro where German and Italian submarines and seaplane bases are to be found (42/566); in region 1267 on 27 August, a damaged Italian torpedo boat, *Paolina*, is to be found.

22

MY THIRD STAY IN MOROCCO

Sophie, George and I would depart for Morocco on the evening of 11 August. That morning FREDO, who would be keeping in touch with BANULS and MUSTAFA during my absence, brought our passports and visas. Commissioner Begue had apparently 'sworn not to leave Algiers unless accompanied by Łubieński in handcuffs' and as yet he had found no trace of him. We had a farewell drink. 'Guard him well!' I toasted. I paid a lightning visit to Lacaze, who provided me with the fuel and oil figures for the whole of French North Africa, which I immediately relayed to London (42/559). Then a final briefing with my two colleagues in the afternoon to give them my last paternal warnings.

At the railway station, I was intrigued by a well-dressed Arab in European clothing who had been observing us for some time, and tried to remember whether I'd seen him before. I decided I couldn't remember him and began watching him discreetly as well. He walked past our carriage as though checking which compartment we occupied.

The train left, our tickets were checked and we settled down for the night. Suddenly, around midnight, I was awakened by a terrific scream from Sophie. I leapt to my feet. The door of the compartment was slightly open; I rushed into the corridor, but it was empty. Sophie, who was lying on the top bunk, told me that as she was falling asleep she had heard what sounded like the door of the compartment being opened very quietly. Gazing into the face of our Arab 'friend', his arm outstretched towards the rack where my briefcase and our suitcase lay, she had shouted out in fright. I asked the guard to close the compartment door properly and to look for him. Needless to say, he was never found. Fortunately, I didn't have any notes on me or in my briefcase; everything I needed for the Agency's work had already been sent on to Casablanca by Boyd.

At Oujda station, on the morning of the 12th, the policemen whom I already knew helped settle our border formalities. Our little dog Arthy, a two-month-old wire-haired terrier, was greatly admired. The remainder of the journey passed uneventfully. Sophie and George lapped up the scenery while I scanned the newspapers and schemed how to fit everything into our trip. There were so many intangibles on which their realisation depended.

I wanted, at least, to ascertain the Casablanca outpost's work, the organisation of the Intelligence network in the territory and the possibility of installing a hurdy-gurdy in Casablanca; to take a look at the factory in Agadir and find out from Laskar the possibilities of his engaging in Intelligence work there; to go to Tangiers and speak to Colonel Eddy; and, last but not least, to be able to rest for a few days and stop thinking about being on a merry-go-round. It was impossible to guess how everything would work out.

VINCENT welcomed us at Casablanca station. He had found us accommodation at Mrs Goworowska's flat – she and her children were going to a summer resort near Casablanca for a fortnight, and I would be able to work there undisturbed. Hospitable as ever, she greeted us warmly, then left almost immediately with her family. I would see VINCENT later.

The whole of the following day (the 13th) was left free to show Sophie and George the town. I made some phone calls. Laskar was not at home but would be returning in a few days; Marcel would come to see us on the morning of the 15th and we'd arrange a programme for our sojourn in Morocco. All morning until lunch we toured the town in a horse-drawn cab and then spent the afternoon on the beach. The weather was marvellous with a light wind blowing from the Atlantic cooling the intense heat of the sun. I was, as the Soviet slogan said, 'gotov k trudu i oboroniyu' ('ready for work and for defence').

On 14 August I met VINCENT at the Polish Office, where we could work undisturbed since its nominal director, Mr Torre, hardly ever made an appearance. VINCENT's reports included the political and economic situation in Morocco and information on military formations, airports, coastal fortifications, air defence emplacements, ammunition stores, military installations and ships at Casablanca port.

Checking it against information already received, it appeared that Casablanca and the garrisons in northern Morocco (Fez, Meknes, Rabat etc.) had been well covered. Information on southern Morocco was, however, still very deficient. VINCENT complained that there were problems involved in visiting the south. There were no Polish people there and it was difficult to justify his trips. Moreover, communications were difficult. Regarding the naval aspect, the information on ships docked at the port was adequate; that on the day-to-day movements of merchant ships was rather sparse.

VINCENT had three Jewish informants in Tangiers, Polish citizens who supplied him with counter-intelligence on the Germans and also acted as intermediaries when changing dollars. He already had a few agents in Casablanca and Rabat, who were given Agency numbers 1951–7. The Honorary Consul, Mr Torre, helped him a great deal and had provided very valuable information. He wanted to meet me, and we arranged a meeting at the Polish Office on the afternoon of the 16th.

I then asked VINCENT about his co-operation with Marcel. He implied that it was not ideal; they did not get on well together and did not trust each other. As Marcel was such a close friend, it was difficult for me to be objective. I told VINCENT that I was very anxious that he should try to be friendly with Marcel, who had been of such great service to the Agency and whom I trusted absolutely. He held a very important and a very difficult position at Rabat; it was thanks to him that Birkenmeier and Boroński had been released from prison. He should ignore stories spread about him by those who were jealous. I concluded: 'Marcel's coming to see me tomorrow, so I'm inviting everyone to supper for a friendly get-together.'

I then asked about the Polish colony in Morocco. There were the old prewar émigrés who had already managed to make money; the wartime ones included a large number of clerks from the Bank Polski, a group of senior career officers and a large number of women who were the wives of servicemen. The only contacts VINCENT had with any of them were within the framework of the Polish Office and were excellent.

VINCENT had problems selecting agents for his outpost. To be fair, in the face of pro-Vichy propaganda, where many people in Morocco still belonged to the Légion or the SOL for opportunist reasons, it was not easy. On the other hand, I wasn't certain of his approach.

Marcel arrived on the morning of the 15th to spend a few days of his holiday with us. We dropped into a café belonging to his friend, a former police commissioner, where, in an empty room, we could talk without being disturbed. He again spoke of Laskar, reiterating that he was completely trustworthy, reliable and a staunch anti-Nazi. I had already invited VINCENT and his wife to supper in Ain Diab that evening and said Marcel should bring Lucienne, which would be a very pleasant surprise for Sophie. He agreed and immediately rang Rabat.

With plenty of time left before meeting Sophie for lunch, we worked out a programme for our stay in Morocco. I reminded him of Laskar's proposal and my desire to visit his fish factory. Marcel then offered to accompany me to Agadir, which would make things much easier because of the regulations controlling journeys to the south. We could stay there for a couple of days, then, after returning to Rabat, he'd take a few days' leave and we'd all go to Marrakesh for a rest and then on to Rabat for the end of Ramadan. It was an excellent idea. It would give me the opportunity of settling all my business and provide excellent cover as well.

Lucienne arrived in time for our lunch at the Roi de la Bière restaurant on the Boulevard de la Gare. The rest of the day was spent on the beach at Ain Diab where VINCENT and his wife joined us for supper. Returning home in the evening, I had the feeling that, although Marcel and VINCENT were far from friendly, the ice had been broken. Marcel had tried hard to be his usual happy-go-lucky and witty self. VINCENT, however, was very stiff and his wife was rather indifferent and cold. They both had the Foreign Office imprint all over them, but there was nothing I could do about it. VINCENT would meet me the following afternoon at the Consulate to see Mr Torre; Marcel would be with us again on the 18th and we'd go to Agadir together.

The following morning I met Laskar at the Hotel Excelsior's café and found him surrounded by what appeared to be his business cronies. Detaching himself from them, he came up to me grinning, and we found an empty corner table. I wanted to discuss our conversation in Algiers and arrange to see his factory at Agadir, providing he still wanted to sell it; I could go there with Marcel on the 18th. In response, he invited me to his home in Casablanca the following morning, where he would explain everything. Then after lunch he would leave for Agadir to prepare for our arrival. It seemed a good arrangement.

Sophie had discovered from Lucienne that Josephine Baker, my fellow godparent, was in a nursing home in Casablanca. She wanted to visit her with George while I went to see the Consul. She would take her some flowers along with all our warm wishes for a speedy recovery.

I arrived at the Consulate promptly and went with VINCENT to Mr Torre's house. En route I asked him what he thought of Marcel. 'He was friendly but you could see he was a policeman!' I laughed. 'It would be difficult to see him as a Foreign Office official!'

Mr Torre awaited us in his office, a short, thick-set man with a marked tendency to corpulence and lively intelligent eyes. He gave the impression of being a businessman, which was exactly what he was since he managed a multi-million-franc enterprise. An Honorary Consul of the Polish Republic before 1939, he was now director of the Polish Office but only nominally, to keep up appearances with the Vichy authorities. Our Governmental Delegate, Count Hutten-Czapski, controlled the affairs of the Polish Office from Algiers, and a consular official from the Polish Foreign office, Przesmycki (alias our VINCENT), was in charge of work on the spot.

After an introductory chat we adjourned to the drawing-room, where, over black coffee and liqueurs, we talked about the events of June 1940, when the first Polish escapees began arriving in Morocco from France. He spoke very warmly of General Maczek and his wife, whom he entertained at his home for several months, before they were able to leave for England via Tangiers in the late autumn of 1940.

On the way back I told VINCENT to continue as usual and, since I'd be sending London's mail from here, his reports could be sent with the others. Sophie, George and myself spent the rest of the day wandering pleasantly through the souks in the Arab quarter. Meanwhile, I was looking forward to my forthcoming chat with Laskar, and an outline plan to reorganise the Agency was beginning to emerge.

Early on the morning of the 17th Laskar and I got down to business at his house. His firm had an agreement with the owners of three motorised fishing boats giving them sole rights to all their catches. The fish were specially prepared and sent to a contractor in Paris. The factory itself was in a district earmarked for the development of the tinned fish industry, near the commercial port and the fishing port that would be created in the future. Agadir's fishing grounds were famous for their plentiful catches, especially enormous shoals of sardines. He showed me documents relating to the firm's turnover, profits and other accounts, which gave me a good picture of the business before seeing the factory the next day.

We moved on to his report concerning his Intelligence cell in Agadir, which was my main concern. Laskar had a few reliable friends on the spot, and he showed me the information already obtained that covered the port and the airport. Realising its importance, I told him I had great pleasure in appointing him the commander of our special outpost Agadir. His codename was SAOUL, his agency number was 1960, and his friends and agents were to be numbered from 1962 to 1967.

SAOUL's outpost was divided into three sections, each being unknown to the others. The unit headed by 'Canari' was surveying the German Armistice Commission and would report on German activity between Agadir and Marrakesh including their conversations and checking their meetings with third parties. The second unit (based on the port of Agadir) was headed by the skipper of the fishing vessel *La Sardine* and was responsible for surveilling movements in the South Atlantic; Ifni and the Rio de Oro coast were patrolled by the other two trawlers, *Le Thon* and *La Bonite*, whose task was to track and report German U-boat movements and to locate their supply bases. The third unit, run by two agents codenamed after La Fontaine's fable 'La Cigale et la fourmi', were specialising in watching the movements of passengers and goods coming in by air, which could be Axis servicemen and spare parts for the submarines.

Our fishing trawlers could reach the Spanish colonies without arousing suspicion since they were frequent visitors; they could establish contacts with other fishermen and even in the ports themselves.

SAOUL was complimented on the work achieved so far, which had developed extremely well, and was instructed to gather information on the military formations in the region, including their morale. His information and reports were to be sent to me immediately via VINCENT (whom he knew personally) at the Polish Office. Letters were to be addressed to 'Mr Roger – Algiers'. All expenses incurred in Intelligence work should be submitted and would be covered by return of post. SAOUL, who was now very excited, would be waiting for us tomorrow evening at Agadir, and had already booked our hotel rooms there.

Returning home, I considered what had already been achieved. In the present situation, an Intelligence cell in Agadir was a necessity. It was the last major centre, port and airport before the southern military zone of Morocco and the Sahara. Axis aeroplanes flying to Ifni and Rio de Oro, and French planes flying to French West Africa, landed there. It was even possible that it might facilitate our entry to Dakar – we would see.

If I managed to purchase the business, then, as owner, I would have the legal right to reside and to move within the area. I could also travel between Algiers and Agadir without arousing suspicion. Moreover, during my absence from Morocco VINCENT, as my proxy, would have a convenient cover for his trips south. Afterwards, his outfit could become part of the Casablanca outpost or a new factory manager would also be head of Intelligence in the region. It could be sorted out later. All this was, of course, dependent on the purchase going through. It even struck me as being quite a good business proposition.

Early the following morning (the 18th) Marcel collected me and we arrived at Agadir before sunset. Laskar invited us to supper at the hotel and outlined his plans. I would be introduced to his colleagues as a businessman and potential purchaser of his factory and we could return to Casablanca on the 20th.

While discussing the legal formalities I discovered to my horror that one had to be a permanent resident of the country before being granted permission to manage or buy a business in Morocco. Fortunately Marcel, as usual, came to the rescue, promising that after returning to Rabat he would obtain identity cards for us stating that we were permanent residents. He warned me, however, that it would not be quick as nobody in Morocco was in a hurry.

We saw the factory, occupying three hectares and stretching down to the main Mogador road, the following day. The single-storey complex consisted of an office building, two halls for cleaning and preparing fish, and special salting and drying plants. At present the factory utilised the simplest methods of production and dealt only in certain types of fish. There were no machines or materials for manufacturing the tin boxes necessary for fish preserves, nor was olive oil used. Production of sardines and other fish preserves could only be activated after the war.

I had no intention of concerning myself with the distant and uncertain future. I was only concerned with our Intelligence needs here and now. Laskar, however, took the opportunity to show us a plan for the future reconstruction of the town. We also visited the port and the fishing boats, which would fulfil our more specialised tasks.

Agadir was the last port in French Morocco, situated at the mouth of the Sousse River, in the most fertile and richest part of southern Morocco. An enormous natural bay, it was ideally suited to be a port. Its name was familiar to me from the Agadir Crisis of

1911 when the Kaiser sent the gunboat *Panther* to probe French nerves – a milestone on the road to war in 1914.

Our sightseeing was completed by lunchtime and we even managed to visit the airport in time to see a German Junkers 88 landing. During lunch I met Laskar's friends (agents 1962 and 1963), who made a favourable impression. Afterwards we visited a large banana plantation owned by the French. I had never seen them growing on trees in such quantities. The irrigation was done mechanically, a good example of what can be achieved in unfavourable conditions.

At the hotel in the evening Marcel and I agreed that the fish factory would facilitate my movements and those of my deputies in Morocco. The price would still have to be agreed and I would eventually need someone as a factory manager. Marcel suggested Josephine Baker's secretary, an energetic and enterprising young man who shared our views and was also a volunteer reserve lieutenant in the French Navy. He seemed just the guy we needed. Marcel gave me his address, and I'd meet him in Casablanca.

We set off the following morning for Casablanca, where I would meet SAOUL on his return from Agadir. En route, we called on Marcel's friend to look at his furniture factory. Surprisingly, our Moroccan host knew Poland well as he had successfully exhibited his cedarwood products at the Poznan Fair in 1938. His warm remarks had the desired effect – I bought a few small items as souvenirs.

In Casablanca I asked VINCENT to bring me his reports for London and told him that he might receive authorisation to carry out all the necessary formalities in my name at Agadir. Report 42/73/tj was prepared and included in pouch 29, which was handed over to Mr King at the American Consulate to be sent to London.

Laskar arrived in Casablanca on the 22nd. After some haggling we agreed on a price and the conditions for the takeover. A lawyer would draw up a preliminary contract and I would take over the factory as soon as the Moroccan authorities gave me permission. The final purchase and sales contract, and payment of the agreed price, would follow in due course. Marcel and Lucienne arrived a few days later and we left for a holiday in Marrakesh.

23

MARRAKESH, CASABLANCA AND RABAT
(SEPTEMBER 1942)

The fortnight I spent in Marrakesh was my first holiday for several years, and was a physical and mental necessity. I had to have a rest and stop continually going over the same problems, which were becoming obsessional. The old town was a wonderful place – extraordinarily exotic with magnificent medieval palaces, mosques and buildings enclosed within its defensive walls. Everything was bathed in a pinkish-red hue, with marvellous views of the snow-covered peaks of the High Atlas. After the war Churchill had the same idea and also rested here.

The La Mamounia Hotel, with its magnificent garden full of flowers, orange, lemon, peach, date and palm trees and exotic vegetation, was also ideal. Being luxuriously furnished and assuring every comfort, it was not surprising that German officers (members of the Armistice Commission) also lived there. Marcel's subordinate, the local police commissaire, organised a series of trips including one to an oasis about twenty miles from town in sub-Saharan desert with hundreds of tall palm trees.

We explored the old city. First, the Sultan's palace, 'Bahia', with its exquisite rooms including those for his favourites; above all, its enormous garden with its great pond where the steamboat brought specially from Paris for the Sultan's delectation had sunk, drowning his favourite. The boat still lay there. Then to Ben Joussef, the beautiful Koranic University. The Sultan's mausoleum was a magnificent monument from the sixteenth-century Saadian dynasty, with its richly gilded and carved cedar dome; the sarcophagi and graves of the sultans and their families were to be found within the crypt. We marvelled at the exteriors of the Koutoubia and El Mansour, two famous twelfth-century mosques, the entrance to which was strictly forbidden to infidels. Inevitably, we wandered through the colourful, densely packed, noisy souks and explored the Casbah.

Undoubtedly the most fascinating and unforgettable place in Marrakesh was the vast square – the Djemaa el Ena ('the square of the dead') with its incessant activity and noise, which continued even when day merged into night. All human life seemed to be concentrated there. One encountered ethnic groups of every variety but predominantly tribesmen from the far southern regions or the Central and High Atlas with their copper, ceramic and leather handicrafts, woollen products and beautiful handwoven carpets in exquisite colours. One could also buy camels, donkeys, sheep and all kinds of agricultural produce and fruit.

These nomads, who came from afar, found everything they needed for their simple lifestyle. Everything was for sale: broken buttons, bent knives, rusty nails, tins, boxes – an extraordinary collection of all kinds of rubbish and junk. It could not be compared to the Kercelak market in Warsaw or the Paris flea market. Rather, it reminded me of similar markets in the USSR, although over there one had to pay an entrance fee regardless of whether one was a potential buyer or seller.

The square was a paradise for women. Here they found everything they needed to make themselves more beautiful – all sorts of scents, perfumed oils and various types of vegetable dyes for the hair, eyes, cheeks and lips. There were also special aphrodisiac herbs, for arousing cold male hearts or where love had died away. All around there were mysterious Arab and Berber women of all types, veiled or unveiled, who one suspected were well versed in these ancient arts.

Barbers also worked on the spot, occupying themselves with beautifying heads or faces or bloodletting by applying leeches to their victims. Dentists extracted teeth with pliers meant to remove nails, the results of which were displayed on rugs. Looking at them one shuddered to think they were human; perhaps they were horses' teeth, intended to advertise their skills. Side by side, sitting cross-legged on rugs, were the scribes, with their copper inkstands, goose feathers and small sacks of soft sand, who would write anything on the spot for a small fee, from love letters to a petition of complaint to the Pasha.

Towards evening, life on the Djemaa el Ena began changing. Acrobats, musicians, dancers, storytellers and actors entertained the dense throngs. Circles of varying sizes, depending on their popularity, formed around them. The crowds were engrossed and strangely silent, with an occasional roar of laughter.

At sunset, when from the minarets of the neighbouring mosques the muezzins called the faithful to prayer, an uncanny silence enveloped the vast square. The crowds fell on their knees, bent over and faced towards Mecca, then burst into roars twice as noisy as before. During the day this activity – the huge noisy crowds, very excited and gesticulating – took place under a blazing sun illuminating the extraordinary range of colours. It was a colourful sight and, after forty years, still remains one of my most vivid memories.

During our stay at the Mamounia, we regularly encountered the Germans in the restaurant. They were distantly polite, especially towards our wives, for whom they opened doors and showed other courtesies. I must add that Lucienne was a strikingly good-looking woman with light blonde hair. As a husband it does not behove me to say too much about my wife; suffice to say that she was certainly no worse than Lucienne. Not surprisingly, therefore, the Jerries couldn't take their eyes off them.

One evening, during supper in the garden, we lost our little dog. The waiters found him curled up in the lap of one of the Germans. Naturally, he was removed forthwith, much to his regret. Had they known who was sitting near them, I doubt somehow whether they would have been so polite.

Our departure drew near and one evening Marcel suggested a trip to see the nightlife of the reserved quarters. A local police commissaire who knew all the nightspots took charge of the expedition.

One of the first places he took us to was a 'ladies' boarding house'. The occupants, on seeing our wives entering, ran away shouting, 'Lala lala!' and hid themselves. The madame of the establishment, encouraged possibly by the presence of the commissaire, who was known to her, received us very courteously with black coffee. Our ladies, curious to see the inmates, had to satisfy themselves with talking to their boss.

Next, we visited a café-bar where the local cabaret was being performed, just in time for an artiste who looked as if she weighed over twenty stone. She was singing 'Madelon', the famous First World War song, and belly dancing at the same time. It was a marvellous sight, which the entire audience applauded ecstatically. Not surprisingly, we returned to the hotel in high spirits.

The ten-day rest refreshed us completely; the change in Sophie was particularly noticeable, and my headaches disappeared. We left Marrakesh on 11 September, and through the train window we could see Arabs and Berbers on beautiful horses riding to Rabat for the Ramadan celebrations. Marcel and Lucienne were returning there while we would be stopping off at the hotel in Casablanca for me to settle some business. We would stay with them in a few days' time.

On my return to Casablanca, I wrote to M. Bayonne, Josephine Baker's ex-secretary, asking him to contact me at the hotel. The following day, anticipating mail from Algiers, I went to the American Consulate and sure enough Mr King handed it to me. I was pleasantly surprised to see Robert Murphy there. In answer to his 'What news, where have you been and how are you?' I replied, 'I was in Agadir in southern Morocco, where I have a fish factory and where my Intelligence service is already at work. I had a short rest, and will be returning to Algiers in a few days' time to resume work.' Murphy, smiling and squeezing my hand, told his consular officials: 'Follow his example! He not only carries out his own special work without any documents, but also his business activities as well! And he has been to places where you are unable to go – even with all your cars and diplomatic passports.'

Then, turning to me, he said, 'Soon you will be witnessing great events'. Since he was leaving immediately for Washington, I wished him *bon voyage*.

The mail contained reports from the outposts, sketches and plans and MUSTAFA's report on the shortcomings in the operation of Central Office's radio transmitter, also his message confirming that Operation Zebra was scheduled for the night of 11/12 September and that everything was normal in Algiers. Having looked through everything, I wrote my report (74/nj), bundled it all together as pouch no. 30 and immediately gave it to Mr King to send to London.

M. Bayonne called on me incredibly quickly and I explained my proposal regarding his management of the fish factory in Agadir. He was happy to accept the post and asked for 6,000 francs a month and a percentage of the turnover, a very modest amount. It was too early to broach the topic of his ancillary job, which would actually be his primary task. A meeting was arranged of all those who would be interested in the factory to discuss co-operation. VINCENT would receive authorisation, as my proxy, to approach the Protectorate authorities in case of need.

I saw Laskar again and he told me about Colonel Eon, an artillery commander who had been supplying him with valuable information from northern Morocco for some time. He was very idealistic and came from an old French military family going back to Napoleonic times. I gave him Agency no. 1961.

During our short stay, we were overjoyed by the news that the British had occupied Dieppe, and thought 'It's finally begun!' Our rejoicing was premature. The tragic news that the commando operation had been unsuccessful and that the Allied losses had been heavy arrived the following day. I checked with the Americans but unfortunately the information was correct.

Thinking about the reorganisation of the Agency, I saw that a primary task (which London was also keen on) was to speed up the passing on of information. This meant that we badly needed a second radio operator for VINCENT's prospective radio station at Casablanca. A Polish operator named Jaskolkowski, released by Agency TUDOR, had been promised since 24 April. I waited impatiently for his arrival, which I associated with the improvement of the Agency's communications between Algiers and Casablanca. But it was not until late October that he arrived in Casablanca via Portugal, and his radio station (codenamed BERNARD) began its test transmissions.

At Rabat we stayed at the Hotel Royale. We obtained our identity cards and Marcel arranged our exit visas for Algiers. He certainly knew how to make our stay as pleasant as possible. Under his auspices we visited the beautiful woods of Mamora, the picturesque gorges of Krifla and Akrech with their orange and lemon groves, and Salé across the Bou Regreg river, which, according to local legend, was founded by one of Noah's sons. We also made numerous trips to the Medina and the Casbah.

More importantly, Marcel had obtained tickets for a special stand, reserved for the diplomatic corps and high officials of the Protectorate, for the Ramadan festivities. During this period it was forbidden to eat during the day; the firing of a gun in the evening signalled that eating could begin at sunset, when, consequently, traffic was very heavy. It was the biggest religious festival in the Islamic calendar and the Sultan of Morocco made a public appearance outside his palace in front of his subjects, receiving oaths of allegiance and gifts from representatives of tribes from all over the country.

I also met well-connected Moroccans occupying important positions in the Sultan's court who were very interested in Poland, which had exported industrial products to North Africa before the war. One of them was holding a ceremonial reception in the traditional style at his house in the evening and we were invited there with our wives. It was a delightful evening. I learned the three-finger technique of scooping up delicious sweetmeat dishes, and Sophie greatly enjoyed visiting our host's harem, especially as some of his wives spoke French.

Although all this was very fascinating, I began to get restless. Above all I was overcome by a terrible anxiety about Operation Zebra. Had it been successful and were the officers safe? Then I began worrying about what had happened to MOUSTIQUE and her colleagues and whether everything was going well with BANULS. I decided that, immediately after the Ramadan celebrations, we would return to Algiers. Our visas were ready but we had to show ourselves at the festivities. I suspected that Marcel had gone to a great deal of trouble to obtain tickets for us and he had convinced me that it would be an extraordinary experience.

The Ramadan festivities took place the day after the party. Enormous crowds had gathered early in the big square in front of the palace, which was surrounded by a high wall with a gate through which the Sultan would ride out. They came from the furthest corners of Morocco, including the Atlas Mountains – Berbers, Arabs and Touaregs – and had spent the night bivouacked in the square. The noise and the traffic lasted all night, the volume increasing towards morning as the crowds swelled.

The reinforced French-Moroccan police attempted to keep order and control access to the platform erected opposite the exit gate of the palace. In front of it a special podium had been built where the Sultan, surrounded by his court, and the French Resident General, Nogues, were to sit. These places were to be occupied by a certain time, after which all the traffic stopped and everyone would await the Sultan's arrival.

Everything went according to plan. Taking our places on the platform, we had an excellent view of the entire square, the gates and the huge crowds that had filled every available inch of space. People were also perched on walls and trees, eager to catch a glimpse of the Sultan; the excitement was electrifying. My attention was drawn to a very large group of riders who had gathered in a far corner of the square. They were colourfully dressed in their ethnic costumes, armed and sitting on beautiful horses with rich saddles and harnesses. Marcel explained that they were warriors from various tribes who had arrived on horseback from all over Morocco. They would stage a charge, shooting at full gallop, just as they had traditionally fought in days gone by.

We were now eagerly waiting for the gate to open. Marcel was in good form, cracking some really marvellous jokes. Suddenly, to the sound of trumpets and drums, the gate opened. First came two eunuch courtiers holding what appeared to be long white scarves, which they began waving in the air. Behind them, in double lines, came the others. Then, coming through the gate, I could see a white canopy being carried aloft by four people and underneath, riding a beautiful sorrel horse, was the Sultan of Morocco. The halter was held by two eunuchs.

On either side of the Sultan came the other courtiers, carrying enormous fans made of white ostrich feathers. Behind them came the high-ranking courtiers and ministers, among them our host of the previous evening. The trumpets blared, the drums beat and the crowds, in response to signs given by the scarves, fell on their knees and uttered cries of joy.

The Sultan approached the platforms and his podium. Only now could one see the magnificent saddle and harness of his horse, covered in gold and inlaid with precious stones, which in the sunshine glistened in a dazzling array of colours. The Sultan himself was dressed in white, and had the hood of his coat over his head in the Moorish style. His face was pale with a dark beard and hair. It looked calm and did not reveal any lust for power; one could even say that it looked rather kindly. As he climbed off his horse, a eunuch approached and he rested a leg on his shoulder. The military Resident of France greeted him with a bow and they sat in the podium together with the high-ranking officials, who stood behind them.

The second part of the ceremony began with a military parade to the music of an army band. First the French soldiers marched past, then the Sultan's guards. There were infantry, cavalry and artillery units, armed with 75mm and old French guns, commanded by French officers consisting of athletic-looking black soldiers obviously chosen for their physique and size. Their uniforms were far more colourful than those of French Republican guards. The whole thing resembled a Hollywood Technicolor epic.

Then came the 'fantasia' – the charge on horseback of fighting Moroccan tribes from the Atlas and the south. Gathered at the other end of the enormous square, at a signal from their commanders they moved in one mass at full gallop. Their swords, raised and ready to strike, flashed in the sun; their war-cries cut through the air. It was a fierce and bloodcurdling sight. Sophie, sitting next to me, grabbed my hand. Nothing, it seemed, could restrain the riders and their horses at that speed. They would fall on the platform and cut it to pieces.

All this lasted only a few seconds. The horses advanced without any perceptible guidance. The riders, holding their swords in one hand and their long, ancient, Ottoman-style rifles in the other, suddenly fired into the air. A moment later they stopped, as if by magic, just in front of the Sultan's podium. Then they broke into a circle and trotted back to their former places. A great sigh of relief went up from the crowd. Marcel was right. I would never see another sight like it again. It was absolutely unique.

Now it was time for the oaths of allegiance and gifts to be offered to the Sultan by the heads of tribes and other representatives, who kissed his hand with great reverence. The gifts were of every conceivable type – beautiful horses, carpets, articles of silver and gold. They were not only difficult to describe but, in fact, difficult to see since the servants took them straight back to the palace. This ceremony took a long time. When it was concluded, the trumpets and drums sounded again. The Sultan climbed majestically on to his horse, and in the same order, but accompanied by even louder cries from the crowd, the procession vanished behind the closing gate.

We returned to the hotel excited and bursting with impressions. We were very grateful to Marcel for the opportunity to see this truly amazing ceremony. He then explained, among other things, that one could tell a eunuch by his headgear; he wore a red fez with a triangular point, rather than the ordinary one with a flat crown. This was the last evening we spent together. The following day (18 September) we left for Algiers and home. Arriving there on the 19th, I immediately reported to Central Office (42/656) that I had returned from Morocco.

24

OPERATION ZEBRA

Returning to the two officers in Gibraltar, Malinowski and Kowal, London now informed us that a third officer, Piotrowski, who had a good command of French, had been assigned to Agency Africa. They were unknown to me but I assumed that they had been given some Intelligence training. I needed to have them working with us immediately, and the Oran commander was asked whether agent 1818 at La Sénia airport could take aerial photographs of the Oran coastline marking the exact location of a site suitable for a clandestine landing operation. These arrived in the Oran outpost's mailbag and Central Office were informed that they would be forwarded with details of the operation.

It was not until 14 August that London informed us that Operation Zebra involved delivering the three officers and collecting the agents from Paris (42/529); Piotrowski's assumed name would be Georges Martin, and they asked what kind of photographs would be needed for his identity papers (6612). The British Admiralty accepted my location and other data necessary for the operation (7020). I then confirmed the conditions and provided the passwords and signals (42/584). Finally, on 1 September, we were informed that Operation Zebra was scheduled for the night of 11/12 September at 00.01 hours GMT (7100).

The Oran commander, who was already keeping the agents from Paris in a safe house, was now informed of the details. Preparations for the new officers' reception were disguised as an overnight camping excursion on the beach. On 11 September a tent for four people was erected at a clearly defined spot on the beach. The Oran commander had identity cards ready for the three officers; only the photographs needed to be attached. He even had the police station's rubber stamp to endorse them. This was possible thanks to Commissaire Labat, who co-operated with our Oran network.

On the night of 11/12 September the Oran commander intercepted the prearranged signals flashing from the ship at sea and replied with the landing signals. Five minutes later a boat bearing the three officers touched land and after an exchange of passwords the agents were on board. Within five minutes the boat had left and the operation was over. The outpost commander affixed the photographs to the identity cards and duly stamped them and the officers now became long-standing citizens of French North Africa who were enjoying a camping holiday on the beach.

On 12 September their papers were checked by gendarmes on the Mostaganem to Oran bus. Everything was in order. On the 15th the outpost commander sent a detailed report, and BANULS reported to London: 'Operation Zebra successful – officers now in Oran'.

The day after my return from Morocco, the 20th, I had a briefing with BANULS and looked through the reports, including the Oran commander's on Operation Zebra. MOUSTIQUE and the other agents had been evacuated successfully and the officers who had arrived were awaiting instructions. BANULS would instruct the Oran commander to escort the officers personally to his flat on the 24th, and notify the Constantine commander to present himself there on that day. He immediately forwarded instructions to both commanders via the post boxes. Details of the new officers' assignments would be issued later on.

MUSTAFA, who was now living in a private flat on Rue Mulhouse, reported that there was a villa in the Hydra district suitable for housing our second radio station, ANTONINA. He was instructed to purchase it for $10,000 and organise it with the help of our Canadian agent 1885 and our second radio operator Mario Marret (agent 1886). ANTONINA was to relieve the overworked ADAM by taking some of its radio correspondence. More important was the security aspect. In the event of the latter being closed down, the former could continue. I also heard the sad news that MACIEJ had departed for France during my absence. We had parted without any farewells and were never to meet again.

On 21 September I had a happy reunion with Mr Boyd and received my mail from London and Casablanca. He asked me my opinion of the leaders of the resistance group, from which I deduced that Robert Murphy had direct contact with them. They were useful in fashioning public opinion and spreading propaganda among the troops and the young, but no faith could be placed in their military potential.

Robert Murphy, by virtue of his position as Minister of the United States Embassy at Vichy officiating in Algiers, had close contacts with high-ranking officers of the North African Army Command and leading officials. Obviously these circles provided him with a certain amount of information on the political and economic situation in North Africa. I had no idea whether it was accurate or whether it reflected the real feelings of the French and the Arabs and the attitude of the Army. Frequently the higher echelons had no idea what the lower ones thought or felt. It wasn't really my problem and I had my own sources of information.

I studied London's mail. Central Office's evaluation of our material resembled a headmaster's report. Very good marks for our counter-intelligence and for our reports on the order of battle. They liked our guidelines for broadcasting propaganda via the BBC and requested us to continue sending material of this type. Extracts from these documents with appropriate comments were sent to the heads of our outposts.

Pouch no. 31 was prepared and handed over for despatch in the evening. It contained the results of my trip to Morocco and maps of North Africa on which all the airfields were marked. Also, a plan for the reorganisation of the Agency and our radio communications network including a list of our Intelligence outposts numbered consecutively from 1 to 8 (Dakar would soon make 9). A request for exit visas for the Łubieńskis was also enclosed. I wanted to move BANULS out as soon as his duties had been taken over by one of the new officers.

In the late evening d'Astier, who had heard of my return from FREDO, came to discuss the general political situation in Morocco. Gaullist elements existed there but they were unorganised and with no overall control. There were individual cells led by energetic people who helped with the evacuation to England but they had made little headway with their propaganda because of the strength of the Légion and the SOL.

D'Astier again thanked me for my help in organising the resistance movement and for establishing links with London. He mentioned that I would be recommended for the Légion d'Honneur for my work for France. Privately, I did not assign any significance to these flattering words. Extravagant praises and empty promises are used when necessary; it was nothing new and I would experience it again. As for d'Astier, his own perverted definition of gratitude would manifest itself after the Allied landings.

In the morning there was a warm greeting from FREDO. He brought some interesting intercepts of telephone conversations at the German Consulate, from which it appeared that things were becoming difficult for them, and was delighted at London's reaction to our counter-intelligence information. Commissioner Begue, who was still in Algiers, seemed to have become more friendly towards him and had given FREDO instructions to search for the radio station.

MUSTAFA brought several telegrams from Central Office. One warned of the necessity for caution as Agency Africa was very important and the Allied General Staff were very keen that its work should continue (7756). This confirmation of our role and the Agency's work within North Africa was very encouraging. Another requested continual information on fuel stocks, diesel, oil and petrol (both civilian and military), which I would have to obtain from Lacaze.

I prepared instructions for the Oran and Constantine commanders, explaining the need to attach Intelligence Officers to their outposts and their roles. They were intended to be their deputies, control agency reports and request important missing details from the agents' reports. Their presence should increase the pace of our work. A briefing session for the afternoon of the 23rd was arranged with MUSTAFA and BANULS.

FREDO dropped in again in the morning of the 23rd and brought another important intercept, this time from the Italian Consulate. The Italo-German Armistice Commission had given the Vichy Government permission to increase their military forces by 50,000. Also information that German armoured formations and aeroplanes had been located near Derna in Libya and Mersa Matruh in Egypt.

That morning, I visited Lacaze at Shell and obtained information on the quantity of fuel stored in North Africa as at 1 September 1942. Additionally, forty-five tons of synthetic petrol for the air force in Morocco had been unloaded in port 1651 and 100,000 litres of gas oil, which was being kept at Shell depots. Eight hundred tons of diesel from Dakar had been supplied to navy storage tanks in Santa Cruz.

On my return, there was yet more mail in my post box from the outposts and new messages to London were prepared. One, recommending that BANULS and MUSTAFA be decorated with the Cross of Valour for their work in very difficult conditions and at the risk of their lives, was intended as a surprise for them. A supplementary list of French ships was given in my report 79/tj. All this would be handed over to Boyd the following morning as pouch no. 32.

My officers arrived in the afternoon for a briefing. Tomorrow (the 24th) Ragache would bring the new officers to Algiers and take them directly to BANULS's flat where the Constantine commander would be arriving. For security purposes, BANULS would then take the new officers at noon to MUSTAFA's flat, where I would listen to their accounts, which would determine where they were to be posted. BANULS would then take them back to his flat again, after which they would leave with the head of whichever outpost they were assigned to.

Handing in our pouch at the American Consulate on the morning of the 24th, I felt that Boyd seemed relieved. They hadn't received any of our mailbags for about a month. There was no time for a chat. I was in a hurry to get to MUSTAFA's flat.

The new officers arrived punctually. I wanted to give a formal flavour to their registration and to emphasise that, although they were working as civilians, military discipline prevailed. They were to be interrogated individually to determine their personal details, army career, participation in the Polish campaign and, importantly, their training at the Intelligence School. I wanted to know the topics studied there, their familiarity with a hurdy-gurdy (if any), knowledge of the French language and of North Africa, and the guidelines given to them by JANIO, the director of Polish Intelligence.

Lieutenant Żorawski (codename MISTRAL) reported first. A naval man, he was married, but his wife and child remained in Poland. He would make himself understood in French. Second Lieutenant Piotrowski (COLT), a bachelor, had graduated from a commercial college and had an excellent knowledge of French and English. Corporal Majewicz (SLAV) was married, with a wife and child in Poland, had worked in a bookshop in Poland and could make himself understood in French.

While their military careers and participation in the Polish–German Campaign of 1939 were different, their Intelligence training had been identical. They had volunteered and had landed up in the Intelligence School. General Sikorski, the Supreme Commander, had inspected the school and assured them that, since their work would be responsible and dangerous, their time in Military Intelligence would be treated exactly as if they were in the front line.

As a result of their knowledge of French they were attached to Agency Africa. They were familiar with the hurdy-gurdy but had no experience as operators. JANIO had told them that they were to search for agents and build up their own network as soon as they received detailed instructions in North Africa; he had given them advice as to how this should be done.

I assigned them as follows: MISTRAL, as a naval man, to the Oran outpost because of the naval base of Mers-el-Kébir, and SLAV to the Constantine outpost. I kept COLT in Algiers as an Intelligence Officer of the Agency who would take over from BANULS. Not only could he pass as a Frenchman and had documents made out in the surname Martin, but he was also best suited to the task.

I gave them a general briefing in which they were told, among other things, that they should forget about the briefing at Central Office and about their 'guidelines'. They would be attached to Intelligence outposts where the head was a Frenchman. They were definitely not to look for outside contacts with agents. This was the function of the commander of the outpost. Their duty would be to look through all Intelligence reports from the outpost's agents and, where important details were missing, to demand further information. All original Intelligence material secured was to be sent to me. While the outpost commander arranged the movement of the couriers, they would prepare the mailbags.

I would now expect comprehensive reports from the outposts and not have to ask for additional data. I assumed that they had been taught in school what Intelligence reports should look like. Only after some time, when they had got to know local conditions and the agents, would they be permitted to extend the scope of their work and then only with my permission. I hoped that their relationships with their colleagues would be friendly and wished them luck in their work. Before we parted, BANULS handed me two mailbags brought to Algiers by the Oran and Constantine commanders.

As a postscript, my three new officers had boarded HMS *Minna* at Gibraltar and had remained on board from May to 11 September 1942. In the event, they only worked for the Agency from mid-September until the Allied landings on 8 November 1942. Thus I never had the extra help that I had counted on.

That evening, while listening to the BBC's French-language service from London, I was deeply shocked to hear some words directed against 'Commissioner Dubois in Rabat'. The campaign, obviously inspired and led from the Casablanca area, consisted of innuendoes and lies and was motivated by envy and spite under the guise of patriotism. It is very easy to do someone an injustice, especially in wartime; far more difficult to repair it. That it was happening here in our service really upset me.

I was incensed by this treacherous attack on Marcel and sent a lengthy report to London on the situation in Morocco and

Commissioner Dubois's help and close co-operation with us, which had begun in Marseilles in October 1940, long before anyone in France had thought about lifting a finger against the Germans; the broadcast was unjust and harmful and I demanded that it be retracted (42/82/tj).

Central Office replied that the matter had been cleared up and that Commissioner Dubois was 'well thought of in London' (8796). Unfortunately this did not protect him against further innuendo. The damage was only finally undone after several years of investigation and effort. It was also connected with the dossiers it was known that Marcel had built up on the murders of Gaullist couriers in North Africa carrying large sums of money – a matter so sensitive that, over forty years later, I am still reluctant to divulge the details.

Pouch no. 33 was handed to John Knox on 25 September and included a detailed description of Operation Zebra (42/81/tj), an outline of the Agency to be effective from 1 October 1942 (42/83/tj), and my report on French military preparations in Morocco and Algeria, the aim of which was the strengthening of French defences as demanded by the German–Italian Armistice Commission (42/84/tj).

FREDO had reported that Admiral Darlan would be flying to Algiers between 11 and 12 October to carry out an inspection of the North African armies. German pressure on the Vichy authorities was being stepped up. According to our information, originating from Air France, in case of alert and mobilisation the air force would be concentrated around Marrakesh and, in the event of war, all aeroplanes and civilian crews would be directed to Blida airport to 'Transport Group 15' (42/680 and 42/687). Achiary, now our Setif commander, reported that the Germans had demanded that all French counter-espionage units be wound up. Apparently, a Gestapo or SS functionary attached to Geissler's headquarters at Vichy had received permission to inspect the spy dossiers of BST throughout unoccupied France.

Moreover, the Germans were demanding large quantities of meat and cereals, though French North Africa had already supplied an enormous amount of the latter from the current harvest. They were also demanding almost immediate delivery of 400,000 hectolitres of alcohol, manufactured from wine – hence its shortage on the market. According to my findings large quantities of rubber were shipped from North Africa to France during 1942.

The first mail prepared by MISTRAL and SLAV arrived from their outposts and there was a noticeable improvement in the reports, which were more comprehensive and detailed. During September eighty telegrams were received from Central Office (the name 'Dakar' being continually repeated) while 112 were sent, containing the usual military, naval and general information. When, as was my habit at the end of the month, I studied my tracing paper showing the disposition of army divisions and the defence fortifications in North Africa, I concluded happily that we had information on all the military units, batteries and coastal fortifications, and the exact amounts of ammunition stored, bombs and military equipment. I was now convinced that London, being in possession of all this data, was familiar with the exact military situation in French North Africa. As usual the latest information on the movements of ships and conditions at the naval bases was also supplied. During September, four more agents (nos 1889, 1831–3) were received into the Agency.

The Agency's work continued relatively smoothly – which is not to say that there was no danger. The unknown threat hung over us permanently. Within Algiers alone there was a galaxy of enemies – Gestapo and Armistice agents, Vichy's special counter-intelligence commissioner (Begue) and his men, the local Sûreté, the Légion, the SOL and a host of other collaborators, Axis agents and informers. One example may suffice.

One day MUSTAFA came to see me unexpectedly with radio messages he had received that morning, which I immediately began to decode. Shortly afterwards BANULS also arrived unexpectedly with urgent information from the outposts. During our conversation the doorbell rang. As usual, Sophie answered the door. I heard French voices and she ushered someone into the next room. After a while she appeared in my office and whispered, 'Inspectors from the Prefecture. Give me a bottle of brandy.' I gave it to her immediately.

BANULS had grown pale, which was not surprising as the police were looking for him. MUSTAFA also looked shaken. The coded telegrams that I had just received, a cipher book and other very compromising documents were spread out on my desk.

Luckily Sophie was entertaining the inspectors with brandy next door and engaging them in conversation. Thus I had sufficient time quickly to remove the compromising papers and hide them securely. On my desk appeared Floc-Av's commercial documents. BANULS stood behind the heavy curtain next to the balcony door. I looked out into the street – the house was not surrounded – then quietly opened the balcony door. If they entered now, BANULS would have passed unnoticed along the balcony into another room and the kitchen and would have been able to leave without being seen.

BANULS stood behind the portière while the inspectors were in the flat, which was quite some time. When they left, Sophie told me that the ostensible purpose of their visit was to ask whether she received any 'refugee aid'. The brandy had prolonged their stay and made them reluctant to leave. It could have ended in disaster.

Similarly, my laconic references to handing over mailbags to the Americans, and my visits to the Consulate and Murphy's office, may have conveyed the misleading impression that there was no danger. The reality was quite different. The buildings in which they were housed were surrounded and watched by Gestapo agents and the special French police. Each of my very frequent and highly necessary trips with the Agency's mail could have ended in arrest. I could have been caught red-handed with overwhelming evidence of our espionage work, which would have compromised the American representatives as well.

One had to try to provide for all contingencies. When leaving home, I always left instructions about what to do if I failed to return. For many reasons I maintained these contacts on my own. Before visiting the Consulate, I spent some time watching the agents outside the building and establishing their routine. The situation inside the Consulate itself can best be illustrated by the fact that the Consul General had to turn to me to check the credentials of one of his new employees.

Once, when bringing our pouches to the building on the fourth floor of which the Consulate was housed, I reckoned the coast was clear. I entered, fully intending to use the lift, but at that moment my instinct suddenly told me to use the stairs. As I approached the fourth floor two men were sitting on the window ledge next to the lift doors. I recognised them as police informers. Ignoring them, I walked up to the next floor, came down in the lift, and quickly disappeared out of the building. My mail was not handed in that day. Situations like this cropped up all the time. They were impossible to foresee and their safe resolution depended almost entirely upon luck.

BANULS arrived unexpectedly on the early evening of 5 October. He had been buying cigarettes a short while ago and the French owner of the shop (which was in the same building) said that two unknown men had questioned him. They had wanted to know how long BANULS and his wife had been living there, and their habits. Filled with foreboding, I made an immediate decision. Handing him some money, I said, 'Go immediately to the railway station and buy tickets to Oran. You're lucky, there's a train going there today. Leave immediately. Say nothing to anyone in the house. If anyone asks say that you are going to Bône to see your family. Report to me before you leave!'

BANULS, dazed, took the money and left immediately.

At 9pm he came to report that by a stroke of luck he had met a Frenchman in front of the ticket office who had sold him two tickets to Oran. BANULS's wife was waiting there with their luggage and the train was leaving in half an hour. The flat was 'clean' – he had left no traces, and was taking the keys with him. I wished him good luck. The Oran commander had a safe house there and he would receive instructions through him. I went to the station to check that everything was OK.

It was a relief when the train pulled out. I informed MUSTAFA and COLT of these new developments. Agent 1850 would be informed via his post box. All the threads were now cut and I calmly awaited further developments.

The next morning FREDO told me that Commissioner Begue had

gone berserk and had given his inspectors hell. He had had BANULS in his hand, yet the bird had flown; obviously he had waited too long. Apparently one of his men had, by sheer chance, overheard a conversation between BANULS's wife and a salesgirl in one of the large department stores on the Rue Isly. He had followed her and recognised the address of the house. They suspected that she was Łubieński's wife and began watching her. They waited for BANULS but failed to recognise him. It was only when they saw them leaving together that they guessed he had changed his appearance. The concierge and the grocery owner were interrogated. The former remained silent but the latter unwittingly let the cat out of the bag. Begue then set up a trap at BANULS's flat which had misfired.

A telegram was immediately sent to Central Office requesting them to evacuate BANULS. The correspondence dragged on for some time. Finally the British stated that he would have to sneak into their consulate in Tetuán, and report with the password: '*Nous sommes les amis de Stanislas*.' Meanwhile, BANULS stayed in a safe house in Oran and helped MISTRAL with his work. He only returned to Algiers after the Allied landings and then left for England with me. That, however, was still a long way off.

25

DAKAR AT LAST!
THE EVE OF THE ALLIED LANDINGS

London continually sought urgent information on the French Fleet, still powerful despite the British attack at Mers-el-Kébir. While the *Jean Bart* (its armaments as yet unfinished) was at Casablanca, its sister ship, the ultramodern and heavily armoured *Richelieu*, was at Dakar. Doubtless the earlier, disastrous Free French operation there was still on their minds. They again pressed us for information on its air and coastal defences, fuel stores and the morale of its sailors.

Our new agent 1889 (ALBERT) was the most suitable candidate. On my instructions, the Algiers commander convinced him of the necessity to go to Dakar. His departure formalities were settled, he was given appropriate instruction, and on 5 October I was able to report that we had sent an agent there (42/716). An explanation of the French markings was also sent as instructed: W = submarine chasers; T = torpedo boats; X = destroyers.

Meanwhile, our new officers were working well. Had they arrived earlier, our work would have been far easier. COLT, who had taken over BANULS's work, was excellent. He had found himself a room and was soon at home in Algiers.

On 2 October FREDO informed me that Italian soldiers taken prisoner in Libya by the British had arrived in Algiers from Casablanca. How they managed to get there was a mystery. Were they saved from a British ship sunk in the Atlantic? Nobody knew.

For some time Algiers had been rife with rumours, which were now spreading alarmingly. They spoke of preparations for an armed insurrection, the organisation of a secret army and an anticipated American occupation of French North Africa. It reached the point where our concierge, Mrs Wasilicz, who helped Sophie with our receptions, asked her whether they were true. Her son, a student at Algiers University, was attending meetings and preparing for an uprising. Naturally Sophie played it down. While it could be seen as the bravado of irresponsible young people, it could also prematurely disclose carefully prepared plans.

A few days later MUSTAFA told me that agent 1885 had boasted to him that, on Mr Knox's instructions, he was to find suitable landing places for the Allied invasion. This agent, whom I did not altogether trust, was a Canadian and a permanent resident of Algiers who had been accepted into the network at MUSTAFA's request. However, FREDO also reported the rumours circulating in town. I therefore resolved to discuss the matter with Minister Murphy. It was a ridiculous situation and the Gestapo must surely have known about it by now. Perhaps they presumed they were feelers put out to spread confusion about the real direction of the Allied attack. In the event, fortunately, the Germans did not appear to draw any positive conclusions from it.

The General Government and the Vichy regime must also have known about the rumours but appeared to have discounted them. Nevertheless, orders were given to strengthen the defences. General Nogues, the Resident Minister of Morocco, informed Vichy that the Americans were looking for landing sites in Morocco (42/606). The lighthouses on the coast near Oran were extinguished (42/616). The Armistice Commission in Algiers ordered the construction of fortifications and shelters at the Maison Blanche airport and the troops defending it were reinforced (42/713). Our Casablanca outpost reported an observation balloon moored over the town with a German and French crew (42/665). Information from the Admiralty was of orders to close the ports at night and of submarine patrols. Agent 1818 reported mobilisation at La Sénia air base and, on Admiralty orders, there were coastal and sea patrols. Furthermore, the military were to occupy defensive positions at night near certain ports. All this urgent information was immediately sent to London.

Meanwhile, Central Office instructed us to work out and send our Agency budget for 1943 (8075). Did this mean that we'd still be working here next year? In which case, why the rumours of a landing? I assumed that our General Staff and its Second Bureau were better informed than myself and therefore sent a draft budget to them with report no 42/89/tj.

While handing over pouch no. 35 on 9 October, I took the opportunity to discuss the rumours with Mr Boyd, who at first dismissed them. However, when I pointed out to him Nogues's telegram to Vichy, the orders issued by the Admiralty and the High Command of the French North African Armies, agent 1818's remarks, as well as the stories told by agent 1885 (whom he knew personally), Boyd became obviously flustered. Taken together, all this could ruin any preparations and cause much loss of life. It was extremely imprudent, to say the least. Boyd was compelled to agree. The French resistance group were responsible, or rather irresponsible – they leaked secrets like a sieve. However, it was far too late to do anything about it.

Now that we had two radio stations (ADAM and ANTONINA), we could send far more telegrams. From the radio correspondence, it was obvious that someone in London was in a hurry and that the final act was rapidly approaching. I tried to hide my own excitement and continued working as usual.

Many messages were now being sent to London on military installations, coastal and air defences, naval strength, new airfields and the air force, all vital to any operational plans. Also sent was detailed information on the naval strength at sea bases in French North Africa. Central Office asked us to confirm whether German U-boats were using the Moroccan ports of Lauteza and Fedala. Hitherto none had been discovered, but our Casablanca outpost was recharged with this urgent task. Meanwhile, the Agadir outpost reported on the coastal defences and a hydroplane base being constructed at the port.

The Algiers commander and agent 1884 conveyed the

information, originating from French North African Army HQ, that the Vichy Government had quarrelled with Germany. Laval had resigned and the Germans were threatening to occupy the rest of France and French North Africa. Apparently, they had two divisions on stand-by at Tripoli for this contingency. London asked us to confirm it by return, adding that the British had received similar information.

This was difficult. It was a considerable distance from Algiers to Tripoli and we had no contacts or means of communication. The information was gathered from various sources over a long period, and it was not until 20 October that we could confirm that the Italian concentration was not a threat to Tunisia (42/774).

The Casablanca police arrested another Pole, a Mr Komar, a former clerk at the Bank Polski in Warsaw, whom they found poking his nose into matters that were not supposed to concern him. He had nothing to do with the Agency's network and had been recruited by our Intelligence either in Lisbon or Madrid to show 'results'. I intervened with Marcel; it was sorted out satisfactorily and he was freed.

A special conference was held with the participation of General Vogel, Head of the German Armistice Commission in Wiesbaden, and the Head of the Italian Armistice Commission in Turin. The Germans demanded that the French should lodge an official request for German troops to be sent to 'defend' French North Africa; General Nogues was said to have opposed the demand (42/846). Meanwhile, eleven submarines and three destroyers had arrived in port 1651 from Toulon (42/770).

In response to my request to send guidelines for co-operation with the Arabs, which I considered very necessary, Central Office replied that they would have to consult the British first (8249). It seemed strange that our Headquarters seemed unable to show any initiative of their own. Similarly, as I subsequently discovered, nobody on our Supreme Commander's Staff knew, in spite of all the information we had sent them, about the decision to occupy North Africa.

From the moment ALBERT was sent to Dakar, I waited impatiently for news from him. He was an elderly and respectable Frenchman, an officer from the First World War, familiar with military matters. I did not believe that anything harmful could have happened to him. So when, on 18 October, the Algiers commander informed me of his return, I immediately arranged to meet him the next morning at my flat.

My conversation with Albert lasted several hours. The material he had brought back was extremely valuable and contained everything we needed and that London had asked for. After studying it, I realised the reasons for the failure of the Gaullist attack on Dakar the previous year, which Churchill omitted to provide in his memoirs. The most important was the lack of accurate Intelligence on the strength of the Dakar defences and naval artillery ammunition, particularly that of the *Richelieu*.

According to my new information, it appeared that the *Richelieu*, immobilised in the port by British naval gunfire, had, at the time the combined British and Free French fleet left Dakar, only sufficient ammunition for its 15-inch guns for one final salvo. It would then have become an immobilised tin can, to be shot up at will. Presumably, had the British and Free French known this, Dakar could have been occupied. Again, this only illustrated the value of obtaining accurate Intelligence in wartime.

Among other things, Albert's information contained:

1. An evaluation of the general political and economic situation in Dakar and the mood of the French and the blacks.

2. Coastal defence plans containing heavy artillery emplacements.

3. Air defence plan with anti-aircraft artillery batteries.

4. Defence plan of the town and port of Dakar together with sketches.

5. Ships at the port, their ammunition supplies and equipment.

6. Special description of the *Richelieu*, taking into account the damage incurred; 15-inch guns in turrets and ammunition supplies.

7. Quantity of fuel reserves and ammunition stores.

8. Strength of the territorial armies and their organisation (two infantry divisions, nine tanks).

9. Field artillery dispositions.
10. Air force: bases and airports.
11. Plan of the town of Dakar showing the places where British artillery shells landed and numbered according to rounds.

Albert was warmly thanked for his work, which deserved a high award. I visualised him as head of the Agency's Dakar outpost and I intended to accompany him to Casablanca, from where, thanks to Marcel, who had provided me with contacts, I could easily obtain an entry permit to Dakar. A sudden change of circumstances made me abandon these plans. Meanwhile, twelve urgent messages to London were prepared (42/779–90) and a special report (42/96/tj) was sent in pouch no. 36 on 21 October, which Boyd promised to send immediately.

Central Office was also informed that seventy Polish soldiers coming from the Middle East on a British ship torpedoed outside Casablanca were rescued but interned in a camp at Ouet-Zem in Morocco (42/700). I connected this incident with the rescued Italian airmen in transit through Algiers. Close contact was maintained with our Governmental Delegate, Hutten-Czapski, during all the time I was in North Africa, and he provided very valuable information. He endeavoured to improve conditions for our soldiers imprisoned at the Mechara camp and later moved to the Colomb-Bechar camp as forced labour on the construction of the Alger–Niger railway. After considerable effort, he managed to get the Polish camp moved to southern Morocco where conditions were better. Just after the Allied landings the soldiers there were sent to Britain to rejoin the Polish Army.

As can be imagined October 1942 was a busy and difficult month. We received eighty messages from London and sent 141 concerning the military, naval and economic situation in French North Africa.

A sense of excitement, expectancy and anxiety began to pervade Algiers, reinforced by rumours and propaganda spread by *Combat* communiqués from the war fronts, which spoke of heavy battles at Stalingrad and a British offensive in Libya, which heightened the anti-German atmosphere. People longed for their situation to improve.

I was aware of the secret conference that took place at the aptly named town of Cherchell, near Algiers, between the American general, Mark Clark, and the leaders of the resistance movement on the night of 21/22 October. I assumed that London knew about it and it was not, therefore, reported. Pouch no. 37 despatched on 3 November did, however, include a plan of the port of Le Havre received from an engineer recently arrived from France, and was followed by pouch no. 38, bulging with mail from our outposts.

The new situation created problems with the French. On 5 November MUSTAFA reported that our Canadian agent 1885 had demanded that all our radio communications in French North Africa be handed over to him. He was 'mobilising them' by order of Colonel Jousse, the military commander of the resistance movement. When faced with opposition, agent 1885 turned directly to our operator (Joseph Briatte – 1845) and told him that henceforth he was forbidden to take orders from a foreigner. Briatte, however, would not agree to his demand. Agent 1885 left station ADAM and returned later with an invitation from Colonel Jousse for talks on 6 November.

I decided not to participate in them. MUSTAFA would attend and declare, in my name, that the radio station worked for the benefit of the Allied General Staffs in London. If Jousse broke this communication, they would hold him responsible.

On the evening of the 6th talks took place at agent 1885's shop between Colonel Jousse, Captain L'Hostis and MUSTAFA. The Colonel introduced himself as 'the Military Commander of the Resistance Movement personally known to Eisenhower', and asked for our radio to be put at his disposal. MUSTAFA explained my instructions, adding that our station had been working with London for two years. The Colonel reluctantly agreed. Using bitter language, he instructed agent 1885 to divest himself of his 'obligations' to organise radio communications for the resistance group.

The incident was reported to London. I did not attend because Jousse should have known from the leaders of his group about the services I had rendered when it was being formed. If he had wanted help, he should have done it through them or approached me directly, not through agent 1885 and at the very last moment. It now appeared that this agent's motive in collaborating with us had been to reap personal benefits and to achieve a favourable position with the Americans and in the organisation of the resistance group.

In my second message on this incident, I spoke clearly about the planned military action and asked for instructions. Central Office told us not to become associated with any such action, to carry out Intelligence work exclusively and not to give up our radio communications to anyone (8855 and 8857). On the 6th, London was advised about the port of Philippeville's defences, which Italian officers had just inspected.

Meanwhile the atmosphere in Algiers became increasingly heated. Mrs Wasilicz, our concierge, saw Sophie that evening and was very agitated. Her son was going to a rendezvous on the night of 7/8 November to collect arms as the Americans would be landing on the morning of the 8th. As a result, I decided to go to Murphy's office the following morning to find out exactly what was going on.

On the 7th I spoke to Boyd who confirmed that 'tomorrow morning' (the 8th) a landing would take place and that an Allied fleet of several hundred ships was nearing North Africa; it was a *fait accompli*. Robert Murphy repeated the information, adding that a very powerful sea force had been mounted, which the Germans would be unable to oppose. Was I in contact with London, and would I be able to stay in touch with them all day tomorrow? Depending on developments, it could be extremely important. Normally we communicated with them twice a day, but I would order a full day's alert, just in case it was necessary. London were immediately contacted and asked to stay in close contact with us.

The same day Admiral Darlan had flown to Algiers to visit his sick son (42/852). A military alert at the La Sénia, Blida and Maison Blanche airfields was reported; it was also reported that sea convoys had been observed approaching the Algerian coast (42/853). All traffic in port 157 had been suspended and ships at sea were ordered to return to the port; submarines there and in the port were standing by for battle (42/854). These messages outlined clearly the developments taking place, which would determine the fate of French North Africa.

Ragache, as Floc-Av's representative in Oran, was visiting the firm that day. MUSTAFA and COLT were informed of the impending developments, as was the Algiers commander. MUSTAFA would issue special instructions to our radio operator concerning the all-day alert. I told everyone at home about the Allied landings that would take place the next day.

That evening I was too excited to listen to the radio communiqués properly. Tomorrow at dawn the operation would commence that I had thought about and anticipated for two years and for which we had all worked so hard. I had assured Colonel Solborg that North Africa would be occupied within twenty-four hours. Supposing it was unsuccessful? In order to assuage my doubts, I had a good look at my special map on which all our information had been marked but in such a way that it was only understood by myself. I ascertained with satisfaction that there wasn't a single division, fort, coastal battery or airport that we had not reported on in precise detail. I was convinced that London had all the information necessary for preparing plans for the occupation of North Africa. Probably no General Staff would be able to obtain such detailed information in the future. My certainty grew that the Allied landings would be successful and, if there were no mistakes, they could occupy all of French North Africa within twenty-four hours.

Looking at the map and reflecting on our work as a whole, I felt that each mark on it had its own history. I thought about the strange good luck that seemed constantly to follow and protect me, facilitating the Agency's activities. It was particularly striking with the people to whom I owed the most. As well as being my most trusted colleagues, they were also my most loyal and closest friends.

First was Marcel Dubois, who began working with me in Marseilles in 1940; it was thanks to him that I found myself in Algiers and able to organise the Agency's work. Then, André Achiary and his successor, Lofredo, in Algiers – how valuable their co-operation had been. I had placed Jean Lacaze in a dangerous position, yet he had offered us financial help at a critical time and had then supplied invaluable information on supplies of liquid fuel in North Africa. SAOUL's information from southern Morocco was immensely valuable.

All of them, for purely idealistic reasons, were still exposing themselves to grave consequences, the danger being reinforced by the responsible positions they held. Moreover, there were also the members of our Agency, its network and their associates, all of whom had worked with dedication. They had distinguished themselves without any shadow of a doubt. There were so many that not all of them were known to me personally. I calculated that there must have been over 2,500 of them.

Sophie interrupted my thoughts.

'If you want to get up at the crack of dawn and follow events, then you ought to go to bed now! It's already very late, you know. It's way past midnight!'

That night, however, sleep was virtually impossible.

26

8 NOVEMBER 1942: OPERATION TORCH

The Allied landings on the morning of 8 November 1942, took place at coastal sites from Morocco to the Tunisian border: to be more precise, from the coastal environs of Casablanca, via the port of Oran, to the Algerian coast up to and including the port of Bône. Tunisia lay too near the Italian theatre of war, from which Axis air attacks were possible. Presumably the Allies had taken into consideration the possibility of an attack by the Italian Navy grouped in the Adriatic. In the event, there were no Allied landings on the Tunisian coast.

I hardly slept and was woken up more or less at dawn by the sound of individual gunshots. George and I went up to the roof of our house, where we had an excellent view of the bay of Algiers and the sea. A slight fog over the sea hid the horizon; the day promised to be clear and sunny. Later, it appeared that the Allies had carried out a surprise landing on the beach at Sidi Ferouche, to the west of Algiers, exactly the same place where the French Army had landed in July 1830 and then occupied Algiers. Meanwhile the fort had not fired a single shot. Troops were landing to the east of Algiers and proceeding towards the town. There, armed members of the resistance movement occupied the main Post Office building, containing the telephone exchange, and attempted to occupy other government buildings.

At the same time an Allied torpedo boat managed to enter the port, disembarked commandos and attempted to occupy it with the help of the resistance. Batteries of the Jetée du Nord in the port and from the Kouba fort opened fire. From the rooftop I saw the torpedo boat pulling away and returning fire. Surrounded by smoke, it reached the open sea safely. The French, having been alerted, mopped up the landing party, later flushing the insurgents out of the Post Office building. I saw the commandos and resistance fighters who had been taken prisoner being led up the Boulevard Laferrière, surrounded by soldiers and armed members of the SOL. In the streets crowds were shouting and gesticulating excitedly. Among them were members of the Légion and the SOL with weapons and armbands. The gunfire had ceased.

In the meantime talks were apparently going on behind the scenes between Robert Murphy and Admiral Darlan, who, as Marshal Pétain's deputy, had assumed complete control and ordered that French North Africa be defended. From the morning radio we heard about General Giraud's appeal to the French North African Army, and that an American, General Eisenhower, was its Allied Commander.

General Giraud was not a national hero. He was known in some circles as a courageous officer who, at the age of sixty-five, had recently escaped from German captivity. Most people knew him as just another general whose name did not strike any chord in their imagination. Certainly there had been no propaganda turning him into yet another saviour of France. His appeal had little significance, whereas one from de Gaulle would have been more effective. Nobody talked about him, however; obviously some political shenanigans were going on somewhere.

Ragache, still unaware that I was head of the Agency, came to see us in the afternoon with some unpleasant news. De Gaulle's followers were being arrested and mobs were destroying shops and homes. Darlan was reacting and issuing orders in Pétain's name. The leaders of the resistance had not issued any directives nor shown any initiative and its members had gone into hiding.

He came again in the evening, bringing current rumours – of battles in Casablanca and Oran and of secret talks now in progress. We listened to the BBC news; no details of the operation itself, only that the landings had taken place. I had stayed at the flat all day waiting for reports that never came. There was no more shooting and the crowds had calmed down. Nobody seemed to know what was going on. According to the latest rumours, Governor General Châtel, returning from Vichy, had landed in Constantine with an appeal to the French to 'fight and defend their honour'. Similar appeals ended with the words '*Vive le Maréchal!*' Others spoke of battles being over that had never taken place. Nothing was known for certain. Arabs arriving in Algiers spoke of the enormous strength of the Allied landings and of military equipment and vehicles being disembarked without any opposition.

There was no real change, however, and the same individuals were still in power. Later on we discovered what was happening. Admiral Darlan had signed an armistice on the night of 8/9 November. General Juin, Commander of the French Armies, ordered a ceasefire.

Operation Torch took the Axis completely by surprise. In Algiers the Armistice Commission and the staff of the German Consulate were imprisoned. The Italians, operating from the Hotel d'Angleterre on Boulevard Bugeaud, did not surrender immediately. The Americans surrounded it and, not wishing to use force, cut off their power and water supplies. The Italians were sent to a POW camp and the Americans installed their own officers' mess there instead. Such are the fortunes of war.

The Allied landings were a great success. In Casablanca the grateful French hastened to bestow the Légion d'Honneur on Colonel Solborg. This time, however, he did not bother to contact me in Algiers.

The Allied landings and Admiral Darlan's ceasefire order were reported in the press on the 9th. General Nogues disobeyed; he had received a direct order from Pétain to disregard 'the traitor Darlan' and continue fighting.

Anglo-American troops entered the town in the morning. I watched the motorised artillery and tanks from my balcony. The public went mad with joy, kissing soldiers and presenting them with flowers. The berets of the Légion and the SOL had vanished like magic. MUSTAFA and his wife arrived together with COLT, excited like us.

MUSTAFA was given three telegrams to send to Central Office:

1. Our report that Agency Africa had accomplished its task, work had been suspended, and we requested further instructions, i.e. to whom and where I should report (42/855).
2. A request for Polish decorations for our agents (42/856).
3. Informing them that General Stachiewicz was presently in Algiers (42/857).

We were in an ambivalent position. Not knowing London's intentions, I did not want to carry the can. Murphy and Eddy knew all about us, so did the British. If they should need us, they knew where to find me. I could not impose myself on them and would await instructions. Meanwhile, after two long years, it was now possible to go into the streets of Algiers without fear. I regretted that Sophie's dream could not be realised – I had left my Polish uniform in France.

Sitting in my office in the evening and looking through our material, I reflected on the Agency's current situation. It had made a substantial contribution to this first Allied victory by supplying their high command with all the necessary Intelligence. I had advised Colonel Solborg correctly that North Africa could be occupied within twenty-four hours and that French resistance would only be symbolic. What else was there to do here? I had no intention of becoming involved. Nor did I want to carry out counter-intelligence work for which the Americans and the French were better qualified.

The railway was not working. I had no contact with our Tunis, Constantine, Oran, Tlemcen, Casablanca and Agadir outposts and no idea how to bring my officers to Algiers. I assumed, correctly as it turned out, that they would find their own way there. Meanwhile, I waited for instructions from London or for some sign from Murphy's office, without which I would be reluctant to expose the Agency.

Bearing in mind that Algiers was the political centre for all of French North Africa and West Africa, the internal situation was confusing, to say the least. Before 8 November the resistance movement had united all the anti-collaborationists and opponents of the Vichy regime. The struggle was against Germany, Italy and Pétain, who personified collaborationism. De Gaulle was its standard-bearer, and it united the most disparate political elements – radicals, socialists, right-wing nationalists, royalists and communists; it encompassed Frenchmen and Jews born in Algeria and those newly arrived from Metropolitan France.

The moment the Allies occupied French North Africa, a new factor appeared on the scene – Admiral Darlan, taking the resistance leaders by surprise. All the old collaborationists were now behind him – the PSF, the Légion, the SOL and most of the high-ranking career officials. Not surprisingly, therefore, after 8 November the resistance ceased to be a link joining those of different political persuasions.

Amid this chaos, Darlan appeared to represent some kind of authority. It was hardly surprising that the Americans should speak to whoever could guarantee an end to the bloodshed, and General Mark Clark therefore signed an armistice with him. Darlan's motives were difficult to discern, but, in the event, he maintained authority until his assassination on Christmas Eve 1942. The German response to Operation Torch was to land their troops in Tunisia and occupy Vichy France on 11 November 1942. Only General de Lattre de Tassigny offered resistance at Montpellier and at Toulon French ships were scuttled.

The Allies above all wanted to maintain calm, especially with the Germans next door in Tunisia and with heavy battles still raging there. Their most urgent task was to get French North Africa to join the Allied struggle and to organise new French military forces. General Giraud was nominated by Darlan as Commander-in-Chief of the French Armed Forces in North Africa. The Americans supplied a considerable quantity of arms and equipment to this new army. Thus AFHQ only intervened in military matters.

Many patriotic Frenchmen were intensely dissatisfied when they realised that 8 November had brought no fundamental changes. The old gang, including Châtel and Nogues, were still in power. Vichy's racialist laws were not revoked. Darlan was building up and extending his control. Worse still, some of the ex-resistance people (particularly royalists) were to be found at his side, including Lemaigre-Dubreuil, Rigault and Henri d'Astier de la Vigerie. Each played his own game and awaited a suitable moment.

Under Darlan's auspices, Légion propaganda now depicted Pétain as a great patriot and as a prisoner of the Germans. Others in the resistance – socialists, radicals and Gaullists under the *Combat* banner, including Capitant, L'Hostis, Moatti and Achiary – moved into the opposite camp. Slogans directed at Darlan appeared ('Darlan to the gallows!') which were hastily removed by the police. Numerous arrests of resistance members, including many Jews, followed. Achiary, now returned to his old post in Algiers, was co-operating with the Allies, helping them to sweep German and Italian spies from Algerian territory.

The local community were mostly unaware of what was going on. General dissatisfaction was, however, increasing, especially as living conditions had deteriorated considerably after 8 November. A privileged elite with a strong currency appeared – the Allied army, which bought up nearly everything. Conditions were exacerbated by the fact that supplies were not arriving fast enough from the United States. I overheard remarks such as: 'What did we need all this for? Nothing has changed for the better. The same people are in power and we have nothing to eat!' The unruly behaviour of the American troops, later mitigated by strong military police action, did not help either.

On 24 November Darlan established his so-called Conseil Impérial, consisting of General Nogues (Resident Minister in Rabat), Boisson (Governor-General of French West Africa), Châtel (Governor-General of Algeria) and Giraud (Supreme Commander and High Commissioner). Admiral Esteva, the French Resident Minister in Tunisia, was out of the running since it was still occupied by the Germans. They formed an administration with Rigault as Secretary for Internal Affairs and the Press (i.e. censorship), d'Astier as Secretary for Police and Security Affairs, and Lemaigre-Dubreuil as Secretary of Economic and Foreign Affairs.

All this stabilised Darlan's authority, which began to cover French West Africa, and there was no mention of either de Gaulle or a republic. Allied policy vis-à-vis General de Gaulle and the Free French was difficult to understand. Within Agency Africa we were all his supporters. Roosevelt's radio speech in November, disavowing Darlan, gave the Vichyites at his side something to think about. Meanwhile, the Free French radio continued its propaganda from London. *Combat* reappeared in Algiers, attacking Darlan; its editor, fearing arrest, went underground. This situation lasted from 8 November to the end of December 1942.

Meanwhile, my own situation was becoming awkward. While awaiting orders, I instructed the Algiers, Oran and Tlemcen outposts gradually to wind up their work. Setif had closed down the moment its head, Achiary, returned to his former post in Algiers. Casablanca closed down of its own accord. Tangiers, the centre of international espionage, was left for counter-intelligence work. Constantine could not be contacted, neither could Tunis, which was in German-held territory. Only the Agadir outpost continued its activities because of the need to observe Ifni and Rio de Oro. Lofredo, our counter-intelligence head, was now helping the Americans to get rid of Axis agents.

Central Office's orders were ambiguous: to stay put 'until the action had been completed'; to report on the North African situation and await further orders (8937); also to forward lists of those to be decorated, with justifications and proposals, and the reasons why General Stachiewicz had gone to Algiers (8978).

Six messages were sent to London on 11 November requesting more precise instructions. I wanted to know what role we should assume now that the landings had taken place and where and to whom I should report. Their queries were also answered: a list of prospective awards would be sent in a mailbag; an explanation of why our hurdy-gurdy hadn't played on the 8th; General Stachiewicz had been invited to Algiers by Colonel Lapara and events had found him there (42/858–63).

On the 13th Mr Boyd invited me to his office. There I met Lieutenant-Colonel Clark, of British Intelligence, which was independent of AFHQ. This was my first and last conversation with Clark, although I subsequently supplied information to others in his outfit and it was reported to Central Office. Agency Africa's network consisted entirely of Frenchmen; only its leaders were Poles. Thus instructions to supply information on individuals collaborating with the Axis or Vichyites could result in personal scores being settled or in other vendettas. In any case, not every agent would agree to spy on his fellow Frenchman. This sort of work was not my cup of tea, even though it might be necessary. Two long reports on the internal situation were sent to London. They, in turn, asked me to send my own proposals on the Agency's future role in North Africa and the name of the Allied Intelligence Chief in Algiers, together with his ideas on the subject. Obviously Central Office had no plans nor any contact with operations in London. Feeling that there was nothing more for us to do here, I sought permission on the 14th to come to London to report on the North African situation and explain the Agency's position. They instructed me to assemble all my Intelligence Officers in Algiers and await orders.

We again began to play the role of a telegraphic agency, receiving messages from the Polish Foreign Ministry, e.g. from Minister Raczyński to Consul Friedrich in Algiers. I could, however, now reveal myself to the Polish community without any qualms. I met Father Solowiej, its spiritual leader, who later helped me considerably in my work with Polish POWs press-ganged into the Wehrmacht, and also Consul Friedrich and his staff.

Count Hutten-Czapski, the Government Delegate, informed me from Casablanca that the local Allied Command did not want to send our soldiers at the Erfoud camp to the Polish Army in England, and London was therefore asked to intervene (42/871). Central Office told us that the British would sort it out and, sure enough, by early December the entire camp found itself in Scotland.

London also told me that, at British request, Colonel Clark should be provided with counter-intelligence information, but agreed that organising our own network was undesirable. At last they acknowledged our work: 'The General Staff of the Commander-in-Chief would like to thank you and the Agency's officers and colleagues for information supplied to the British authorities, which greatly contributed to the success of the operation in North Africa (Head of the 2nd Bureau)' (9101).

I visited Jean Lacaze at Shell to thank him for his valuable co-operation. We would meet again before my departure for England, as he wanted to ask a favour.

Our two spare hurdy-gurdies (BERNARD and ANTONINA) had to be sorted out. We were now without operators and I had no idea whether we would need them. Central Office were vague as usual and suggested that we search among our soldiers, but none fancied staying behind while the others were evacuated to England. In the event, the two radios were closed down and we reverted to ADAM in Algiers.

Having no transport, I had to remain in Algiers and await instructions. Like everyone else, I greatly admired the splendid equipment of the American forces. I met many servicemen of Polish descent and our conversations were unintentionally amusing.

The 17th was full of surprises. MUSTAFA brought some Polish airmen he happened to meet on Rue Isly to see us – Major Krol, a well-known ace, and two of his officers. When Major Krol was flying to Algiers he had not been informed that a Polish Intelligence cell existed there. There was no end to their questions, while we wanted to know what was going on in London. Then, suddenly, BANULS and his wife and MISTRAL arrived from Oran in an American jeep.

This was the sort of occasion that rarely presented itself and it had to be celebrated accordingly. Among my special stores were two rare bottles of brandy, an 1831 and an 1863, only intended for exceptional circumstances.

The 1863 bottle was not going to last long. A wonderful aroma filled the air, and my airmen downed their glasses in one go. Such philistinism was heartbreaking. I hid the bottle and substituted another, which nobody noticed. All our dear guests were entertained until the morning, when black coffee was much in evidence. Major Krol, who was returning to London, took my pouch containing supplementary information for the head of our Second Bureau.

On the night of 12 November the Luftwaffe carried out its first air raid over Algiers. The port and the ships were unscathed;

only the civilian population and the town itself were affected. The sky above Algiers resembled a spider's web, thin criss-crossing fiery threads with exploding shell clouds. Streaks of light from powerful searchlights swept across the dark sky. Once caught by the intersecting beams of light, an aircraft became a sitting target for the incredibly noisy anti-aircraft guns and rarely escaped.

The daytime air raids, on the other hand, created an amazing amount of smoke. Batteries in the upper part of the town created a giant artificial smokescreen that floated downwards, completely covering the town and port. Even after the all-clear it blotted out the sun for a considerable time. These surprise inland attacks were carried out from the south, from occupied Tunisian airfields. In spite of heavy losses, the Luftwaffe persevered with them and they affected the civilian population more than the Allied troops. The air defences were powerful since in addition to the land batteries there were also the guns of the ships always anchored in the port or in the bay. Those who had experienced the London air raids agreed that they had never heard such a rate of fire even during the worst days of the Blitz. The effect here was much greater.

At 9 pm on 21 November, as we were about to sit down to supper, the air-raid siren sounded. Normally we paid no attention to it. This time our dog Arthy, who was usually calm, became very agitated. Sophie, who had a feeling of foreboding, begged us to go down to the cellar if only to quieten him. A few minutes later there was an enormous booming sound – a bomb had exploded very close to us. The house shook and plaster fell off the walls, which luckily remained standing.

Upstairs, our flat was a picture of devastation. The doors and windows were torn out of their frames, the furniture was smashed, and broken glass, splinters and plaster covered the table, which had been laid. The bomb had fallen directly in line with the wall of the house, slicing off balconies and windowsills as if guillotined, and exploded on the pavement. Had we remained upstairs we would, at the very least, have been badly injured. Minutes later, having heard that a bomb had fallen on the house at the corner of Rue Isly and Rue Chanzy, a breathless MUSTAFA came running in. After carefully locking the flat behind us, we spent the night with the MUSTAFAS. Central Office were informed that we had moved to 7 Rue Mulhouse. The flat was a write-off. After staying with them for a fortnight, we found another at 5 Rue Negrier.

Around this time there were many Polish merchant ships, including the *Batory*, *Sobieski*, *Kosciuszko* and *Lewant*, in Algiers port. We entertained the crews at our new home and were invited on board in return, which provided a very pleasant distraction.

Central Office wanted to send MISTRAL to Poland (9245). He was eager to go and, in response to my query about BANULS, I was ordered to send them both to London. The problem was that the Agency did not have any funds, nor did I have the appropriate Allied contacts in Algiers. In the event they finally left with me in December 1942.

In spite of British co-operation, it was not until 8 December that Major Tree, from Colonel Clark's outfit, came to see me and it was agreed that I should keep in touch with him. Around the same time Boyd told me that Colonel Eddy wanted to see me and I called on him. The Americans wanted me to be in charge of Intelligence in Morocco (particularly on the Spanish colonies), and to collaborate with him in Algiers and Tunisia. We laid down the principles and Eddy told me: 'We have full confidence in you. Let's say that Morocco is within our sphere of influence. Let the British look after Tunisia!'

Central Office were informed and replied by return: the Agency was to continue working, the decision to co-operate was approved and I was to await instructions (9606).

During this period I continued to receive messages from the Polish Foreign Office for their government and consular delegate in Algiers. Among them was one relating to Polish gold that was then in Dakar. Others concerned a completely different field of activity and were 'very important and urgent':

Obtain data on the Italian information service and military Intelligence (9354); extract from the publication *Guide Côtière* information re coastlines of Sardinia and Sicily (9603); Sardinia, data needed – order of battle coastal defences, airports (9608).

Hopefully, therefore, one could discern the direction that the Agency's future activities might take. Moreover, Central Office informed us that we would receive a budget advance for the first quarter of 1943 (9601) and that we should notify them of its arrival and the exchange rate.

Conditions were now far more difficult. I did not have the means to perform new tasks. I was known and constrained by the Allies and their Intelligence services, which had all the human and technical resources at their disposal. Each organisation vied with the other to obtain its own small triumph and one had to be careful not to antagonise them. This became even more apparent later on when I also began co-operating with French Intelligence.

At present I had no contact with AFHQ in Algiers, which was based at the St George Hotel, and had not received any instructions to report there. My status was therefore highly ambiguous. The Allies were particularly concerned with Tunisia, where heavy battles were raging, and had severe organisational and logistic problems. In this situation nobody would say anything about the Agency's future work without a clear order from above.

Meanwhile, co-operation with Eddy and Clark was moving slowly. My first task was to look for agents who knew Italian and could help fulfil my new orders. Anti-fascist Italians from among the North African immigrants would be ideal. The head of the Constantine outpost would try to find and recruit them – not a very easy task.

SLAV, the only missing Agency officer, turned up unexpectedly in early December. While sitting on the jetty in the port of Bône, he had been recognised by officers on board HMS *Minna*, which carried out Operation Zebra. He was taken on board and brought to Algiers. Its captain, Lieutenant MacCallum, wanted to meet me personally and SLAV brought him and his two officers along. He told me that, of all the similar operations in which his ship had been involved, Zebra was the best organised and its execution had been the swiftest. We became very friendly and entertained them at our home almost every day. In return we were invited on board. The fortunes of war intervened – the *Minna* left Algiers in June 1943 and never returned.

A meeting of the heads of the Agency was arranged for the morning of 15 December at MUSTAFA's flat. All our Intelligence Officers would be present except VINCENT (Casablanca) and the Tunis, Setif and Agadir commanders, who would be unable to attend. They would finally meet their chief at long last. I wanted to thank them for their work, inform them that they were being recommended for Polish decorations and request applications for awards to their most deserving agents. Our future role would also be discussed.

MUSTAFA would prepare wine for the end of the briefing session. I would be waiting in the next room and he would inform me when the meeting was ready to commence. I could just imagine Ragache's face when Floc-Av's commercial manager made an appearance.

Promptly at 11am MUSTAFA reported that they all had assembled. After a while I emerged from the adjoining room. As anticipated, Ragache looked bewildered. We shook hands.

'So, it's you!'

'Yes,' I said with a huge grin. 'It's me – we've known each other for a long time!'

'I'd never have guessed!'

I told them that, until I received further orders, the agency would continue its work. None of them would be discharged but, if any wished to resign, then obviously their wishes would be respected. Any information on Axis agents or collaborators should be sent to me personally as the post boxes would cease functioning as of today.

The Oran commander told us about events there on 8 November. General Bergeret had given orders for its defence and the French Admiralty ordered the port entrance to be blocked. Agent 1819 had executed his orders in such a way that a clear passage was left through which he, as a port pilot, was able to lead Allied ships into the port. According to agent 1818, during the defence of La Sénia airport, an Allied officer was temporarily taken prisoner and a plan of its defences was found on him. The airport commander told his officers that there was a traitor in their midst. The plan had, indeed, been sent to London, and it was gratifying that it had been put to good use. The Constantine commander told us that there had been no resistance there – Châtel's appeals on his return from Vichy had fallen on deaf ears.

Maurice Escoute, the commander of our Algiers outpost, asked to be relieved of his duties. His place was taken by Robert Ragache, who moved quickly into our safe house near the railway station.

I met Mr Boyd more often now and he complained about the difficulties the Allies were having with Darlan's representatives. There were no more pouches but he handed me the post from London. Mr Knox was immediately called up into the American Army and officiated at AFHQ as a Lieutenant-Colonel. Robert Murphy had become a political adviser to General Eisenhower.

The American representatives had little idea of the popular mood, and the British understood even less. The resistance movement had officially ceased to exist on 8 November. Within a short time, however, the so-called 'Association de la Libération Française du 8 Novembre 1942' had been formed, which soon swelled with imaginary 'freedom fighters' who at first enjoyed many privileges. The same was happening among us. Human nature is the same everywhere.

We often encountered Henri d'Astier de la Vigerie, now Secretary General of the Police, in the Le Paris restaurant. Our conversations were polite but short. Obviously my presence, as a foreigner who knew too much, now made me an unwelcome visitor. I continued to keep in touch with Achiary, L'Hostis and some of the others who were violently opposed to Darlan. Those close to him would like to settle old scores. Trying to maintain a semblance of neutrality and not get involved in internal political affairs was not easy. When the *Combat* people asked me to send pieces of information to de Gaulle in London, I could not refuse.

The Comte de Paris, the Pretender to the French throne, had arrived in Algiers with the help of the royalists. Forbidden to reside in Metropolitan France, he owned land in Morocco where he resided permanently with his family. The royalists' hope rested on President Roosevelt's speech that described Darlan as 'a provisional and temporary authority'. Thus, the moment he left, they would introduce someone who was not politically active, who stood above political parties and who, in their opinion, would be able to unite all patriotic Frenchmen.

Perhaps this would be feasible elsewhere. It would be unsuccessful in France with its strong republican tradition. I had no idea whether they were aware of their lack of support. The Arab question was becoming a serious problem. Central Office informed me in November that the British were unable to lay down any guidelines.

27

DEPARTURE FOR ENGLAND –
SIKORSKI'S STAFF – TIME IN LONDON

In mid-December 1942 Central Office ordered me personally to present my comprehensive report on the Agency's work. I asked Major Tree to arrange passages to London for BANULS and his wife, MISTRAL and myself. We would be sailing in the first sea convoy to Britain. I would travel as William Ramsey, a British citizen, and would be notified twenty-four hours in advance.

I prepared recommendations for awards and a report on the evacuation of our soldiers from France, which presumably London would also want to see. MUSTAFA was left in charge and given guidelines, such as not to become involved in internal French affairs or counter-espionage but to limit himself strictly to military matters; to maintain contact with Colonel Eddy and Lieutenant-Colonel A. J. Morris, who had replaced Colonel Clark; to observe any political changes and to inform me of them.

On 22 December Major Tree informed me that at 8am the following day he would drive me to the port and put me on the ship. BANULS, Marta and MISTRAL would also be there. Thus I had a whole day for my farewells, which included the staff of Floc-Av, Jean Lacaze (who gave me a letter to one of Shell's directors in London) and my remaining Intelligence Officers, with whom I had a last briefing. The rest of the day was spent with Sophie and George, whom, unfortunately, I would have to leave behind.

Major Tree collected me on the 23rd, drove me to the SS *Arundel Castle* and handed me over to the ship's captain as a VIP for whose safety he would be held personally responsible. I was installed in cabin no. 1, with a personal steward at my disposal.

The SS *Arundel Castle* was a giant passenger ship adapted as a troop carrier; its shops and bars made it resemble a small town. Exploring the decks, I bumped into MISTRAL and BANULS, who had just embarked. We were the only 'civilians' on board and Marta was the only woman. The others were British 8th Army men, including high-ranking officers going on leave for the first time. Naturally, everyone was intrigued by these civilians who ate at separate tables in the officers' mess, especially the one who occupied cabin no. 1. I described myself as 'an Englishman born overseas' (which is why I couldn't speak the language) and said I was visiting my 'mother country' for the first time. It was highly unlikely that anyone believed me, but at least it kept them quiet.

The convoy gathered all day in the enormous Bay of Algiers and manoeuvred into line for its journey to Britain. Nobody knew its size or the strength of the escorting vessels. Passing the Straits of Gibraltar on the evening of the 24th while at supper, we heard the radio announcement of Admiral Darlan's assassination. While never imagining that the problem would be solved in such a violent manner, I could guess who inspired and was morally responsible for it. I presumed that MUSTAFA's message elucidating the matter would be waiting for me in London.

The weather was favourable to the point of monotony. The voyage was without any unpleasant surprises either from the air or from U-boats, and took seven days. On 31 December we found ourselves in the Irish Sea, and well before midnight the ship docked at Greenock. Loudspeakers announced disembarkation on 1 January.

In the morning, finding myself at the end of a queue of officers, I paid no attention to the loudspeakers calling 'Mr William Ramsey' to present himself to the 'Immigration Commission' and BANULS had to point out that they were calling me. I had completely forgotten my new identity. I struggled through the queue and became their first customer. When asked for my passport, I replied: 'I have no passport. On board ship, I was referred to as Mr Ramsey. Actually

I'm a Polish Major, Mieczysław Słowikowski, and my codename in the Intelligence Service is RYGOR from Algiers.'

At this my formalities were quickly settled. When I mentioned that I was accompanied by two of my officers – Żorawski and Łubieński and his wife – they were dealt with in a similar manner. The ship's captain told us that we would have to wait until the afternoon. A special motorboat would collect us from the port.

Thinking about my forthcoming visit to Headquarters and Intelligence Central Office, I assumed that I would have to submit my report to the Chief of Staff, General Klimecki, and perhaps even to the Commander-in-Chief, General Sikorski himself. Probably the Polish Foreign Office would also want to see me to find out about the recent changes in French North Africa.

At 3pm the motorboat collected us from the ship and we left for the port, where we were welcomed with great courtesy by a British Intelligence Officer. Everything had been arranged for us – train tickets, compartment, even a cup of tea at the hotel. Being treated this way created the illusion that one had some place in the enormous war machine. Perhaps only a little cog but at any rate of some importance.

In due course we were driven to the station and settled into our compartment. The train steamed off and began hurtling through the darkness. Blackouts were compulsory and there was nothing to see, so, tired out, we began to drowse. We awoke at Euston Station on the night of 2 January 1943 and emerged on to the darkened platform, where shadowy figures were barely visible. Someone asked in Polish, 'Are you Mr RYGOR?' Coming up close, I saw a Polish uniform; an officer from the Information Corps approached us. Introductions followed, and I was taken to the Hotel Rembrandt, where a room had been reserved. BANULS and MISTRAL were driven off in a different direction.

The officer explained how I could get to the Hotel Rubens, where our staff were to be found. Work didn't begin there until 10am. After a while I was alone. I was in London! It was early, so there were a good few hours of sleep left until 10am. I hit the sack and fell asleep almost immediately.

Our Supreme Commander's Staff and National Defence Ministry were housed at the Hotel Rubens in Buckingham Palace Road, some twenty minutes away. There was a pleasant surprise and the first warm greetings. The military policeman guarding the entrance saluted and said, 'Major, how pleased I am to see you. You do not need a pass!' We had recognised each other even though I was in civvies. He had been a guard at the General Inspectorate of the Armed Forces in Warsaw, frequently on duty in the corridor near my office and the steps leading up to the first floor and to Marshal Piłsudski's private apartment.

It was 9.30am. Work began in half an hour. I sat in the waiting room. None of those arriving were known to me. The Second Bureau, or, to give its official title, the Information and Intelligence Division, was on the fourth floor. At 10am I waited for the lift. Unexpectedly, Colonel Gano, the head of the Second Bureau, stood next to me. He told me that he was happy to see me and, as we went up, I heard a few pleasant words about my work. As we left, he told me to sort out my business with JANIO and he would speak to me later.

I did not know JANIO, the Director of Intelligence, personally, but had heard that he was the best head of the German Section we ever had and was highly esteemed by the British because of his work on the German Navy. Our meeting was very cordial. He greeted me with these words:

I'm pleased to meet you. You've done splendid work! Our British hosts cannot praise you enough, which naturally helps us considerably in our relations with them. I know that you've had great difficulties in your work. You must now have a rest and sort out your personal affairs. Major Ptak, whom you probably know, will sort out the financial details with you. We'll talk about your future Intelligence work before your departure.

What could I say in reply? Naturally I was also pleased to be in London and meet my boss, about whom I'd heard so much. I thanked him for approving my work and that of my colleagues in Agency Africa. Thus our talk finished. JANIO's parting shot was to invite me to supper in the evening. I was to come to his office at 7pm.

These two conversations with my bosses were something of an anticlimax. I went down to the officers' mess, where I met a few colleagues and friends. They bombarded me with questions about where had I been and when and how I had arrived. Their curiosity had to be satisfied, if only partially. This was fine the first time but subsequently became very tiring. Some of their questions, particularly about my new assignment and whether I would be staying in London, could not be answered because I didn't know myself, which, of course, only intrigued them even more.

Being free until 7pm, I wanted to visit other acquaintants, who might be able to tell me something interesting. While meandering about on different floors, finding friends and arranging meetings, I stumbled on TUDOR (Major Zarembski), now in charge of the Soviet desk in the Studies Section. We were both delighted. He invited me to visit him at home as it would be a pleasant surprise for his wife. We arranged to see each other the following day to discuss everything.

At 7pm I met JANIO. We ate at the Ambassador Club, run by one of our counter-intelligence people, which was fairly empty. The food was good and was washed down by a considerable quantity of drink. Our conversation became increasingly friendly. JANIO touched on many extremely confidential matters and from henceforth we were on Christian-name terms. The supper dragged on since new guests were continually arriving and joining us at our table.

The next morning (3 January), JANIO, who had asked me to visit him daily, informed me that there was no news from Algiers and that Major Ptak would sort out my ration card, clothing coupons and finance. Over lunch he told me that I had been allocated a nice room in the Green Park Hotel in Half Moon Street, off Piccadilly, which was quite near the Rubens. Since I was a complete stranger in London, it seemed a good idea.

My sojourn in London was limited to the area around Victoria Station, Piccadilly and High Street, Kensington. Once, while delivering Lacaze's letter to the Chairman of Shell, I ventured into the City, where, being invited to lunch to give an account of the economic situation in North Africa, I had to work for my keep.

Although wartime scars were visible everywhere, the bombing itself made little impact on me. Perhaps it was because the city was so huge, and when the air-raid sirens sounded one never knew which part was under attack. I also became acquainted with London's fogs, which, coupled with the blackout, bound me to the solitude of my hotel room for many a lonely evening. My inadequate knowledge of English made contact with Londoners difficult. Nevertheless, they made a great impression on me as a foreigner. In spite of the enormous destruction, life went on. Trains, buses and the Tube functioned normally, and the morning pint of milk was still delivered. On many partly destroyed shops and offices the 'business as usual' sign indicated that it would be difficult to break British morale. Only the newsreels of 'Uncle Joe Stalin' (which brought loud applause from the audience) irritated me, and I began avoiding cinemas.

Having nothing else to do, I explored the neighbouring streets. The rest of the day was spent wandering around the corridors of the Hotel Rubens and its officers' mess, where I could meet someone to talk to. Otherwise I was left entirely to my own devices and had no idea why I had been brought to London. Virtually nobody at the Polish Army headquarters exhibited any interest, apart from a personal one, in my activities in French North Africa. Nobody was interested in seeing my written reports on our work in France or the names of its participants and their achievements.

Reconciling myself to my fate, I put my papers back into my case and began joining in the political discussions taking place. They mostly concerned General Sikorski's policy of 'minimum friction with our Soviet ally', and his alleged blind faith in British and American goodwill, and whether it went against Polish interests. The most bitter concerned the Russo-Polish Pact, which Sikorski had signed, presumably under British pressure, after Hitler's invasion of the USSR in June 1941. This involved an 'amnesty' for Polish troops taken prisoner by Stalin in 1939 when he was Hitler's ally. It reached its climax in February 1943 when, in a special issue, the Polish army newspaper *Walka* published an open letter to the President asking him to dismiss Sikorski because his 'subservient and defeatist attitudes were leading Poland to disaster'.

One day I met Roman Czerniawski (WALENTY, ARMAND) and he told me about his activities after TUDOR had sent him to Paris with his agent 'La Chatte'. After the collapse of his network and his arrest, he managed to escape from the Gestapo and, after many adventures, managed to reach Britain through Spain and Portugal.

TUDOR, whom I met frequently, described the reasons behind the Paris cave-in and his own escape from the south of France. It appeared that Czerniawski had finally become independent of TUDOR's Marseilles network when he received his own hurdy-gurdy and was placed under JANIO's direct control from London. In October 1941, he was brought to Britain for organisational discussions but was caught by the Germans while parachuting back into France. In the arrests that followed, 'La Chatte' assisted the Gestapo. TUDOR was informed by the radio operator, who managed to escape, that the Germans knew everything. Winding up his headquarters at Mimosa in Marseilles, he went into hiding at a villa in Aloche. From then onwards the leadership of Agency TUDOR changed hands. Romeyko, and then Sliwiński, headed it before it was wound up.

Some time after TUDOR's flight to Britain, he was contacted by Czerniawski, who had just arrived from Portugal. TUDOR then disclosed to me, in great secrecy, that Czerniawski had confided to him that he had been 'turned', and that he had agreed to become a German agent (codename BRUTUS), in return for the lives of his arrested French agents and his mother. Much later it was revealed that he became a double agent, working for the British in their 'double-cross system'.

TUDOR elaborated General Sikorski's policies towards the USSR, while Stalin was still insisting on the Curzon Line. The Allies wanted the Poles, at all costs, to come to an agreement with Moscow. The Red Army was bearing the brunt of the fighting and was more important to the British than the London Poles.

From my conversations with TUDOR and others, I also gathered that our Central Office and the General Staff as a whole were not fundamentally interested in Agency Africa's work. In their opinion, Central Office merely acted as a supplier of translated material to British Intelligence. It was the British, through our Central Office translators, who passed their Intelligence assignments on to me in Algiers.

28

CHURCHILL'S REPORT – AN EYE-OPENER –
THE FINAL DECISION

The 5th of January 1943 was a day full of surprises. Somehow I had arrived later than usual at the Hotel Rubens. JANIO said that the British wanted to have a chat with me. I should report immediately to Commander Dunderdale (codename WILSKI), British Intelligence's chief liaison officer with our section, who awaited me in his office. One of our young officers took me there. Turning left at the hotel exit, it was only a few minutes' walk along Buckingham Palace Road.

Commander Dunderdale received me at once and ordered an officer to assemble all his personnel. Meanwhile, in perfect Russian, he expressed his pleasure at being able to meet me in person. Praising my work highly, he said that the head of the British Secret Intelligence Service was recommending me to the War Office for a high British decoration.

After a while the room began to fill up with army and naval officers who, presumably, were in some way involved with the activities of Agency Africa and in the preparation of Operation Torch. Commander Dunderdale said, 'Gentlemen! I am privileged to introduce Mr RYGOR, whose work is very familiar to you.' (This was followed by applause.) He then introduced the officers individually. His welcome made me speechless, especially after my lukewarm reception at the Rubens. After a short while the officers left and I was alone with their chief.

Dunderdale said:

Sir, you were brought to London at the insistence of General

Menzies, the head of the British Secret Service, who wishes to have your report on the internal situation in French North Africa. Our officers there lack your experience in these matters, and most of their estimates are obviously second-hand.

He expressed his confidence in my judgement and added that the General would like to have my appreciation of the situation there. This would be used in his next report to the Prime Minister, who needed it prior to his conference with President Roosevelt, which would take place somewhere this month and would include a discussion of the North African problem. As time was short, we should get down to work. He called his secretary, who took down in shorthand his English translation of my verbal report in Russian. It encompassed, among other matters:

1. A general outline of internal politics in French North Africa prior to the Allied landings on 8 November 1942.
2. The development of the internal political situation after the landings and the role played by Darlan and other French leaders.
3. The orientation and actions of political parties and movements, namely 'la resistance' and Combat.
4. The background to Darlan's assassination on 24 December 1942, and an account of the French royalist party.

I also answered Dunderdale's questions concerning various French personalities. Finally, my own opinion was expressed and the names of several prominent Frenchmen suggested for influential positions. I emphasised that this should be treated as an interim period until power in French North Africa was turned over to the Free French under de Gaulle's undisputed leadership. My report was derived from the information collected by our Agency and represented a cross-section of opinion.

Our conversation was interrupted by a telephone call from General Menzies, inquiring whether the report was ready. Dunderdale assured him that it would be ready in less than half an hour and that, in his opinion, it was interesting, penetrating and clear-sighted.

A short while later our prolonged chat ended. The verbal report was ready. Dunderdale asked me to prepare a written memorandum on our conversation as soon as possible. I knew that he was pressed for time; nevertheless he did not want our meeting to terminate abruptly. He promised to show me, in the near future, the huge map of North Africa hanging at the War Office with all my Intelligence information marked on it from which Operation Torch was planned. This inevitably reminded me of Colonel Solborg's description of his own visit there. Dunderdale escorted me to the door. Shaking my hand, he added, 'I'm sorry that you are not British – for what you have done for Britain, you wouldn't have to work again for the rest of your life!'

I left in a daze. The contrast between the importance attached to our work by the British and the sheer indifference shown by our General Staff was staggering. Quite obviously Central Office had nothing to do with the decision to bring me to London. It was the British, not the Poles, who were interested in someone capable of helping prepare Churchill's meeting with Roosevelt. It proved that Central Office were only acting as translators and postmen for Agency Africa's messages, which went to General Menzies, and they had not even bothered to analyse my reports. Ironically, although the Poles were instrumental in bringing about Torch, they knew nothing about its planning whatsoever.

The implications of Commander Dunderdale's remarks were sinking in. I had never thought of myself as a British agent but had fondly imagined that I was working for the Polish General Staff. JANIO would have some explaining to do. Preoccupied with my thoughts, I missed the hotel and found myself outside a small cinema. Distracted, I entered, unaware that it showed mainly newsreels, and those from the Eastern Front. The audience were enthusiastically applauding the shots of 'Uncle Joe'. I left, in an even more confused state, and returned to my hotel room to brood in solitude.

I had more than sufficient time at my disposal to grill JANIO for an explanation of our relationship with our British hosts. While he skilfully wove his way round the questions, I pinned him down on my secret report detailing my discussions with Colonel Solborg. He had read it but had, at the time, dismissed it as 'an unauthorised venture into grand strategy'. He admitted that Operation Torch had developed in an identical way and that he had been wrong to destroy it. He added: 'The Polish General Staff are not interested in the existence of Agency Africa. It neither occupies itself with operational matters nor has it been advised on them by the Anglo-American Joint Chiefs of Staff. Furthermore, it hasn't asked about them.'

This was a clear and unambiguous reply; everything had been answered; only the British and the Americans were interested in my work. Our Foreign Office were not much better either. Despite my continual memoranda, they had no conception of the political situation in Algiers. As late as April 1943, we received a message from Count Raczyński's office stating: 'Do not link yourselves with de Gaulle. The Commander-in-Chief backs General Giraud.'

My visit to London was very disillusioning. At least the witch-hunt for those responsible for the Polish debacle in 1939 had been abandoned. Possibly this was due to the realisation that the French had suffered an even greater defeat. In the event, thousands of files, collected with such fervour in our Paris days, now lay, thankfully, forgotten.

I felt uneasy and began keeping to my hotel room. My protracted stay was unexpected. I was sick of doing nothing, especially as it seemed that my mission was accomplished. I missed the excitement and the nervous tension. I longed to return to the African sun, to my friends, to the service and, above all, to my family. The delay was blamed on obtaining permission from General Giraud. The French were now in the saddle and apparently had no further need for the Poles in North Africa. The new 'official' agency would take much longer to form than the secret one.

One good thing, however, was my growing friendship with JANIO. He appeared to be alone. Possibly he had a wife somewhere in Poland but he did not tell me and I did not ask. His solitude reminded me of MACIEJ (Ciężki), but his lack of friends among the Rubens staff remained a mystery. Gradually a picture of him emerged.

Janio never refused anyone a favour. Typically, he once told me, 'Any person may become useful one day – you never know who and when!' Coming from Polish peasant stock, he was as cunning as he was shrewd. Well-educated, he had fought for Poland's freedom since his youth. Somehow he had become entangled in Intelligence and, quite instinctively, became one of its best proponents.

Before the war he had run an agency on North and Central Germany from the Polish town of Bydgoszcz and his achievements were extraordinary. The separation of East Prussia from the rest of Germany forced the Germans to come to an agreement by which they could send passenger and freight trains through the Polish Corridor. Janio's men had come to a financial arrangement with some Germans whereby a Polish expert was 'allowed' on to their train at the first station in Polish territory. He opened certain letters and even shipments of Wehrmacht weaponry, photographed them, then left at the last stop before the border crossing. These operations provided much valuable information.

After the Polish defeat in 1939 Janio made his way to France, where he obtained valuable information on the German navy from his prewar agents whom he had planted in various *Kriegsmarine* garrisons and naval bases on the Baltic and the North Sea. With the fall of France he came to Britain, where the Polish Army was being rebuilt under British auspices. The British soon remembered that he was responsible for their information on German battleships and were eager to co-operate with him again.

Janio confided to me that he was in trouble. He was receiving anonymous letters containing threats and slanderous accusations concerning his alleged pro-German sympathies, and even allegations of treason. He was duly interviewed by the Military Prosecutor and cleared of any suspicion. The two letter-writers, former Intelligence Officers who had been removed from their posts at the Rubens, were exposed, arrested and sentenced to a term of confinement. Later, Janio, not wishing the gossip to continue, asked to be relieved of his duties and to be sent to the front. He was killed at Monte Cassino in 1944.

Meanwhile, Mustafa began sending reports from Algiers on

the new situation created by Darlan's assassination. Arrests of republicans and radicals (including André Achiary) had taken place, while Robert Murphy was entertaining the Comte de Paris, the Pretender to the French throne. Other messages reported Governor Châtel's replacement by Peyrouton, who had been tipped in my report; General Nogues had gone into self-exile in Portugal. MUSTAFA was instructed to approach Murphy with our information on North African personalities, which may have had a hand in Achiary's release. This was reported on 19 January, together with the arrest of Henri d'Astier, Giraud's Minister of the Interior.

There were two important items in the first pouch from Algiers. One was a detailed description of Darlan's assassination on Christmas Eve by a twenty-year-old monarchist, Olivier Bonnier de la Chapelle, the son of the editor of the local evening newspaper, *Les Dernières Nouvelles*, and a member of the Chantiers de la Jeunesse. The second was an assassination attempt on myself some twelve hours later by an unknown sniper.

Apparently the shot was fired from the Government building opposite our house in the Rue Berthezène into our ground-floor flat, and passed an inch from SLAV's head. He was sitting near the table with Sophie, George and COLT with his back to the window and, having replenished the glasses, was in the act of reclining in his chair when the shot rang out. Since SLAV was frequently mistaken for me, and my London trip had been secret, I was the obvious target. The Allied Military Police were alerted; Achiary came immediately and discovered that the bullet was of French make. The investigation led nowhere. It was obvious that the instigator had tried to get rid of someone who knew too much about him.

On 29 January MUSTAFA reported the sad news that our flat had been destroyed in an air raid. Sophie and George were safe but SLAV, who occupied the second-floor flat, was seriously injured and was in hospital.

JANIO's disclosure that my return to Africa depended on General Giraud's agreement reminded me that, when preparing my trip to London, I had collected evidence of patriotic Frenchmen working for their country via Agency Africa, and that their names should be submitted to the Free French. However, JANIO informed me that Free French–Polish relations were 'very cool' (to put it mildly) and, since the Allied landings in North Africa, de Gaulle had almost severed them completely. He even advised me against visiting the French General Staff while in London, since our authorities would certainly frown on it. He explained that Sikorski was always on Churchill's side when it came to a dispute with de Gaulle, who very wisely always put the interests of the Free French first.

I now discovered that the names of Agency Africa's agents admitted to our service and reported to Central Office were not disclosed to the Free French authorities – only to British Intelligence. I immediately protested to the Polish Second Bureau that I had unwittingly inherited a situation with which I did not wish to become associated. In fact, I became the scapegoat and, on my return to Africa, was exposed in my new work to difficulties created by disappointed French patriots who, quite honestly, were fully justified. I now realised that the chosen sentences demanded by my French agents as proof that their work was known to the Free French and transmitted by the BBC were nothing but an elaborate and cynical confidence trick.

It continued to trouble me. The French Algerian authorities did not reply to any of my communications in which I tried to put the record straight. Finally, on 8 August, I managed to contact Major Pelabon, the technical director of Jacques Soustelle's Special Service in Algiers, with a complete list of my main French colleagues working for the Free French.

This was not, however, the end of my humiliating experiences. When it came to the greatly deserved Polish decorations, Gano agreed to issue only eleven Crosses of Merit out of my proposed ninety. This pusillanimity contrasted strikingly with the lavish treatment received by Agency TUDOR.

Later, in fact just after the war, it became common knowledge that Gano had friendly and business relations with some of Agency TUDOR's officers. They formed a company ostensibly to explore and exploit minerals in the High Atlas in Morocco. Rumour has it that they were searching for gold. They found nothing and Gano died at the home of one of them. Had they asked my advice, they could have saved themselves considerable trouble. If there was any gold in Morocco, I would have known about it. Nevertheless, it was clear that the plethora of decorations lavished on Agency TUDOR was an example of back-slapping (or rather chest-slapping) among old pals.

At last JANIO informed me of Gano's decision. The Agency would continue; they wanted me to return to Africa and begin new work. Gano had talks with the British, who raised no objections, providing the French agreed. MUSTAFA's latest radio messages revealed that our old friend Colonel Rivet had become Chief of French Intelligence, and it was his permission that would have to be obtained. Anticipating a favourable response, my colleagues in Algiers were advised to search for accommodation for our new Agency, which would now become official.

Meanwhile, Gano and I participated in several working lunches with highly placed British and French people at the Dorchester Hotel. The discussions related to my anticipated work and the current political situation. Among the confidential gossip was an inquest on the Casablanca Conference and the dispute between Giraud and de Gaulle, who had both participated.

At last a reply from Algiers – General Giraud's staff had agreed to Agency Africa. On 21 February 1943, after a briefing at Central Office on the Agency's future work, my departure was finalised. This time, unfortunately, Łubieński would not be accompanying me to Algiers as he was being retained at Central Office. Later he was sent to our Madrid Embassy as press attaché, a post ridiculously inadequate to his talent and to his proven ability.

In the event I was given a service-type passport, a British exit permit and a financial allocation. I was also offered an unusual luxury – a deputy. Not knowing any of those whose names were suggested, I agreed to Captain Lucjan Jagodziński, formerly in our service in Germany. We would be flying with the Americans. This time Central Office had done their best. The rest was up to me.

29

ALGIERS, THE TEMPORARY CAPITAL OF FRANCE – GENERAL DONOVAN

Algiers had become the provisional capital of Free France. De Gaulle's arrival was awaited and in the meantime power rested in the hands of Giraud and his provisional government. Giraud was neither a statesman nor a politician and those who pinned their hopes on him were disappointed. As a leader, he was an artificial creation, virtually unknown to the local French and unaware that their loyalties lay elsewhere.

Politically, little had changed. The Gaullist faction Combat were still demanding radical changes and issuing inflammatory leaflets. The Allies, on the other hand, were content with the situation and increased their representation. Macmillan represented the British; Morawski became Polish Ambassador with Major Dziewanowski as our Military Attaché.

Membership of this big happy diplomatic family was swollen further with the arrival of a huge Soviet delegation headed by Comrade Bogomolov, an old hand at the game who had once been Ambassador to Poland. The Russians had no existing interests in French North Africa, and the sheer size of the Russian circus indicated only one thing – subversive work among the Arabs. Soon the first flowers appeared. At the end of Ramadan they hired the Aletti Hotel and organised a 'celebration' where Soviet Moslems addressed their Algerian counterparts in comradely Arabic. Achiary was alerted to the new danger to France and was advised to monitor the local communist party's contacts with the Bogomolov faction and their propaganda among the Arabs.

General de Gaulle's advent to power led to little improvement and he began with a series of errors. Having a grudge against Roosevelt and Churchill, he was now turning towards Stalin and, while the other Allies were preoccupied, the Russians were grabbing their chances. Achiary did not fully understand my fears for the future and appeared to be over-optimistic.

The French generally were disillusioned by the Allied occupation. Algeria not only had to feed itself but had to assist in feeding the Allies as well. It became hard to buy anything, even on the black market. Fortunately Captain Jagodziński came to the rescue by finding a 'restaurant' where one could get a decent meal. Actually it was a small abandoned shop in the Rue du Tanger, hidden from the street by tired curtains ornamenting a dusty window. Inside, some of the customers sat behind a long counter facing a row of four tables pressed against the opposite wall. The tables had tablecloths. Those behind the counter ate without any bourgeois niceties. At the end of the shop was a kitchen with a large table in the middle where food was prepared, and which served the most favoured clients.

Strangely, the more austere the culinary conditions of her customers, the more highly they were thought of by the proprietress-cum-cook. Randolph Churchill and Hutten-Czapski, who clung to the kitchen table, were the elite. We Poles behind the counter were second-class and, sadly, the French seemed to come last. This bizarre hierarchical order was the brainchild of Auntie Brass, a short, plump Dutch woman of indeterminate age with ginger hair, a round owl-like face and a sharp nose, who was an incredibly good cook. Her existence consisted of running the 'restaurant', and making the life of her sister, who served as a waitress and unpaid informer, as miserable as possible. Nevertheless, we always had a good time there.

Once, during a very late dinner, an embarrassed Auntie Brass sought my assistance. Randolph Churchill was in her kitchen; he had had a few drinks too many and was requiring more. She therefore proposed that he be demoted forthwith to a place with us behind the counter. We obliged and, without any further ado,

Randolph was not only among us but had been invited back to our flat for a drink. It turned out to be very friendly and amusing. As it was far too late for him to return to his quarters, we put him up in our guest room.

In the morning, over a hearty breakfast, I disclosed to him the purpose of our sojourn in North Africa. He, in turn, told me that his father was sending him to see Tito in Yugoslavia. As this was after the Allied landings in Italy, it gave me a sudden shock. North Africa, Italy and now the Balkans – all the pieces were falling together. Solborg's words came to mind, 'Our talk will bear all the fruit we desire.' Churchill and I met sometimes at the restaurant, but one day he disappeared and I never saw him again.

Some time after my return from London I met Colonel Eddy and Mr Boyd at Murphy's old office. Eddy, who was now stationed in Algiers, frequently visited us and was very interested in my work. He admitted that he had followed it very closely from my reports and made no secret of the fact that he was the one who sealed my pouches before they were sent to Lisbon. The only reports he missed were those in Polish. He loved *objets d'art*, and his most frequent refrain was 'How much?' He was always urging us to sell him some old pieces of family jewellery, which Sophie carried around with her as our last security.

At that time I was planning our expansion in Italy and becoming interested in the prisoners of war in Tunisia. Among them were Poles press-ganged into the Wehrmacht. My plan was to separate them from the Germans and then pump them for information. Eddy was responsible for clearing French North Africa of hostile elements. We collaborated with each other and he used my network. Later he was transferred to the Lebanon.

Several reports were despatched urgently to Central Office, together with the Polish Military Attaché's post, presumably to be handed over to the British as usual. Among them was information collected by Ragache on Darlan's assassination, and a clandestine letter written by Bonnier de la Chapelle to his parents on the eve of his execution and smuggled out of his death cell. Reading it made one feel pity for the naive young assassin who put his faith in the unscrupulous leader of the royalist plot. Bonnier assured them that their action had been well planned and that he would not be shot. Their leader, who was in a position to organise everything, had promised him that in the event of his arrest he would face a court-martial and a mock execution would follow. A doctor would testify that he was dead, he would have a mock funeral, and then return later as a hero. The plan was adhered to with one exception – the execution was a real one.

This clandestine letter explained Bonnier's happy-go-lucky attitude during his short trial, in which he accepted total responsibility. He implicated nobody – it was all for France – and he died because it was intended for him to die. I was certain that, knowing too much, I had also been chosen to share Darlan's and Bonnier's sudden demise. Strangely enough, I had a presentiment that I might be repaid in this way.

Maison Blanche airport now became an important staging-post for the Allies. It gave me the opportunity to meet General Sikorski and his Chief of Staff, General Klimecki, before their tragic deaths in Gibraltar on 4 July 1943. After Sikorski's death, I entertained our new Commander-in-Chief, General Sosnkowski, en route to Italy to inspect the 2nd Polish Corps at Monte Cassino.

My good friend Colonel Leopold Okulicki also passed through Algiers after being recalled from the Italian front. We discussed our common acquaintance, Zygmunt Berling, who, refusing the 'amnesty', had remained in Russia and had recently been promoted to General by Stalin. Okulicki told me that the NKVD officer releasing him had said, 'You are lucky to have escaped from our hands. If we catch you a second time you won't come out alive!'

The next time I met him was in 1944. He was now General Okulicki and was awaiting his plane to Italy and a parachute jump into Poland to take command of the underground Home Army. As we embraced each other he said, 'I know what is awaiting me. We shall not see each other again. That is my fate!' His words were tragically prophetic. Arrested by the Russians, together with seventeen other Poles, he was eventually placed on trial in Moscow and sentenced.

During early June 1943, Colonel Eddy told me that his boss, General Bill Donovan, head of the OSS, had come to Algiers. Knowing our Agency's work, he wanted to see me, and I was invited to a reception that the Americans were arranging for him.

Donovan was very polite. He invited me to sit next to him and began by expressing his admiration for our organisation, which reminded me of Solborg's remarks the previous year. I was then asked about aspects of the political situation in Algiers and the French and Arab attitude towards the war. He seemed, however, mainly interested in ways of preventing a third world war. In his opinion, Europe was the cause of the trouble, which, he confessed, was still an unknown quantity to many Americans.

I ventured to suggest that, apart from anything else, many of the problems were the result of American isolationism, the economic motive behind American foreign policy and the failure of the League of Nations. Radical changes would be required to prevent a future war. Among them, Europe ought to be reorganised on the lines of the United States with some sort of federal government. The colonies should be liberated, including those of the Soviet Empire, since the Soviets were aiming at world hegemony and the imposition of their system.

Donovan interjected: 'But with whom then would the United States trade?' I replied that it might prove more profitable to trade with the newly liberated nations.

'You may be right but it would take time, and there would be great difficulties.'

'Yes, I know, but that doesn't mean that we shouldn't try.'

Colonel Eddy, who had been listening attentively, cut in: 'The Poles are already working for a third world war. They do not want to come to terms with their Eastern neighbours!'

I replied: 'You will see for yourself, Colonel. The next war is being prepared by you, not by me!'

Eddy was about to reply but Donovan interjected: 'It's not as simple as you think, Colonel!' The others agreed with him.

After the reception, he took me to one side and said with a friendly smile, 'You should join our service, Major. We need people like you.' I told Donovan that I was honoured but, for the moment, I was still fighting for my country.

When we met again in 1944 I asked him, 'Do you know the terms of the agreement reached between Roosevelt, Churchill and Stalin at the Teheran Conference? It is well known that the Germans, via Radio Wanda, have been broadcasting to our troops at Monte Cassino telling them not to fight for the Allies who sold Poland to Stalin at Teheran.'

Donovan said that he was not personally present at Teheran, but considered that it was German propaganda to demoralise our troops. Later it was disclosed to me that the information broadcast to the Polish troops at the front was true. German Intelligence had received detailed information on the Teheran Agreement from their agent 'Cicero', the trusted valet of the British Ambassador to Turkey.

30

THE END OF AGENCY AFRICA

The rest of my story is something of an anticlimax. On my return to Algiers, my first task was to inform Central Office of our future work. According to my orders received in London, I was expected to start Intelligence work in Italy and continue co-operation with the Allies in North Africa. The conditions and possibilities of our work were forwarded to Central Office in a secret report dated 2 March 1943.

The possibilities of work in Italy were very slim. Regarding North Africa, in accordance with my discussion with Colonel Eddy and at his request, the Constantine, Oran, Algiers and Moroccan outposts continued, the number of agents being reduced to a minimum. Their tasks were counter-intelligence, anti-sabotage and internal political information on public opinion and the local administration. These reports were transferred directly to Colonel Eddy at G-3.

The interrogation of prisoners of war of Polish nationality who had been captured in Tunisia provided an important source of primary material. The information obtained was sent to Central Office; my officers translated these reports into English for Brigadier Strong in Britain and Colonel Eddy, and into French for Colonel Rivet.

The work of our outposts in North Africa was very sensitive in relation to the Allies and our French hosts. It was limited to the minimum in order not to compromise our good relations with them. Some of our agents had to be leased to Colonel Eddy without offending the British. Because of the lack of a relevant order from

Washington or London establishing the relationship of the Agency with the local Allied military authorities, we found ourselves in a very difficult position. I was forced to horse-trade my reports and our agents' services for American favours, such as petrol for our cars, to keep the agency going. The lack of an official stamp upon our activities produced a situation whereby several of our agents preferred to join the American and British services, where their work was more appreciated.

Our POW work was greatly assisted by the aid furnished by Hutten-Czapski and Father Solowiej. The latter proved invaluable in obtaining access to the prisoners, since, in the early months following the landings, we were not given any official recognition by Allied HQ. This situation, mentioned previously, arose from the impotence of our Central Office. Colonel Sloane, acting on General Eisenhower's direct orders, refused to allow us passes to the POW camps.

Nevertheless the information that we managed to obtain from the POWs was so valuable that Colonel Sharp of G-2 arranged a meeting with General Bedell Smith, Eisenhower's Chief of Staff. As my English was poor, I took Lieutenant Piotrowski (COLT), who was fluent in English and French, as my interpreter. General Bedell Smith was already acquainted with our work and I convinced him of the necessity to interrogate the Poles immediately they were taken prisoner. By doing so, we would be able to obtain the enemy's disposition at any given time, which would be of immense value.

The material extracted was incredibly rich and varied – not only from the front but also from the territories under Nazi rule. We obtained details of Hitler's Atlantic Wall fortifications and those in Italy, armament dumps, army stores and food and clothing supplies, including those intended for the Eastern Front.

There were thousands of items, which were sifted, compared and assembled into concise reports with maps and plans. When one considers that the work was performed by only ten officers, the results were extraordinary. As a result, I became very friendly with Colonel A. J. Morris of British Intelligence's Interservice Liaison Dept (ISLD), who was a very pleasant change from his predecessor.

He told me that the authorities in Cairo were very interested in our work on the Polish POWs and, in fact, they sent a high-powered representative to Algiers to discuss it with us.

Despite our partial recognition, we were not allowed to work with the Allied armies on the Sicily front, and I approached General Patton, the Commander of the 7th Army, directly. Colonel Sharp, who again offered me his help, flew to Sicily on 19 August to enlist Patton's support. This was eventually obtained, and I was able to inform London that a conference with Lieutenant-Colonel MacMillan, the head of CSDIC (the Combined Services Detailed Interrogation Centre), would be held on 22 September. This became possible only because of the direct intervention of General Bill Donovan, whom I had met earlier (see Chapter 29). The meeting with MacMillan was a success. We would collaborate directly on the interrogation of prisoners but at the same time keep our freedom of action in Intelligence matters, particularly in Italy. The Agency was admitted to CSDIC, a cell of the Army Chief of Staff and G-2, quite an achievement considering Eisenhower's coolness towards us.

We now organised our Italian outposts – two groups of officers attached to the British 8th and American 5th Armies. Majors Tafelski and Jagodziński were the commanders; Captain Kokorniak with 2nd Lieutenants George Malcher, George Rieger, Majewicz (SLAV) and Wadowski were the officers. They were undoubtedly the source of very important and up-to-date information on the enemy's disposition.

With the arrival of the Polish 2nd Corps in Italy, our outposts were transferred to their Intelligence Department. Obviously, as the number of Polish prisoners dwindled, our work would come to a natural end. Nevertheless, a good start had been made, based on the elementary psychological fact that once an individual is approached by a compatriot, many things become possible. Similar cells were created and operated successfully after the invasion of France in 1944. My personal contacts also paid off. Although having very little real authority, I was frequently asked by Eddy or Rivet to intervene in some backbiting incident among the Allies. As a neutral party, my role could be said to have been useful right up to the end.

Well after my first visit to London, news arrived via our Embassy that eight Crosses of Merit were being awarded to my French agents and to Lieutenant Rombejko (MUSTAFA). They were well below the number requested, and without citations. To make matters worse, the Gold Cross of Merit was not awarded to Ragache, who thoroughly deserved it. Only after my continual demands did Gano agree to issue three more Silver Crosses, which were also without citations. I tried to cover up this premeditated snub by having the missing citations issued by our Algiers Embassy and sealed officially. We had a little ceremony of our own. The ten Crosses had to go a long way, as everyone deserved a medal.

I had finished my job. The Allies were well advanced into Italy and our Intelligence outposts for the interrogation of prisoners were now operating under the auspices of the Polish 2nd Corps. During my second trip to London in February 1944, to receive my OBE, the question of terminating our activities had already been raised. Since my return to Algiers in March 1944, contacts with agents were curtailed and our work in Morocco and Tangiers had ceased. It was agreed with Central Office that Major Adam Świtkowski would be sent to Algiers as Polish Intelligence's representative at Allied HQ.

Our Military Attaché handed me the liquidating instructions, signed by Major Ptak and dated 7 August 1944. On 1 September 1944, exactly five years after Hitler's attack on Poland, it came into effect. My departure from Algiers was set for 8 September 1944. I was sorry to leave North Africa but was physically and mentally exhausted. Five years of living on one's nerves were enough for anyone, and I badly needed a rest.

Just before leaving, my friend John Boyd, the American Vice-Consul in Algiers, sent me a letter, which I cherish. He wrote: 'When I look back upon the dark days of 1941–2 in North Africa when it was hard to tell who were friends and who were our enemies, to me you were a ray of sunshine in the delicate work you were performing under such trying circumstances.'

On my arrival in Britain, I reported to our HQ at the Hotel Rubens. From previous discussions with my former chief, I gathered that there was no place for me in the Polish Second Bureau. I was too tired to worry about it. After a holiday, I was posted to Crieff as Chief of Staff of the Infantry Training Centre, where I began writing these memoirs. I liked Scotland very much.

EPILOGUE

Nearly seventy years have elapsed since the Allies landed in French North Africa. When Churchill heard on 8 November 1942 that the invasion had been successful, he ordered the church bells to be rung. At the time the British and the Americans regarded it as the first great victory over Nazi Germany, turning the tide in the Allies' favour.

Stalin had wanted a second front in Western Europe. The Red Army, recovering from the unexpected German attack in 1941, was still suffering heavy losses at Stalingrad and elsewhere. In reply to Stalin's continual demands, Roosevelt promised a second front in Europe in 1942.

As Churchill makes clear, the American representatives, General Marshall and Admiral King, arrived in London for a conference in July 1942, bringing with them the 'Sledgehammer' plan for a second front in Europe, which was opposed by the British. During these Anglo-American staff talks, Roosevelt, replying to General Marshall's telegram on 24 July 1942, suddenly gave instructions for the Chiefs of Staff to prepare a completely new plan for an occupation of French North Africa with General Eisenhower, an American, as its commander. Why did Roosevelt suddenly change his mind? Which of his advisers was the most influential?

Could it have been Colonel Solborg, who toured Western Europe and North Africa as an OSS representative? He was delighted by our conversation on 15 June 1942, and left immediately for Washington. Churchill said of Roosevelt's memorandum for Torch:

'He outlined for the delegation the strongest and most illustrious document of wartime politics I have ever seen him do.' Could our conversation, repeated in Washington, have been influential in changing Roosevelt's mind? It was a strange coincidence that many of its points were repeated in the memorandum.

Churchill also relates his talks with Stalin on 12 and 13 August 1942, concerning the second front, at which he introduced the plan to occupy French North Africa. One would assume that Stalin was displeased with this further postponement of a landing in Europe but, much to Churchill's surprise, he agreed. Stalin had not told Churchill his own plans. When, however, the Allies later occupied southern Italy, he demanded at Teheran that Eastern Europe was to remain a Soviet operational zone. Almost half of Europe was handed over to Stalin with only the flimsiest 'conditions' attached, then confirmed at Yalta.

What was the effect of the Allied occupation of North Africa? The military and political benefits were enormous. Firstly, the Germans lost an enormous number of men whom they later needed for the Italian campaign. Egypt and Suez were no longer threatened; the route to India and the Far East was safe; the Mediterranean was again open to Allied shipping; Turkey and Persia were safeguarded, as was the Arabian peninsula. True, the Germans occupied the rest of France but the French fleet had been scuttled and de Gaulle was organising a new army in Algiers with American assistance.

In Allied hands, North Africa became a bridgehead from which attacks could be launched in any direction, posing a threat to Italy and Germany in the Balkans. Moreover, its air bases not only provided cover for the sea convoys but facilitated aerial attacks against Italy and southern Germany. It was also a great moral victory, proving to the world that Hitler could be defeated. The Allies were right to proclaim it as a great victory.

The Allies knew about the increasing German interest in North Africa from Polish Intelligence in Algiers. The German Armistice Commission sent their experts from Wiesbaden to verify its defensive strength. They advised that the Wehrmacht take a more active role; German action was expected. Not unexpectedly, therefore, plans for Operation Torch were prepared in strict secrecy. It was carried out swiftly with a surprise element. Even de Gaulle only found out about it on the morning of the landings, which did not increase his affection for 'the Anglo-Saxons'. At the time it was regarded as a purely Anglo-American victory, and indeed it has remained so to this day. Agency Africa's Intelligence work from 22 July 1941 to the Allied landings on 8 November 1942 involved sending 1,244 frequently multipartite Intelligence reports to London. The Polish contribution has now been placed on record.

As a postscript: the final victory was not ours; it was a 'defeat in victory'. As if to emphasise the shape of things to come, already foreshadowed by the Teheran and Yalta agreements, Polish soldiers, sailors and airmen were not invited to participate in the great Allied victory parade in London in 1945.

Appendix A

POLISH PERSONNEL WORKING IN
THE 'EVACUATION'

1. Karol Badeni (Cadet Officer)
2. Bauer 'Bartek' (Czech citizen)
3. Marta Biskupska (Miss), wife of Henryk (Henry) Łubieński
4. Adolf Bocheński (Cadet Officer)
5. Włodzimierz Mizgier-Chojnacki (Staff Major)
6. Adam C'Kreiza (Lt)
7. Roman Czerniawski (Staff Air Force Captain)
8. Bolesław Dulemba (P.O. radio operator)
9. George Gordon (Lt)
10. Stanislas Gustowski (Major)
11. M. Halski (Lt)
12. J. Iwanowski (Captain)
13. K. Jagielski (Captain)
14. Stanisława Januszewska (Mrs)
15. W. Jordan-Rozwadowski (Cadet Officer)
16. J. Kamiński (Staff Captain)
17. Zygmunt Kiersnowski (Lt)
18. B. Kontrym (Captain)
19. Krasiński (2nd Lt)
20. Z. Krzesimowski (Lt)
21. J. Krzyżanowski (Staff Captain)
22. Kubicki (Captain)
23. Henryk (Henry) Count Łubieński (Lt)
24. W. Neklaws (Captain)
25. K. Osiecki (Captain)

26.   W. Popfewski (2nd Lt)
27.   M. Pruszyński (Cadet Officer)
28.   Joseph Radzymiński (journalist)
29.   Stanisław Rombejko (Lt)
30.   J. Roztworowski (Cadet Officer)
31.   Stojatowski (Cadet Officer)
32.   T. Szulc (Captain)
33.   M. Tonn (Staff Captain)
34.   Wincenty Zarembski (Major) – 'TUDOR'

Appendix B

AGENCY AFRICA, AFR

Intelligence Officers

BANULS	Lt Count Henryk (Henry) Łubieński
RENÉ	Lt George Gordon
MUSTAFA	Lt Stanislas Rombejko
DOKTOR	Lt Jekiel (Polish Navy)
VINCENT	Lt Edward Przesmycki
COLT	Lt A. Piotrowski
MISTRAL	Lt Zorawski (Polish Navy)
SLAV	2nd Lt Majewicz
Lt Piatkowski	

Post-Torch:
Station RYGOR
Major L. Jagodziński, 2nd Lt George Malcher, Major Tafelski, Captain Kokorniak, 2nd Lt Wadowski, 2nd Lt George Rieger

Outpost commanders

1812   Robert Ragache ('Paul') – Oran
1820   Maxime de Roquemaure ('Morel') – Tunis
1830   André Achiary ('Silver') – Setif
1847   Maurice Escoute – Algiers
1849   Michel Kokoczyński ('Michel Rouze') – Philippeville

1850   Paul Schmitt ('Lucullus') – Constantine
1860   Denis Pucheu – Bône
1889   'Albert'– Dakar
1960   Saoul Laskar ('Saoul') – Agadir

<u>CADIX (associated with Agency Africa)</u>
MATHEW   Major Maximilian Ciężki
WHIRLWIND   Colonel Gwido Langer

Appendix C

PRINCIPAL FRENCH AGENTS ASSOCIATED WITH AGENCY AFRICA

RYGOR's list of recommendations presented to Commandant Pélabon, Directeur Technique des Services Spéciaux, Algiers, on 8 August 1944.

List 1

1. Robert RAGACHE
Captain of the High Seas; 7 Rue Clausel, Algiers. As the commander of the Oran district outpost, worked with an attachment without limits, directing the activities of the network in a highly intelligent manner and furnishing information of the utmost importance to the Allies without regard to the personal dangers involved. Decorated with the Silver Cross of Merit with swords.

2. Paul SCHMITT
Commander of the Constantine district outpost. Proved extremely valuable, furnishing precious information to the Allies. Director of the daily newspaper *Alger-Républicain* in Algiers. Decorated with the Silver Cross of Merit with swords.

3. André ACHIARY
Commander of the Intelligence outpost in Setif. Commissaire of Direction Surveillance du Territoire in Algiers. His activities as an associate were always highly appreciated. Decorated with Silver Cross of Merit with swords.

4. Louis GIORGI

Captain pilot, postal sector 99021. 51 Avenue du Parc, Cité Marval, Oran. An active and faithful associate. Commander of the outpost at La Sénia airbase. Apart from technical information, has regularly supplied us with lists of officer personnel and their political affiliations. Furnished plans of airfields, their defences, aeroplanes and the fighting readiness of the French Air Force. Decorated with Silver Cross of Merit with swords.

5. Joseph BRIATTE

Radio technician and operator of ADAM radio station in Algiers. Has faithfully and continually assured the radio link with the Allied High Command in London. Decorated with Silver Cross of Merit with swords.

6. Michel KOKOCZYŃSKI (Michel Rouze)

Commander of the Philippeville outpost. Earlier was a deputy commander of the Algerian outpost. Chief editor of *Alger-Républicain* in Algiers.

7. Maurice ESCOUTE

Commander of the Algiers Outpost. 9 Rue Trollard, Algiers.

List 2

1. Pierre LAMY

Captain of the High Seas; 9 Rue du Fondouck, Oran. Captain of the coaster vessel *Forfait*. Supplied information concerning the African coast and reported the movements in ports and other maritime information. Decorated with Cross of Merit with swords.

2. Achille GUERIN

Captain of the General Staff of the Oran Division. 33 Rue d'Arzew, Oran. Military information.

3. Maxime de ROQUEMAURE
Commander of the outpost in Tunisia. 11 Rue Mogador, Algiers. Decorated with Cross of Merit with swords.

4. Jean FORIELMEYER
Pilot in the port of Oran. 8 Rue Stora, Oran. Guaranteed us information on the movements in the port of all ships and their cargoes. Decorated with Cross of Merit with swords.

5. Mme Jeanne RAGACHE
7 Rue Clauzel, Algiers. Regular courier between Oran and Algiers. Wife of Robert Ragache.

6. Pierre ADDA
20 Rue Henri Martin, Algiers. Deputy commander of the Algiers outpost. His missions were particularly delicate and audacious.

7. Henri DOUMENC
Bursar at the High School in Constantine. Deputy commander of the Constantine outpost, later at Setif. Organiser of the local network, supplied regular and effective results.

8. Inspector LOFREDO
Inspector at the DST. Ensured the protection of the network in Algiers. Commander of the counter-intelligence outpost. Decorated with Cross of Merit with swords.

9. Gabriel LABAT
Commissaire of police in Oran department. Commander of the protection of the Oran network.

10. René RAMON
Corporal in the French Air Force; a gunner. 2 Rue Ramier, Oran. Now in Free French forces in Britain. A faithful associate. Information on Air Force fortnightly.

11. Lt-Colonel RICHARD
Military information from Oran district.

12. Jean DUPIN
Chief Navigational Officer of Compagnie Generale Transatlantique, 23 Boulevard Front de Mer, Oran. Responsible for reporting cargo traffic especially of rubber and molybdenum.

13. Henry PUAUX
Magistrate at Tlemcen. Supplied very useful information. Second-in-command of Tlemcen outpost.

14. Dominique FILIPINI
Pilot in the port of Nemours. Regularly supplied precise information on the sailings of ships and mineral cargoes. Commander of Nemours outpost.

15. Denis PUCHEU
Manager of railway at Bône. Deputy commander of Constantine district with special responsibility for Bône outpost. Among our local associates, his task was the most difficult. He fulfilled it with excellent results.

16. Pierre COLONNA
Inspector of Algerian railways. Rue des Dames, Constantine. Courier to Algiers. Among his numerous duties was the recruitment of agents and informers. Penetrated French Nazi-type organisation SOL as commander of a platoon. Very intelligent and audacious. Engaged with enthusiasm in all allocated duties.

17. Albert DOMINICI
Inspecteur of the Police Spéciale in the department of Philippeville. Post office box and courier between Philippeville outpost and its centre in Constantine. Resided at 2 Rue General, Faudras, Oran. Information from Philippeville region, railway network and the port. Decorated with Cross of Merit with swords.

18. André DIEHL
An employee of the Algerian Railway at Constantine. Courier to Algiers. Recruitment of agents and informers. Important information on rail traffic. Rue Pierre Curie, Constantine.

19. Louis DEROCHE
Head of a dept at the Governorship General in Algiers. Extremely active. Valuable reports on economic and administrative matters.

20. Eugène BONFANTI
President of the Council at the Prefecture in Constantine. Prefect Commissaire to the Government in Algiers. Responsible for selecting various economic and administrative information.

21. General FLIPPO
As a Colonel, was pensioned off from the army for his Gaullist sympathies. Brought back into service and promoted after the Allied landings. Responsible for political activities in the military field; responsible for preparing a military coup in Algiers in the event of an Allied landing.

22. Captain Gaston NOUGARET
Commander of the Bougie outpost in the district of Constantine. At first a company Captain at Bougie. After the Allied landings, became deputy commander of a battalion, 3rd RTA in Guelma. Various military reports. Responsible for organising an armed coup at Bougie on orders from Algiers.

23. Charles MAIRE
Secretary at the Commissariat Central in Oran. After the landings, became chief of the Guardians of the Peace in Oran's central commissariat. An associate of M. Labat in our Agency's security service. Helped facilitate movements of agents and reported on all police searches.

24. Jesus PERES
Director of agricultural co-operative in Beni-Saf. A conscientious supplier of information on movement of ships in the port, and on the economic situation in the region.

25. M. HOSTEIN
Courier between Algiers and Oran, later in the region of Algiers. Arrested in January 1942, deported to Tunisia, released after Torch landings. Joined a British special unit, taken prisoner, transferred to Italy, where escaped to Algeria to join the Army. Extremely serious and discreet.

26. Pierre GRIFFI
Radio specialist. Executed by the Italians in Corsica.

27. Dr Roger SAOUL
Courier between Algiers and Tunis. An employee of Air-France at Dakar.

28. Pierre MALVY
Ex-Director of Prefect's Cabinet.

29. Mme Aimée SCHMITT
Wife of an outpost commander, various duties, liaison, reception of couriers.

30. CAMPODOMICO
Pilot in the port of Algiers. Conscientious surveillance of the port. An extremely serious informant providing important information.

31. Marcel DUBOIS
Special Commissaire in Rabat.

32. Jean THOMAS
Works engineer in Algiers.

List 3

1. Inspector SCHMITT
Inspector of DST. Served as a warning agent. Chosen by André Achiary to watch over Commissioner Begue. Placed in Oran by Achiary to investigate the deaths of Gaullist couriers and scrutinise the activities of Commissaire Freddy. After the landings, worked in armed forces security.

2. Alain THIRION
Director of the National Society of Oil and Petroleum. Living at Rue de Besançon, Oran. Supplied information on fuel situation and stocks.

3. M. FLANDRIN
Employee of Algerian Railways. Ecole Berthelot, Oran. Supplied monthly statistics on rail traffic and was removed from his position. Served as our post office box for the towns of Sidi-bel-Abbès and the port of Mostaganem. At the moment, employed as Personnel Officer at the newspaper *Oran Républicain*.

4. Jean GERBAUD
Lawyer at Oran and later at Tlemcen. Courier between Tlemcen and Algiers.

5. André BOLLUIX BASSET
Barrister, Oran. Post office box.

6. M. BIANCO
Employee of the port of Oran. Maritime information.

7. Bernard SERRIS
Director of the society L'Entreprise Maritime et Commercial in Oran. Rue Alsace-Lorraine, Oran. Maritime information.

8. M. GASSER
Doctor. President of the Délégation Spéciale of the town of Oran.

9. Georges GUERON
Industrialist at Tlemcen. Post office box.

10. M. ABEILLE
Financial Counsellor at Tlemcen. Commander of the Tlemcen outpost.

11. M. SIERRA
Spanish refugee. Ex-major in the artillery and former chief of the Services des Investigations at Valencia. Information on Spanish affairs and on the Falange. Also on German agents in Spain.

12. M. BONNET
Doctor in Sidi-bel-Abbès. Assembling of information and post office box.

13. M. FERRARIS
Retired teacher. Correspondent of *Oran Républicain*. Courier between Oran and Sidi-bel-Abbès.

14. M. DURAND
Public works engineer at Mostaganem. Commander of the Mostaganem outpost.

15. M. BLANC
Ex-station-master in Sidi-bel-Abbès. Reports on railway traffic.

16. General TUBERT
General of gendarmerie in Algiers.

17. Captain ANGLADE
Customs captain in Oran.

18. Mme BLANCHOT
Office employee. Rue Durmond d'Urville, Algiers. Post office box.

19. Jean DUCROT
Reports from the port of Algiers.

20. M. ROTH
Reports from the port of Algiers and on the coastal defences of Algeria.

21. Jean LACAZE
Director-General of French North African Shell Company in Algiers. Information on stocks of oils and petroleum in Algeria and on supplies of American petrol by French to Libya.

22. Saoul LASKAR
Commander of the Agadir outpost. 4 Passage Soumica, Casablanca, Morocco.

23. M. BLANCHOT
Editor in the Prefecture of Oran.

24. Henri GARRIVET
Commercial employee in Guelma. Commander of the local sub-outpost, also post office box and courier to Constantine.

25. Dominique CIANFARANI
Retired headmaster at Philippeville. General activity and information; courier to Constantine.

26. Marcel PIETRI
Doctor. Rue Robault de Fleury, Constantine. Post office box.

27. François ADGER
Student. Now in Free French Forces. Various information and missions.

28. Gilbert HIMOUN
Doctor. 14 Rue des Frères Beraud, Constantine. Post office box.

29. M. CHOURAQUI
Doctor. 2 Rue Lastienne, Algiers. Post office box.

30. M. BROCARD
Owner of the bar-restaurant 'Des Familles' in Bougie. Information: maritime and various. Assembling reports; post office box in Bougie and courier to Constantine. Now deceased.

31. Captain SIMONPIERRI
Liaison in Setif. Post office box.

32. M. CASANOVA
Railway employee in Constantine. Information on railway traffic.

33. M. NOUVET
Railway employee at Tébessa. Very active in Tunisian outpost. Reported on Tunisian arrests.

34. M. GUIDICELLI
Railway employee in Ouled Rahmoun. Information on railway traffic.

35. M. CHANU
Teacher in Constantine. Now conscripted into the army (29th Regiment T.A. in Koléa, near Algiers). Information on the activities of the authorities.

36. Maurice BESSON
Rue Khermissa, Souk Ahras. Organiser and commander of the outpost in Souk Ahras in the Constantine district outpost.

37. Mohammed el AZIZ KESSOUS
Journalist. Boulevard Bru, Algiers. Now living in Jemmapes. Reported on co-operation of certain important Arab personalities with the Axis.

38. Auguste PICCIOLI
Employee in port of Bône. Information on movement of ships.

39. Eugène BONNET
Railway employee in Bône. Information on movement of traffic.

40. Henri ANSELME
Railway employee in Bône. Post office box. Various services. Courier.

41. Louis DURANT
Bône. Various services. Courier to Constantine.

42. M. FIOCARD
Teacher/Instructor, now Captain Pilot. Contacts with the resistance movement. Surveillance of Italian Armistice Commission and Axis elements.

43. René ESPY
Railway employee in Bône. Penetrated the SOL on orders from Denis Pucheu (see list no. 2, no. 15).

44. René DAGUET
Railway employee in Bône. Liaison, various information, post office box.

45. Charles STORA
Doctor in Algiers. Post office box. Arrested in February 1942.

46. Henri DUBOUCHET
Surgeon. 119 Avenue Michelet, Algiers. Information on stocks of medical supplies. Post office box.

47. M. ALCAY
Doctor. 10 Rue Michelet, Algiers. Post office box.

48. Henri LABBE
Liaison.

49. Mario MARRET
Agency's radio operator, station ANTONINA.

50. Inspector PELISSIER
Sidi-bel-Abbès. Inspecteur of DST. Now armed forces security.

Appendix D

ADDITIONAL LIST OF PRINCIPAL FRENCH AGENTS ASSOCIATED WITH AGENCY AFRICA

The following names, submitted by the outpost commanders, unfortunately arrived too late to be included in the list of recommendations submitted to Commandant Pelabon in August 1944 (see Appendix C).

1. Joseph ROBERT ('Joseph') (no. 1887)
Supplied precious information from Tunisia.

2. M. 'ALBERT' (no. 1889)
Commander of the outpost at Dakar. Held an important post in the General Governorship of Algeria. Information of invaluable importance on the French military dispositions in Senegal, coastal defences of Dakar and the port, also on the battleship *Richelieu*.

3. Colonel EON (no. 1961)
Commander of artillery in Morocco. Active in Laskar's outpost in North Morocco. Important information on defence. Now promoted to General.

4. Lieutenant E. BAYONNE (no. 1967)
Manager of fish-processing plant at Agadir. Lieutenant in the French Navy. Former private secretary to Josephine Baker.

5. 'Le Thon' (no. 1962)
Skipper of the fishing trawler, Laskar's Agadir outpost. Responsible

for surveilling and patrolling coast of Spanish colonies of Ifni and Rio de Oro, reporting movements of German U-boats.

6. 'La Bonite' (no. 1963)
Skipper of the fishing trawler, Laskar's Agadir outpost. Responsible for surveilling and patrolling coast of Ifni and Rio de Oro, reporting movements of German U-boats.

7. 'La Sardine' (no. 1964)
Skipper of the fishing trawler. Responsible for surveilling movements of German U-boats in the South Atlantic.

8. 'La Cigale' (no. 1965)
Member of Laskar's outpost specialising in surveilling Agadir airport.

9. 'La Fourmi' (no. 1966)
Member of Laskar's outpost specialising in surveilling Agadir airport.

10. 'Canari' (no. 1968)
Member of Laskar's outpost specialising in surveilling German Armistice Commission.

11. 'Canadien' (no. 1885)
Canadian citizen domiciled in Algiers. Helpful in organising ANTONINA radio station. Member of Laskar's outpost specialising in surveilling Agadir airport.

INDEX